The
Business
of
Woodwork

To Bette ... partner, colleague, grandmother of my grandchildren, and special friend ... whose encouragement, support, and gentle blue pencil made this Book possible.

$75

The
Business
of
Woodwork

Bill Norlin

Woodwork Press
Distributed by Quality Press
2002

iv

Library of Congress Cataloging-in-Publication Data

Norlin, Bill
        The Business of Woodwork
        1. Industrial Management.   I. Title.
92 - 83706

ISBN   0-9635117-7-7

Third Printing
Printed in the United States of America

Contents

Contents

This time, like all other times is a very good one, if we but know what to do with it.

-Ralph Waldo Emerson

Introduction

This Book tells you things you need to know about the Wood Manufacturing Business. It will make your Work more rewarding and more enjoyable.

It can be helpful to ALL Woodworkers, whether in Office or Plant ... to ALL Companies, large or small, young or old ... because it answers the most-asked Woodworker questions.

Working with wood creates a special joy. When hand and tool touch a fine piece of wood, good things begin to happen. As we learn to shape parts and put them together, an enormous satisfaction and pleasure is found. Wood gives a texture ... a warmth ... a unique charm not found in other materials. Small wonder, then, those experiencing the joy would entertain thoughts about earning their living in Woodwork. Well, why not ... *it's a great way to earn a living!*

But, it's useful to know a few more things about the *Business* of Woodwork. Loving to work with wood is a great start, but not quite enough. Woodworkers are quick to learn, and *do* learn, but the process can be somewhat uneven and take too long. This Book wants to speed the learning process. Woodworkers will do better with some Business Knowledge.

Presented are truths gleaned from more than 40 years of hands-on real-life experience, including lots of trial and error you won't have to repeat. Hands-on experience with the tools and materials, with supervision and managing, with negotiating and training, with ownership and finance, and in-plant consulting. *(Meeting a payroll over time teaches special lessons.)*

You'll learn what a Business really means ... to the Owners, to the Employees, and to the Community. Wherever your place in the scheme, this overall perspective will be helpful. Presented is a System of Fundamentals basic to Success ... for any size Woodwork Manufacturing Business ... in any stage of its existence.

The good news ... there is a symmetry between the audience for fine woodwork and our ability to produce it. People *do* appreciate the value of woodwork, and are willing to pay for it. *Woodwork can be produced profitably.* The Book shows practices which can improve the odds significantly.

The Business Practices set forth, here, are true and tested. Tested in real life, with real people, in real situations. They are uncomplicated and easy to learn. They address the way we Market, and the way we Produce. And they address all of the Events which must occur, and explain about the kinds of People we need to accept accountability for those Events.

The Book is about making Money ... with explanations about the principal reasons Woodworkers don't make more Money. Which are:

1. Poor understanding of Overhead Costs.

2. Underestimating Material Waste Factors.

3. Failure to have a clear understanding of Project requirements. *(Customer expects one thing, Woodworker produces another ... resulting in re-work, slow-pay, no-pay, reduction in price to get paid.)*

4. Simply not asking for a decent Price.

5. Not knowing how much it really costs us to produce something. *(No Job Costing to track true performance, poor shop practices resulting in inconsistency ... an Operation takes 2 hours one day and 4 hours the next.)*

The Book addresses the Philosophical question: Why should we be in the Woodwork Business? There *are* good answers. We can satisfy both egotistic and altruistic inclinations. Something for us ... something for everybody. The opportunity to craft things of beauty, and to prosper should satisfy the self. The jobs created, our being a good citizen in the community, a customer to other businesses, a taxpayer ... all prove we make a large contribution to Good Order.

Most of all, People's lives are enriched by what we do. The beauty and the usefulness of our products enhances most any space people enter. Where they live, work, worship, study, shop, play ... whatever ... beautiful wood products make the space more enjoyable. The lives of the people producing the woodwork are enriched, as well. In addition to earning a living and experiencing the joy of accomplishment ... lasting, rewarding careers are shaped.

CHAPTER ORDER

Our chapters discuss the sale and delivery of goods and services by way of a Transaction. The Chapter topics are not arranged for order of importance. **They're ALL important.** There will be considerable overlap. Chapters on Marketing, Managing, Manufacturing, etc. will, of course, focus on those topics. But, there's Managing involved in every event ... Manufacturing certainly requires Operations and People ... and everything we do is a part of Marketing. We feel the Operations can be better understood after examining the events of the Transaction. Good People can be recruited and trained more effectively when we can clearly describe their Tasks and Responsibilities.

You will find recommendations concerning the way we make the Contact ... prepare, present, and follow up a Proposal ... plan, schedule, and Manage a Project ... purchase the materials ... Manufacture the Project skillfully, and efficiently ... then collect the Money. Shown are Methods, Checklists to assist thoroughness and accuracy, various Forms to use in the Transaction, and helps in making Policy. As all *these* methods are shaped, so too are things like: the Operations, Plant Layout, plus Recruiting and Training the People to make it all work.

These recommendations are not just for large companies. They fit for all sizes. The fundamentals set forth are appropriate for a shop with 3 craftsmen, or with 100 craftsmen. For manufacturers just starting out, or those who have been in business for years. If a small, young company wishes to retain the option to grow ... these Methods should be installed now. It's easier when you're small.

All the recommendations are drawn from a reservoir of real-life experiences ... those of many Woodworkers. We're sure they'll work for you, too. So read, think it through, apply as it fits, and do well!

Work hard. Work Smart. Be Prosperous. Enjoy your Life.

1

What is a Business?

Or, the question could be: What is a Business, and who gets to be one?

The need for a Business isn't questioned. Everyone needs goods and services that are supplied by Businesses. Most everyone needs to be gainfully employed to put bread on the table, so many work for a Business. But, we seldom examine the parts, or wonder about the differences, or what shapes a Business.

A Business is a Building, Equipment, and People. But, it has to be more … it has to have a Purpose. Its purpose is to fill a need, or to supply a demand. It finds out what people want to buy, and then figures out how to deliver it. The fulfillment is an event called a Transaction.

That's what a Business does. It supports the Transaction. The size and shape of the Business is determined by the complexity of the Transactions, and their frequency. A Business becomes a blend of Marketing, Managing, Manufacturing … and, of course, Money. A Business buys and sells … hires and fires … makes things … pays taxes … the list goes on … all in the support of (and supported by) Transactions.

The nearby illustration shows Events of a typical Transaction. They're ALL important. Depending on their execution, each has the potential to make us money, or lose us money. The better we understand the Events, the better prepared we'll be to effectively perform them. The loop (or spectrum) begins at Marketing (Contact, Evaluate, List, Cost, Price, and Close). Managing guides the Project through the steps to Collection. Manufacturing occurs in that part of the spectrum, too. Then, the Measurement of performance … both physical, and financial (How did we do on Productivity? How did we do on Cost?). Results of the Analysis and

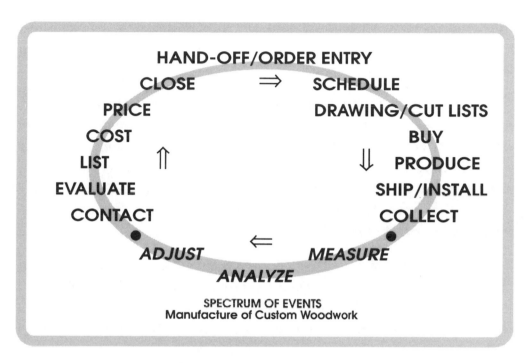

HAND-OFF/ORDER ENTRY

CLOSE $\Rightarrow$ SCHEDULE

PRICE DRAWING/CUT LISTS

COST BUY

LIST $\Uparrow$ $\Downarrow$ PRODUCE

EVALUATE SHIP/INSTALL

CONTACT COLLECT

ADJUST $\Leftarrow$ *MEASURE*

ANALYZE

SPECTRUM OF EVENTS
Manufacture of Custom Woodwork

Adjustments are then fed into the Marketing process as we begin the trek around the circuit, again. Through the Book, we'll be examining all aspects.

Whether we are designing a new Business, or analyzing our existing Business … it is useful to examine OUR typical Transaction, and how well we handle it. A successful Business is the one who can handle Transactions efficiently and effectively. The many events of the Transaction need to be structured and organized. The People, the Skills, the Knowledge, and Productive Capability should move in a smooth sense of direction and purpose.

But, there is another dimension to explore: A Business is much more than just the apparatus to support the Transaction. A Business not only serves the community by providing goods and services, it does more. It also offers jobs. In fact, it offers careers. Our Business is a good citizen in our communities in other ways, as well.

We're customers to other Businesses … no small contribution. We're taxpayers, adding our share to support all the important government functions. And we're good Citizens and good Neighbors. We volunteer time, energy, and substance to many worthwhile community projects. *But there's even more.*

There is a far greater good about Business that is little understood. *As Businesses, we provide what is probably the most viable entity in existence that assists people in building a fulfilling, satisfying life.* That's a pretty strong statement, but I think it stands up under scrutiny. There is no shortage of theories on what makes people happy, but I've observed one plan that works for most. The happy people I'm talking about know the *joy of accomplishment.*

They've discovered that if you apply your efforts to learning, and then apply what you've learned to step up and do a job, it brings a true satisfaction. It's yours to keep. No one can take it away. It's real, and it lasts. They keep Learning ... Keep Working ... and Stay Happy!

Significant evidence shows if we are:

>   Given a job to do—

>   Put in a good working space—

>   Given good instructions—

>   Provided good equipment and supplies—

>   Shown recognition ... and given fair rewards—

We will have achieved what most of us want and need.

And, businesses who provide these things do themselves a favor, as well. As Business owners and managers, we have the opportunity to build into this Win-Win situation simply by being good managers. It's not a trade-off ... it's not "either, or" ... *we can be practical and profitable at the same time.*

BUSINESS GOALS - EMPLOYEE GOALS

That's the point, here. The goals needn't be far apart. People want to learn and grow ... both as persons, and as professionals. They understand the process includes diligent application of skill, enthusiasm and energy. All we need is a sensible business plan which they can enter wholeheartedly. What is good for them can also be good for the business. The Business provides the opportunity ... the People respond. We're not assuming the responsibility for people's lives, and their happiness. It's still up to them ... the individuals. Essentially each of us is responsible for our own happiness, or unhappiness. And, certainly we are responsible for our decisions and actions. However, it costs a Business little or nothing to provide a good climate. And People will respond. The folks we need, need us, as well. The good ones will quickly recognize and appreciate our efforts.

So, look around. Observe the Business you're currently involved in. The Business which employs you. The Business you want to start. The Business you already own. A Business is a marvelous entity. It can do fine things for many People. Let's get a better understanding of what we do, and why we do it.

And then, let's do it better.

2

Computers

Everyone in Business should have a Computer ... at least one.

Computers do too many things too well to be ignored. Computers will extend each key person's effectiveness and productivity by about 50%. And that's just the beginning. Due to the superb abilities to store and retrieve information, plus the lightning-fast calculation, the 50% increase in effectiveness is not only fast, but accurate. Then, to put the frosting on the cake, all documents can be printed out with a great, professional appearance. *One more thing: Consistency. Add it up ... legibility, accuracy, speed, professional appearance, consistency.*

Computers will be discussed in virtually every chapter, complete with examples, so it is appropriate to give a bit of background, plus some suggestions for getting started.

Are we replacing pencil and paper? Not at all. We will ... we must ... remain proficient with pencil and paper. *In fact, we must be able to do everything with paper and pencil before the computer can be of value to us.* But, if we do know what we want done, and can do it with pencil, the computer can make life much easier, and more fun.

Will it reduce paper work? Not necessarily. In fact, computers are capable of producing enormous amounts of paper. We're not bringing in the computer to eliminate paper. The proper amount of Paperwork is key to good Business. The trick is to produce just enough ... and then stop. Too much is a burden, too little can be disastrous. The computer is a great tool to help us produce the correct amount.

HOW DOES IT WORK?

My strong recommendation is that you remain a woodworker and not become a "computer person." Therefore, I also counsel against hiring "computer people" and trying to teach them the woodwork business. Better to teach woodworkers about computers. Which suggests a starting point. Start modestly! Stay away from programmers, and others with a "main-frame" mentality. They want everything to be too big and too complicated (and expensive).

I'm talking about off-the-shelf hardware and software. Desktop stuff. If, indeed, we eventually work into something more elaborate, that's fine. But that's not the place to start.

Start with the *output*. We need many features, which makes it tough to decide which to do first. Accounting and word processing would be close to the top, but so would using a database to log all contacts, then track them on through to sales, invoicing, etc. And, of course, a spreadsheet for calculating bid costs, or tracking Cashflow, is vital. Fortunately, there's a "good-news" solution.

SOFTWARE

The Output starts with Software ... the Applications (or Programs) enable us to work with Words, Numbers, Related Facts, and Pictures. Since we need them all, let's start with a "combination" program which includes multiple capabilities. I recommend ClarisWorks™ ("street price", about $200) run on an Apple Macintosh™. Add a modest Accounting package (several can do the job for under $350), a drawing program (MacDraw® II from Claris™ will do fine), and we're in business. ClarisWorks™ includes a Word Processor, a Database, a Spreadsheet, a Graphics Program, and a Communications Program.

We get the capability to write letters and proposals ... put names, addresses and phone numbers into a Database which allows retrieval in many useful forms ... a Spreadsheet, which is an electronic columnar pad in which to enter numbers and formulas for rapid read-outs in all sorts of calculations. The Graphics program permits drawings and illustrations, even uncompli-cated Page Layout (Letterheads, and other Forms, for example). The Communications portion of ClarisWorks™ provides the software for exchanging information on a network (across the office) or phone lines (across the country) to On-line services, other modems or faxes.

HARDWARE

Start with a machine which is easy to learn, and fun to use. Although you could even "get by" with less, go for a Macintosh™ Classic II 4/40 (4 megabytes of RAM, and 40 megabyte capacity hard drive) as a minimum. (Current Street Price, under $1,500.) Get a Printer with good quality output. They're available for under $1,000, but they'll be kind of slow. Build up to a faster one when you can.

BACKGROUND

Talking about computers is difficult. Much of what you try to say will be changed by the time the words are in print. Even more of what you try to say is tough to quantify. There would seem to be too much opinion and not enough fact. I'm not doing it with the expectation that the words will be timeless. I'm not saying that there is only one way to do a thing (anything). I'm sticking with the consistent theme of the Book. I will talk about what works (for myself, and others). I will try to explain why it works. *I do so to assist you in making your own decision.* I don't deal in absolutes. It is of no value to say, "you MUST do this," or "you MUST NOT do that." I am happy to suggest you do, or not do, a thing … with a careful explanation of why, to be of use in your decision process. But it is only A way to do a thing … NOT *the ONLY way*.

I want to talk about computers, because they can be so instrumental in your success. Yet so few woodworkers are getting full benefit from them. Many woodworkers don't even have them. The good news is that a lot of trial and error by the pioneers has advanced the state of things considerably. Past years of hype, confusion, and disappointment have faded. Hardware and Software now available are useful, reliable, and economical. They are easy to learn, and fun to use … as long as we don't start with the most complex.

There are essentially two worlds in business desktop computing … Macintosh and MS-DOS. I have worked with both. In fact, the DOS machine was the first. We now do everything on a Macintosh™. The DOS world dominated early. An 800 pound gorilla (initials IBM™) presumed that anything called a "computer" should come from one source. They had great respect, and a solid reputation. They were noticed. But, their personal machines didn't always sparkle. Other DOS machines provided many more innovations and quality features, but none dared question the DOS operating system. Those machines handled text and numbers quite well. But people wanted pictures, too.

A brash little machine called a Macintosh™ offered to do pictures. It also came with a "mouse" with which you could "point and click". Many folks thought pointing and clicking was easier than trying to remember more and more keystroke sequences to move from here to there, or open up file folders. In fact it was kind of neat to see what you were doing, instead of having all those mysterious things happening behind the screen. For me, the difference was dramatic. One machine was "daring" me to come up with instructions acceptable to the DOS system. The other one smiled and said, "come on, let's do something … let's have some fun."

Apparently, I'm not alone. Many, many independent studies show that people get up to speed on a Macintosh™ much quicker. You and I might hang in there and get meaningful work out of either machine … particularly when we've spent serious money setting up. But it's just possible that some employees would see it differently. After a certain amount of struggle, they might be inclined to ask, "who needs this aggravation?"

The Macintosh™ visual effects, graphics and drawing capabilities, pointing and clicking, etc. did not go unnoticed. Now, the DOS world has Windows®, by another 800 pound gorilla, Microsoft™ … who was also responsible for MS-DOS in the first place. In fact, the differences are beginning to blur. Many software developers offer products for both worlds, and they translate across easier and easier. The differences will probably continue to fade, but differences remain. So, to sum up: I continue to invest in Macintosh™ equipment because the gorillas are still 5 or 6 years behind, and I don't expect the lead to fade quickly.

THE TEST

If you *are* considering getting started, you should test the theory for yourself. DO NOT start with the cheapest *hardware* you can find. Start on the other end. **Again, start with the *output*.** Letters, Letterheads, Drawings, Financial Statements, Forms, Proposals, Cashflow Charts, Cutting Lists, Estimating Charts, Financial Charts, etc. This Book is full of them. You'll find them in many chapters. The whole Book and everything in it was done with the sort of applications we're talking about. Insist that the sales representatives show you the output. Find out which Applications do it the best. Find out which Machine runs those particular Applications. *Then you decide!*

"Computer" people will sneer at my suggestion of a modest start. They will say it's not "powerful" enough. (Translation: it doesn't have bells and whistles you don't need. It doesn't require much disk space, nor RAM (Random Access Memory), and doesn't create huge files.) Well, they're wrong. I know, because I have those "powerful" applications, too. I keep spending time (for familiarization) and money on upgrades for various Programs for which I will probably never have need for more than 20 or 30% of their capabilities. They keep growing because each developer is trying to outdo the competition, as well as impress the "experts" who write the magazine articles. "Computer" people will also say you should stay with the DOS world because there are thousands more Applications available. Let's put that in the proper context. You will probably eventually require 6 to 8 Applications. You will look at, and "test drive" the top three in each category. Which means you need 24 Applications to look at. Thousands are not required.

And if I'm wrong, you still have lost very little. You've begun with an uncomplicated system that's easy to learn, and it didn't cost much. If you outgrow any part of it (I hope you do … I hope business is that good) you're still O. K. You can easily transfer any and all files into the new (more "powerful") Application without losing any special effects you have created.

Same with the Hardware. Unless you start with an obsolete model, your modest beginning will always be of use … probably right in your own Plant. Or else, at home, or as a trade-in.

So, what are we waiting for?

3

Marketing

Marketing is not a part of what we do ... everything we do is part of Marketing.

Marketing is the process of finding what people want to buy, learning to produce it, and then telling people about it.

In the Chapter, *What is a Business?*, we established the purpose and focus of our efforts; i.e., we build the Business to support the Transaction. The type, size, shape and frequency of the Transaction then determines the size and shape of the Business. Then, why not stipulate: ***The purpose of Marketing is to improve the quality of the Transaction.***

Marketing should strive to produce *more* Transactions. *Better* Transactions. *Bigger* Transactions. *More profitable* Transactions. Therefore, the shape of the Business, the Plant, the People, the equipment, the Products ... everything we do is Market driven. ***Hence, everything we do is (or should be) part of Marketing.***

Marketing is Definitions. Of course, Selling is a critical part of Marketing. But how do we determine what we're supposed to be Selling? We must define our Market (the People who need our Product). We must define our Product (the blend of Goods and Services we intend to offer).

We are actually defining both Product and Market at the same time. And we should have some sort of definition before we place an advertisement, or make a sales call. How could we sell, or place, if we haven't decided what and to whom?

We don't start at zero. We have a pretty good idea of what our capabilities are, and we already have some sort of experience meeting people's expectations. Something or other in our backgrounds has given us general knowledge of providing customers' needs for fine woodwork. But, we need to understand the importance of refining those definitions further.

Norlin's First Rule of Marketing:

Don't Sell something unless you know how to Manufacture it,

and Don't Manufacture something unless you know how to Sell it.

Broadly, we have two choices: We can produce something we think is neat, and fun to do … and then go looking for someone to buy it. Or, we can go out and find out what someone wants (needs), then go back and produce it.

The second method works better. Whereas the first *can* be done, it involves enormous investments of time, money and effort to fill the warehouses and stock the shelves (fill the "pipeline") … and then only in the *hope* that someone will respond.

It's much better to define exactly what someone needs, make a deal concerning scope, price, delivery, and payment … then go back and manufacture the goods, make the delivery, and receive the payment … that's the way to go. Quickly, smoothly, and easily. It's much better to build to order.

NOT QUITE THAT SIMPLE

The premise is sound, as far as it goes. But there is a serious shortcoming, too. The shortcoming is the vast ignorance of our potential clients. We have just stated that we should only build what the client wants. But, they can't know what they want if they don't know it exists. They probably haven't seen it, yet. There is an astonishing lack of knowledge of what we are able to produce. Their sights are often set much too low, concerning what they can afford to own.

They start with a straightforward "perceived need". They need Cabinets, a Desk, a Credenza, a Reception Desk, some Paneling, etc. But they have only a glimmer of what the choices are. (I'm including both professional specifiers and the ultimate owners.) Time and time again I see prospective customers vastly underestimating the Woodworker's capabilities.

Our Marketing just became Educating. And we're the ones who will have to do the Educating. We are the only ones truly capable of it, for we are the only ones who fully understand. And we're the first, and only ones who know when we've added a new capability.

The first step is to understand the need for further education, and truly believe it. The next step is to act on it. And then perfect and implement our follow-up process. The process is going to continue as long as we're in business. (Yes, you can read it both ways … If we don't continue the process it *could* mean the end of our business).

THE CONTACT — SEE AND BE SEEN

How do we begin the process? How do we do the Defining … the Educating? BY BECOMING VISIBLE. By being out there making CONTACTS. There is much to be done. We must find the folks who need what we know how to produce. We must convince them we will satisfy their needs as to Quality, Value, and Service. We must be prepared to answer their first questions (not always said aloud, but always there).

"Why should I do business with you? In fact, why should I even be talking to you?"

Even if they answered our ad, or saw us in the directory … the question still is there. If we are ready with:

"We build great sound system units out of solid hardwood … here let me show you some", and whip out some dynamite color photos, we've begun to answer the question.

We need to be out there establishing lines of communications. We must be projecting a specific profile (image?) into the community. Curiously, if we've been on the scene for any length of time, the community *does* have a perception of who we are and what we do. They perceive us as large, or small … dumb, or smart … capable, or incapable. Who knows how those perceptions are formed? But they are. Wouldn't it be better if we helped the process by projecting the correct profile, instead?

LOOK AND ACT PROFESSIONAL

Dress up to the occasion, even if it modifies your life-style. Jeans and T-shirts are fine in the plant. Meeting the public needs more. We don't dress up because we think we're important ... it's the occasion that's important. Have a good looking card to exchange. Send thank-you's and inquiries on good looking letterheads. Not glitzy or gaudy ... pleasing and professional. Log all contacts into the computer database. Spell names correctly. Get the address, phone and fax numbers right. Note what was discussed and who does what, next. And then follow up. Each contact gathers facts about who they are, what their needs are, and how soon they are going to place an order. Each contact adds to our store of information concerning what our product line should be. That's the Defining part.

And it's also the Educating part. At each contact, we should teach a little, and learn a little. Carry pictures. Pictures of the plant ... inside and out. Pictures of fine woodwork ... pieces still at the plant, or woodwork installed on the job. Have your camera handy, always.

Get lots of pictures. Show your pictures to your professional photographer whose eye will quickly determine which are the most impressive. She can then approach the work with the right lenses, lighting, etc. and bring back the quality we want for the portfolio.

Do a comparison. The last one I did, I could make up dozens of photo folders for less money than a colored brochure. I didn't need thousands ... just dozens. Plus, the photo route allows more flexibility. You can add or delete photos, plus it's a grand opportunity to make another call and add new items to the prospect's folder.

Start the Defining/Educating process with what you know. If you're familiar with Residential work, begin there. If your background is in Commercial work, start there. Don't try to be all things to all people.

Only a large, established company can *try* to do EVERYTHING! (And they probably shouldn't.) Learn to focus. Learn to excel in a few things, rather than dabble in many. Find a "niche" and really work it. A "niche" can be a production of pieces in a particular species, such as Cherry. Or it can be a narrower range of products, but offered in species not offered by others. Or it can be offering the usual products in the usual species, but delivering *on time!*

A niche is really the only way to go. Do something different, or do something almost the same ... only do it better. In other words, find out what people can't get anywhere else ... and do it! We cut down the competition and take the lead!

Depending on the size of our Team, our skill, the completeness of our Plant and its equipment, we may expand into several niches. That's fine. Just don't keep butting the same brick wall by trying to best other woodworkers who have been serving the same niche for years and years. "Me, too" does not impress.

KEEP SENDING OUT THE MESSAGE

Get out and talk to people. Take along your portfolio. Show how great our capabilities are. Get them into the plant. Plant tours are terrific. Invite a crowd, hire a bus if you have to. Show the Product, and how it's built. Don't be shy ... tell why our products are better! Invite the media, too. Show Specifiers, Contractors, Owners ... any potential customer ... we have great people, a terrific plant, the latest and best techniques. And we have alert, "with-it" management. *We are continually improving Value and Service ... just for them!*

Keep building the Contact list in the database. Begin to distinguish contacts by interests and specialties. Establish mailing lists. Send out Letters, Bulletins, or Newsletters to keep prospects, and customers, up to date. To illustrate the point. Think about your most recent improvement in capability, such as:

PEOPLE

In-plant training has produced crafters with greater skills. Who was notified? When? How? You hired an experienced, respected, well-known

Project Manager to help handle increased business. Who was notified? When? How?

EQUIPMENT

Better Machines improved both quality and efficiency. We're now able to craft products better and faster. We can meet tighter schedules and tighter budgets. Who was notified? When? How?

NEW PRODUCT

A new counter-top material has been introduced. Key crafters have attended the seminar to get hands-on experience on its use. We know how to treat edges, joints, scratches, etc. ... in short we're ready to do a thorough, complete fabrication and installation. Who was notified? When? How?

NEW SERVICES

Finishing and Installation are both now furnished. The satisfaction of the end-product and its end-use is assured. We now have control of the quality and the timing. Or, we now have the capability to coordinate more materials. Marble, glass, stainless steel, (electrical ... whatever) can be included in the contract. What terrific news! Who was notified? When? How?

We're never really finished telling the story, are we?

But, isn't it time we started?

Let's tell them ... loud and clear, then do three more things ...

FOLLOW UP ... FOLLOW UP ... FOLLOW UP.

4

The Bidding Process

Let's be clear about the purpose of a Bidding Policy, which is:
***GET SOME ORDERS IN!* ...**
*followed by: **TRY NOT TO GIVE AWAY THE STORE!***

All else follows.

We want results. We want the Order. We want an Order that is clear and concise about who does what, and when. We want the four principle parts covered, which are:

1. What is going to happen? (Scope)

2. When will it happen? (Schedule)

3. When will we get paid? (Terms)

4. How much will it cost? (Price)

When we have agreement on those four, we have a contract. The contract is what we're after. Note that we can Price the Job *only* after the other three parts are known. Do not Price by Scope, alone. Schedule and Terms are definitely a part of Price.

It is probable that virtually all of our Sales Revenue will come from competitive Bidding. The sensible assumption is that we're always bidding against another Price. Even when it appears a prospect is only talking with us, we should assume we are (or will be) bidding competitively. And even when we're not bidding against a specific "real" number, we're "bidding" against a perception of "what it should cost". Therefore, it behooves us to examine ALL aspects of the process and be prepared to make good decisions.

We are proceeding around the nearby Spectrum of Events. We began the Product/Market study and learned about CONTACT in the *Marketing* Chapter.

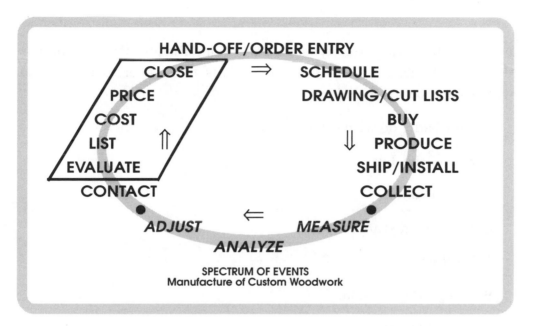

HAND-OFF/ORDER ENTRY

CLOSE	⇒	SCHEDULE
PRICE		DRAWING/CUT LISTS
COST		BUY
LIST	⇑	⇓ PRODUCE
EVALUATE		SHIP/INSTALL
CONTACT		COLLECT
● ADJUST	⇐	MEASURE ●
	ANALYZE	

SPECTRUM OF EVENTS
Manufacture of Custom Woodwork

Now, we're ready for the next steps, which are:

- EVALUATE — Study the various opportunities and pick the best.

- LIST — Make a complete and accurate take-off, properly listing all items we will be expected to furnish.

- COST — Develop the Anticipated Cost for the complete Project.

- PRICE — Determine the Selling Price.

- CLOSE — Prepare and submit the Proposal. Follow up. Negotiate as appropriate. Close the Sale and bring back the Order.

• EVALUATE — Study the various opportunities and pick the best.

Contacts have been made. We have some bidding opportunities. Time to decide which gets our attention, first. Which fits our operation, best. Where should we concentrate our time and enthusiasm. The Evaluation process applies to decisions of what to bid today and this week. It is also a continuation of the Market and Product definition. The week-to-week decisions about which projects are more profitable, and which customers are easier to work with, become a part of our Bidding Policies and our Marketing Policies. There are many points to consider as part of the evaluation process, including:

1. How badly do we need an Order.

2. Size of the Job.

3. Time Frame.

4. Shipping distance.

5. Bid List.

6. Design Professional.

7. Project Owner.

8. Quality of Plans and Specification.

Let's take them one by one.

1. How badly do we need an Order.

If there is a serious hole in our production schedule, we will look at bid opportunities differently. Don't wait too long. Anticipate. The sooner we see the slack period and address it, the more options we'll have. In periods of drought we look at Jobs we would normally bypass. But don't go crazy. Don't get involved with a new product or market that is totally unfamiliar. This is no time to get acquainted with an entirely new Customer. Best Order to fill a hole would be one in familiar territory. Good Bid List, good Design Professional, project type we know well. We can shave the regular markup enough to get the job without buying a pack of trouble. When shaving the markup to get some work, do it with a smaller job, rather than a larger one. Another possibility: look at smaller jobs, and/or work we have done in the past but moved away from because of tedious, time-consuming transactions. Things we've "outgrown". Example: small residential jobs which we found took too much time to put together.

There is hardly anything in the world that someone cannot make a little worse and sell a little cheaper, and the people who consider price only are this man's lawful prey. It's unwise to pay too little.

When you pay too much, you lose a little money … that is all. When you pay too little, you sometimes lose everything, because the thing you bought was incapable of doing the thing it was bought to do.

The common law of business balance prohibits paying a little and getting a lot … it can't be done. If you deal with the lowest bidder, it is well to add something for the risk you run.

And if you do that, you will have enough to pay for something better.

-John Ruskin

By the way, while we're on that subject ... never be afraid to move away from any type of transaction which requires too much valuable management time for their revenue value. Don't fall into the trap of thinking, "But we might need the work some day". That's exactly right ... and that's what we're talking about, now. Here's the difference. We sometimes feel that if we don't stay in a market, and bid it all the time, it will be lost.

Wrong! That's the point. That work is ALWAYS there! We can abandon it and pick it up again as often as we wish. Examples: Dealing with homeowners. Even if they should remain loyal, their repeat business may be 3 years away. And Designers with small projects. The ones who sell lots of goods from big furniture manufacturers, but need a few special items to complete the package. In both cases, loyalty is not really expected, or required, either way. Our stock answer becomes, "We're sorry, we're tied up with large production jobs and can't meet your schedule right now. Maybe we can get together, next time." (Always tell the truth.) But on that day we need the work; we jump on it, figure it, negotiate it, and bring back the Order. Always move to the more profitable, less aggravating jobs as quickly as possible. We can always go back to the other when and as we have to.

2. Size of the Job.

Big jobs are always tempting. At first glance, it appears one big Order can add six months or more to our backlog and give us a chance to relax for a bit. Things are not always what they appear. Big jobs seem to provide huge revenue with the same amount of paperwork and general office activity. They do not. They will require more of your management time and skills than you realize. And they can wreak havoc on production schedules. Even the biggest jobs are still on demanding schedules. They can bring grief to a small Business. Even shop drawings and submittals can be traumatic.

Another point, here. Don't neglect our "steady" minimum effort repeating work. Woodworkers tend to underestimate the amount of steady work coming in from repeat customers. It's great business. Let's not neglect its

Surprising.

I don't know which is *more* surprising. Whether it's the fact that the old "Which two do you want?" question is still as valid as ever, or the fact that so many woodworkers still ignore it.

The fundamental truth remains ... there are three parts to the delivery of goods and services.

- **Quality**
- **Service**
- **Price**

Also still true, you can only have two out of those three.

The customer will ask for all three ... perhaps even insist on it. That doesn't make the request valid.

That sort of bargain is available only when someone is going out of business. (Whether they realize it, or not.)

YOUR RESOLVE:

Sell Quality and Service. Decline to provide all three. Raise the level of Quality. Raise the level of Service. Raise the Price. Make Money.

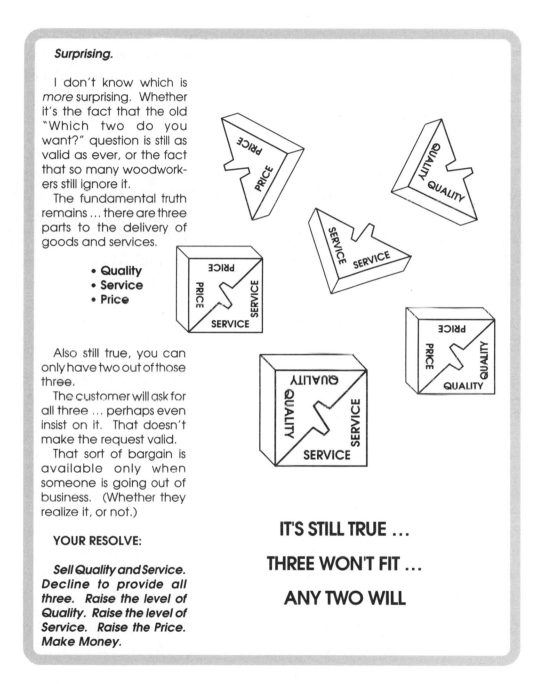

IT'S STILL TRUE ...

THREE WON'T FIT ...

ANY TWO WILL

importance. This steady flow, which just kind of "falls in the door", sometimes runs as high as 30% of our sales volume. It comes from Architects, Designers, Contractors, Stores we've worked on ... all our usual contacts. Part of it is additions to jobs under way. Part is follow-on work from previous jobs. But it's there, it's real, and it should be recognized. Yes, we have to price the work and put it in the schedule, but it is almost effortless compared with "hard" bidding. The point is that a huge job could (probably will) jeopardize that work. We shouldn't allow that to happen.

Now, this "steady" work is totally different from that described earlier! This is the kind we *do* seek and want to retain. It's the kind that fits our Marketing strategy. LOYALTY IS REQUIRED FROM US, to sustain loyalty from them. We should strive to respond quickly to quote requests, plus give the best delivery service possible. (CHECK THE SCHEDULE BEFORE WE PROMISE.) And then follow up, and follow through. Sometimes a policy requirement on this work stipulates quotes from more than one woodworker. Let's be the one who jumps on it, not the one who sits on it. Our strategy should be to bring back the Order before the competition has got around to looking at the plans.

Am I saying we shouldn't try to grow? Not at all. Recommendation: Apply two rules:

   1. Don't bid any job more than twice as big as the largest job we've successfully processed to date. (If we've done a $40,000, stay under $80,000 — don't go for $100,000.)

   2. Don't bid any job larger than 20% of our current annual volume rate. (If our sales volume last month was $70,000, that means an annual volume rate of $840,000. We shouldn't bid a job larger than $168,000.) *(The cap may even be lower, depending on our Working Capital which will be discussed in depth in the Money section.)*

Why such rules? Isn't there a certain risk involved in any hope for gain? Absolutely! The operative word there is "certain". We surely must take *some* risks, but not *all* risks.

Three main reasons: Our management capability, our production capability, and our financial capability. The huge job will probably strain all three dangerously. But, that's not the only reason. A combination of smaller jobs could swell the sales volume to a similar total volume. However, no smaller jobs, even in combination, are likely to carry the same demands as the huge one. More than that, the combination of smaller jobs spreads the risk. If any should become slow-pay (or even no-pay) we might be able to ride it out. With the huge one, maybe not. In spite of best efforts, we can't always judge credit worth. Plenty of high-flyers who seemed to have all kinds of cash have crashed and burned. We don't want to go down with them. And doubling the job size will produce all the excitement we need. Believe it. Doubling gives us all the growth room we need.

3. Time Frame.

Includes 2 parts: Do we have time to bid it, and do we have time to build it. (Follows logically on the size question.) The Bidding Process includes keeping a watchful eye on the Timeline Chart, or similar Schedule Board *(which will be discussed in later Chapters)*. For two reasons: 1) Spot the holes, and fill them. 2) Don't pack it too tight. Good opening dialog might include, "When do you need the price, and when do you need the product?"

This is not to be taken lightly. When we make a Proposal, whether it's a $40,000 school job or a $3,000 sound center, it's not merely putting a price on the job. We are saying, " we will deliver what we have agreed **on this date _____.**" We're not only selling goods and services, we're selling a **time slot.** This must be respected by us, and by the customer.

4. Shipping distance.

Is the job across town, across the state, or across the country? If there's a local slump, those out-of-town jobs begin to look pretty good. Considerations: shipping costs will grow, coordination and field measurements will cost more and consume more of a manager's time. And what about that weekly job meeting requirement? Can we put it all on one truck, or will it need 2, 3 or more shipments? Are shipping costs going to price us out of the job? (These are all worthy considerations, but none should discourage … if we need a job, go for it.)

5. Bid List.

Two Lists: 1) The list of woodworkers bidding against us. 2) The List of people receiving our bid. We *must* know who we're bidding to ... we're *entitled* to know who we're bidding against. Don't be afraid to ask. Either can change the way we look at the situation. If we're bidding to general contractors, and the list includes some firms who have given us grief and not paid their bills on time, we can probably find something better to bid. We *can* prepare a bid without sending proposals to *all* Bidders. But, if we bid 4 and skip 2, we reduce our chances considerably. If *our* competition includes some firms known to disregard specifications and deliver an entirely different level of quality and service from ours ... might we be wasting our time?

6. Design Professional.

We, as professionals, have a responsibility to learn to work with other professionals. In most instances, we can. However, there are a few folks out there that always seem to make jobs more tedious. They're slow to return approved drawings, or make color selections. They send out Change Requests, but then can't get things approved. Or maybe they always seem to be out of town when it's time to get payments approved. Or they insist on using certain inappropriate materials which make our task more difficult. (Like insisting on plywood cores for plastic laminate faced cabinet doors.) It's not simply because they're tough on us. I'd much rather work with a "tough" one than one who is vague and uncertain. I can meet exacting demands. I chafe at having to deal with "wishy-washy". For whatever reason, or combination of reasons, if we are not comfortable working with someone, it's a consideration.

7. Project Owner.

Some woodworkers properly determine they aren't interested in working for certain government agencies. I'm one. It is our right. Or we may grow weary of certain school boards, or church boards. We have every right to make such policies, and stick with them. I would counsel against narrowing the potential customer base too much, but as agreed earlier ... we don't have to be all things to all people. There are some work-arounds. I learned that chintzy inspections and unconscionable paperwork and certifications (government work) can be modified if you're working with a good contractor who will run interference. But if your contractor "opens the gate" and lets the ducks keep nibbling, change contractors or change projects.

   8. Quality of Plans and Specifications.

The quality can vary significantly. If you've opened a sizable set of plans and begin to see evidence of a hasty preparation, stop and think. If further review shows ambiguities and other question marks, think some more. If the thing bids in three days, and we'd be hard pressed for time to think it through, anyway, it may be time to say, "no thanks". Sometimes plans and specs seem to contain more riddles than answers. If there are already 5 addenda and you have been advised there are 2 more on the way, it may be time to bail out.

The quality of the accessibility should be considered, also. Occasionally, we have the loan of the plans for only a few days. Sometimes we don't even get a complete set. Sometimes we have to do a takeoff in a plan room, or in a contractor's office. None of those are quality conditions. The aforementioned opportunities (plus scan machines ... film projected up to a viewing surface) may be O. K. for a cursory exam to see if we want to bid the job. If we're serious, we need the whole set of plans and specs ... and if we're really serious, we want our own. The larger copy machines have improved those options, considerably. A good set of documents that are complete, clear and informative will make the listing, reviewing ... the whole process, go easier. As we compute the cost, we do so with considerably more confidence. A curious "other-side-of-the-coin" ... if the plans are so bad they scare off the competition, maybe we should take a look. Depending on the skill and experience of your team, "different" strategies can be effective.

Clearly, many considerations are required as we decide which jobs we'd rather bid. Probably none, by itself, would be enough to deter us. It's when they begin to add up, that we must take notice. And, again, if we REALLY need the work, all "problems" pale to insignificance. If there's nothing else to bid, the plans just got better. Also, we have time to ask the questions, clear the ambiguity, build in protection against the "what-ifs" … maybe we can make some lemonade out of this lemon. We can call a huddle with plant people and figure out a better, faster, way to build something. We can make some more phone calls and find better prices on material. Extra effort pays off.

THE NEXT STEPS

What we want from our next actions is the "Anticipated Cost" of the "job" (or "project"). Anticipated Cost includes cost of Material, Labor, and correct Overhead Factors (for both Plant Overhead, and Administrative Overhead). You have heard Anticipated Cost referred to as an "Estimate". Let's try to move away from that term. The term "Estimate" suggests an approximation or conclusion made from incomplete analysis or faulty information (a guess?).

Let us tolerate no faulty information or incomplete analysis. "Estimate" suggests vagueness where we need accuracy. There will be a *few (very few)* Cost areas where we won't expect absolute accuracy, but it will be our responsibility to keep those Costs within certain brackets, or ranges. And, further, we (the whole organization) must tighten those brackets as much as possible. This isn't an exercise in gambling … the future of our Business and all its People depends on good performance, here. The fundamentals, and the good practices, can be learned. There is no reason not to learn them.

The nearby Chart showing the Eight Fundamentals is a good place to start. Examination of the 8 Points shows most can be closely identified and controlled. If we can't do *"Accurate take-off and listing"*, and do the *"Calculation of the material required"* without error, **we're not yet in business.** *"Orderly and accurate recapitulation"* should be automatic, as well. (The cost of a computer system can be justified on this function, alone.)

A word about *"Clear understanding of the quality required"* is in order. Our responsibility begins with ascertaining the level of quality "requested" …

THE EIGHT FUNDAMENTALS

Producing consistent anticipated costs with the greatest accuracy possible requires these ingredients:

1. Accurate take-off and listing.
2. Clear understanding of the quality required.
3. Calculation of the material required.
4. Application of the appropriate material waste factors.
5. Determination of labor hours required to produce each item.
6. Orderly and accurate recapitulation of these items.
7. Application of **correct overhead cost factors.**
8. Applying sound judgment concerning special considerations.

START WITH THIS CHART

whether reading prepared specifications, or talking person to person. Much of the time, some clarification is in order. Is the quality "requested" truly required, or only desired? (And is the customer willing to pay for it?) We will do well to inquire. A tremendous assist in this regard has been provided by the publication *"Architectural Woodwork Quality Standards"* from the Architectural Woodwork Institute*. The *Quality Standards* has been in use almost 20 years, is updated regularly, and is now widely accepted. It is virtually the industry Standard.

It speaks of 3 grades of manufactured custom woodwork: Premium, Custom, and Economy ... and each is clearly spelled out. Quality of material, workmanship, finishes, etc. is stipulated, and tests are shown to determine if the quality grade has been delivered. It's about as clear and concise as we could ask, *but still not absolute.* That is, even when a certain quality has been called out, we can't be sure that the performance will be demanded. Remember our question "required, or desired"? As we become familiar with the cast of characters, we will have a better sense of who understands specifications, and insists on performance.

*The Architectural Woodwork Institute is a not-for-profit organization representing the architectural woodwork manufacturers of the United States and Canada.
(P.O. Box 1550, Centreville, VA, 22020-8550)

It's really an extension of the evaluation process. If the Specifier doesn't really understand quality grades and/or doesn't insist on delivery of grades, we may want to find something else to bid, today. We must keep working at it. Don't let it get you down, but don't ignore it.

The mystery of *"correct overhead cost factors"* is explained in this book. *"Applying sound judgment concerning special considerations"* is what you do everyday by thinking things through, discussing the what-ifs with colleagues, then deciding a course of action. *Functional ease in all these things begins with understanding, builds on good work habits, and is polished with experience.*

> **• LIST — Make a complete and accurate take-off, properly listing all items we will be expected to furnish.**

Good Listing begins with a full deck. That is, a complete set of documents ... Plans and Specifications. A word about the ongoing reference to "plans and specifications" and "design professionals", etc.: It's true such terms are a part of larger and more formal bid projects. I'm well aware that not all readers are involved in those projects, right now. However, the principles apply regardless of formality. The more formal approaches spell out excellent examples of points which *every* project contains. It is extremely likely that sooner, or later, you *will* be involved in such a project so it's not too soon to get acquainted. More important, no matter how small the project or its amount of informality ... SOMEONE HAD BETTER WRITE A CLEAR DESCRIPTION OF WHAT'S SUPPOSED TO HAPPEN.

If our prospect has not spelled out each detail, that doesn't mean "anything goes". We must clear up ALL points before we prepare a Proposal. Clear understanding of details (material, joinery techniques, hardware, finishes, etc.) not only eliminates surprises concerning the finished product (and completion date), the understanding also makes it more likely the competing bids will be "apples-to-apples". If the prospect is reluctant to write specifications or have them written professionally, *we* must *still* spell out

SPEC - CHECK   Check List for Project Specifications . . .
a Critical part of a Thorough Plan Takeoff
BIDDING REQUIREMENTS and GENERAL CONDITIONS

Bid Date

Completion Date

Delivery Dates (Phases, East Wing first,

Bldg B, etc.)

Pre-Qualification (Who can bid Millwork?)

What is Approved?

Alternates

Unit Prices

Required pricing by Division, Phase, Etc.

Addenda

Payment terms ... (Retainage, etc.)

Submittal requirements

Penalty clauses

WITHIN SECTIONS

Who installs?

Who finishes?

Factory prep Doors?

Do Sections 6, 8, 9, all agree
on these points?

OTHER

_____

_____

_____

_____

GUIDELINE FOR YOUR OWN CHECKLIST

what we are proposing. If drawings are required, we could offer to provide them … for cash up front, which then may (or may not) apply towards the total price.

That might seem to make it easier for our competition (our spec. sheet, and/ or drawing) but not necessarily. If the prospect is going to someone, anyway, we may be better off if the competitor is on the same page. Best scenario: During the planning, sketching, and specifying we conduct ourselves so professionally, demonstrate our knowledge, and convincingly show our sincere desire to please … the prospect becomes convinced we're the ones for the job, and doesn't even go to anyone else. But, the point: whether the documents consist of 3 pages, or 300 pages, make sure we have all of them, so we can proceed.

We should approach the project with an "aggressive inquisitiveness". We must have an insatiable appetite for every scrap of information, no matter where it is. There are 2 ways we can approach the "take-off" (or "listing"). A good analogy is the way we approach a blind intersection when we're driving our car.

We can say, " I don't see anything ... therefore, nothing is there."

Or we can say, " I'm sure something is there ... therefore, I'm going to keep looking for it." The second approach is highly recommended in both instances.

WRITING IT DOWN

We can begin the actual Listing as soon as we determine we have all the "published" information. We may need more information, but at least we can start with a complete set of whatever has been made available. The next consideration is an orderly process for setting down the information as we discover it. "Orderly process" includes actual pieces of paper used, plus work habits. Each assists and complements the other.

Don't start filling out a Form, yet. Just grab a plain old lined pad for the preliminary notes. I have tried many Forms designed for this step and still haven't found the ideal one for every company and every situation. Head up the top 3 pages of the pad as follows:

The first page says SCOPE, and receives today's date.

(It's the temporary "Cover Sheet" so it will include some Key Job Information in addition to the Scope.)

It will receive the:

- Project Name and Location.

- Design Professional's Name, Address, Contacts, and Numbers (Phone and Fax).

- Bid Date and Time.

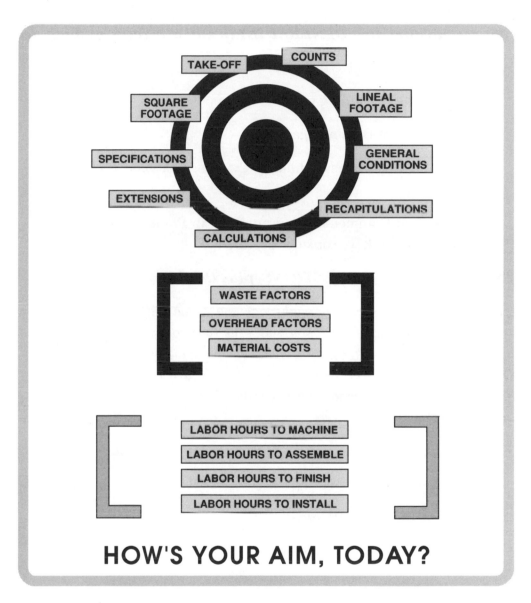

HOW'S YOUR AIM, TODAY?

- Plan Set Number (or specific identification as to Date, Revisions, etc.).

- List of Addenda received (with their Dates).

- All the Items we intend to furnish (or may be expected to furnish). (Again, write it as we find it ... we'll put things in proper order later, and determine whether to "include", or "exclude".)

The Bidding Process

The second page says GENERAL INFO, and also receives the Date.

Information it will receive includes:

- People we're Bidding to.

- People we're Bidding against.

- General Conditions outlined in the Specifications. *(See nearby List.)*

- Notes and Comments about anything in Plans, or Specs. … usual, or unusual, we consider pertinent.

The third page says QUESTIONS, plus the Date.

(Get in the habit of heading each page you touch with some idea of the contents, and the Date. Treat yourself, plus your colleagues, with the great advantage of telling "at-a-glance" what the page is about. Applies to Lists, Drawings, Memos … everything. Don't make yourself, or anyone else read half a page to find out what is being read. The Date quickly identifies the latest page worked on.)

The third page includes questions for anyone and everyone.

- Design professionals.

- Recipients of our Proposal.

- People who do our purchasing.

- Our drafters.

- Plant people.

- Any other associate.

Later we can combine and set priorities. Some questions might require immediate response. Example: we're right at the edge of one of our company policies (size of job, distance, bid list, etc.). We may need authorization before we proceed. It is far more professional (as well as practical) to prepare a list of questions and make 1 phone call, rather than make 3 or 4. The recommendation applies to questions for colleagues, as well. Our teammates don't like being bugged with question after question any more then we do.

All the accumulated information will soon be transferred to other pages, which *will* be "standard" Forms. But at the preliminary stage the Lister should be concentrating on squeezing out all the pertinent information and doesn't need the distraction of looking for the right "box" to put it in. Here's the logic: the information doesn't come in an orderly fashion, so it isn't ready to be transcribed in an orderly fashion. Just grab all the details as they appear, and save the sorting for later. Some bits of information come from the drawings. Some come from the specifications.

There's no magic rule about which to examine first. You might bounce back and forth in the early going. We don't have to finish one before we begin the other. Keep track, though, so we don't miss anything in the switching. This is actually an extended phase of the "Evaluation" process. We're still retaining the right to reject the project if it doesn't measure up. As we discover new facts concerning the job, it's highly probable that the "little red flags" are popping up. (Points which might reduce the desirability of the job, particularly if they continue to grow in number.)

If you think there are many decisions to be made during these first hours into a Listing, you're right. The judgments will come easier with experience. While we're gaining the experience, a good set of Company Policies will help, too. (More discussion on *"Policies and Policy Making"* in the *Operations* Section.)

THE FORMS

About now, we're ready for some "standard" Forms. Somewhere in the Listing process we will have determined we *are* going to bid the job, and we *can* begin to transfer information to the more organized ("standard") format. Standard is in quotes because even our own "standard" is subject to ongoing refinement. That's fine. Flexibility and adaptability will keep us more efficient and more productive. And here's where a Computer can really give us a significant boost ... in several ways.

The person doing the Listing will continue to List, but now some of the information on our 3 beginning sheets could be processed by someone else. At the same time we're Listing the job, and then doing the calculations, someone can be using another database to prepare our Proposal. In the regular database, we will have listed the ongoing cast of characters with whom we do business. The Architects are there. Designers are there. The Contractors are there. Do you see where we're heading?

Our Proposal Form is also there. So we fill in a few blanks rounding out the specifics on this particular job (Name, Location, Bid date and time, etc.). We can "paste" in the Architect's Name and Address (from our file). We can put the bid date into a special box beside each Contractor who will receive a proposal, then "sort" to develop the mailing list. We can add the "Scope" (note, this information is all from our "Scope, or temporary Cover Sheet", plus the "General Info sheet"), and we're ready to mail them out. At this point, we have options:

1. We can wait for prices before printing.

2. Go ahead and print out so that the pricing can be hand written.

3. Or we can mail them out and phone the prices out on bid day. Either way, we have it all set up and ready to go. We have done it with minimum hassle, and we will be making a fine looking, professional presentation. The "Form", once established will print out again and again without error.

Meanwhile, the person Listing has switched to Forms designed to expedite the move to the Spreadsheet(s). The spreadsheet is an electronic columnar pad which can (should) be doing all of our calculations, extensions, subtotals, totals, and summaries.

Our spreadsheet(s) will be set up with the necessary formulas, which will speedily and accurately calculate (and recalculate) our Costs as we enter

	A	B	C	D	E	F	G	H	I	J
1				**JOB TAKEOFF LIST**						
2	Job Name					Bid Date				
3										
4		(Add as many Categories as you wish)								
5										
6	CLASS	ITEM	MATERIAL	QUAN	THK	WIDE	LONG/HI	DETAIL	RM NO	REMARKS
7	(Trim,	(Base, Cove,	(Wood					(A14/6)		(Double Glaze,
8	Sash,	Chair Rail,	Species							Woodlife …
9	Door,	Six-Panel Door,	Etc.)							whatever)
10	Special,	Circle-head Sash								
11	Etc.)	Door Jamb, etc.								
12										
13										
14										
15										
16										
17										
18										
19										
20										
21										
22										
23										
24										
25										
26										
27										
28										
29										
30										
31										
32										
33										
34										
35										
36										
37										

Your own Takeoff List may be tailored to suit any type of product, or products. Using a Spreadsheet gives us enormous flexibility. Column widths can be adjusted instantly. Boxes, Text, any size, shape, or "look" which makes the Form easy to use can be applied. Go ahead and experiment … don't be afraid of trial and error. Print out 2, 3, 4, or more versions and try them in real life. That's another beauty of Computers … the ability to try. Different versions can be created quickly and easily. We don't have to invent the "perfect whatever" the first time.

(or modify) the information. The "Forms" we use are actually printouts of the same spreadsheet we will use for calculating, only left blank. Several examples are shown, nearby. We can pencil in the information as we go through the plans and gather the facts. Later, either the Lister, or someone else who also has a keyboard, can enter the information into the actual spreadsheet for calculating.

We can make up as many "Forms" as we wish (General, Casework, Special Casework, Trim, Paneling, Doors, Door Jambs, Borrowed Light Frames, Special Millwork … whatever our products might be). If the project consists of just one of our products (Cabinets, or Moldings, for example) we can reach for the Form for that product. If there is a mix of products, the Listing can begin with the General Takeoff List (shown nearby).

It can go like this. We List items in any order we chose. We can go room-to-room and List all items in the room (Paneling, Trim, Cabinets) … or, if we prefer, we can List by item, first (all the Cabinets, then all the Paneling, etc.) We can List in any sequence we're comfortable with, because we can then reorganize the information with a "Sort", or "Sorts". Then the Items in each Class can be transferred into their own place on the spreadsheet for further calculation.

We accomplish this by designating this body of information as a "database" within the spreadsheet, and we can "Sort" our information in many different ways. In effect, we can say:

- "Please show me all the Trim."
- "Please show me all the Sash."
- "Please show me all the Doors."
- "Please show me all the Walnut Trim."
- "Please show me all the Cherry Trim."
- "Please show me everything on the 2nd floor."
- "Please show me all the Casework on the 1st floor, by face material, lowers first, then uppers."

We have many options for sorting. After the first sort, we can do further sorts … continually refining the data to extract exactly what we need. If an addendum were to come out changing all the Trim on the 3rd floor from paint grade poplar to cherry, we could make the change and recalculate the whole thing faster than we can say it. And the calculations will be correct. Can you imagine how many keystrokes on our adding machine it would require to do that? (With the chance for error with every keystroke.)

But there's still more. Actually, the same information base we are developing can be used all the way through the job. Since the various materials and species, plus all their quantities has been listed, we can determine all the materials to be ordered when we get the job. Much of the information translates to Cutting Lists and work orders … even to Shipping Tickets, and Invoices. As you begin to work with this concept, you'll see more and more "Forms" which can be developed to satisfy needs and smooth the process of communicating. In actual use, after the Form has been set up the information literally flows into place as instructed. Of course the Forms can be reused every day. People throughout the Plant become familiar with them. There is a consistency and a legibility everyone will appreciate. We'll discuss the Spreadsheet methods more as we get into the Formulas and Calculations for both Material Quantities and Labor Hours required.

In this manner, the Listing continues until every scrap of information has been found and recorded. We have developed an orderly process which can assimilate the facts quickly and accurately. You've probably noticed something else. This structured approach can accommodate interruptions. The Lister can stop for questions, phone calls, etc., and then get right back into it again. The process can even lend itself to a hand-off, if a change of Listers becomes necessary. The process also works for a review by a supervisor, or another colleague. So, we have a method which helps the Lister to be confident and productive … a method which can be handed off … and a method which can be reviewed. We have installed a critical step in the development of Anticipated Costs.

Costing / Pricing

NEXT STEP - TRANSLATING TO DOLLARS

When we're through Listing all the Items which will be furnished, and their exact quantities, we can begin to compute their Cost. We now know the number of Cabinets required, the Lineal Footage of Trim, etc., but that information needs further translating.

> • *COST — Develop the Anticipated Cost for the complete Project.*

For Material, we need to convert to square-foot, or board-foot quantities … enter Material Replacement Costs … consider Waste Factors … and then apply Overhead Factors.

For Labor, we need to apply time values for each Operation performed on the Material, add them up, and then multiply by our computed Hourly Labor Rate. (Which includes the Overhead Factors.)

FIRST, THE BOARDS

Solid wood parts may consist of Moldings with intricate detail worked in them (such as Cove Mold, Crown Mold, Chair Rail, etc.) or they may be S4S (Surfaced 4 Sides) squares or rectangles. Whatever their profile, they will be machined from a rough ripped shape, usually a rectangle. That is, some rough stock (whether 4/4, 5/4, 6/4, etc.) will be ripped into strips which will be further machined to produce the finished dimension or profile. The process is referred to as "rip-and-run". The Moldings (including S4S shapes) may be ripped on a straight-line rip saw and run on a Molder. Or, they may be ripped on a regular variety table saw and further shaped on a jointer and/or a shaper. Our methods will certainly have a strong

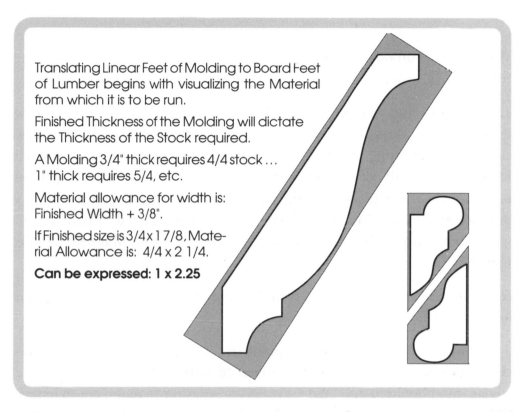

Translating Linear Feet of Molding to Board Feet of Lumber begins with visualizing the Material from which it is to be run.

Finished Thickness of the Molding will dictate the Thickness of the Stock required.

A Molding 3/4" thick requires 4/4 stock ...
1" thick requires 5/4, etc.

Material allowance for width is:
Finished Width + 3/8".

If Finished size is 3/4 x 1 7/8, Material Allowance is: 4/4 x 2 1/4.

Can be expressed: 1 x 2.25

influence our Labor Costs, but perhaps not so much on our Material Costs.

Moldings may be the finished product to be shipped. Or, they may become parts used in other products we are manufacturing. If they are the finished product, we will tally (determine the quantity), bundle, and ship. If they are parts, they will be kept with other parts going to the Assembly Area. There may be other variations, such as end trimming, cutting to length ... perhaps even sanding and finishing. These variations can influence the amount of material required, so our Listings should include such information.

Most woodwork companies do not run their own profile Moldings. They buy them from people who specialize in Moldings. My broad recommendation would be to treat Moldings as a "Buyout" until we have a large size operation. The specialists have the machinery, the space, the material handling equipment, the purchasing power, plus more uses for the "short and narrow" pieces. That makes them extremely competitive. Most give good service, too. But we will expect to run a lot of continuous S4S shapes, and we need to know how to calculate material requirements.

Whether we run our own, or buy out Moldings, we need to observe some fundamental rules.

1. Trim is referred to as Standing Trim, or Running Trim depending on how it is used. Standing Trim is cut to specified lengths (door and window casing, for example, or any other use which requires many same-sized lengths which will not develop well from random lengths). Running Trim is assumed to be attached to solid, continuous backing so that joints may be made anywhere. Therefore, random lengths may be used with minimum waste. Standing Trim costs significantly more, both for Material and for Labor.

Recommendation: Add 20% to both Material and Labor as a start, if you haven't developed historical values.

2. When we talk about lineal foot quantities, use ONE number ... which is **the number of lineal feet we intend to ship.** (Standing, or Running comes into play here, too. We must decide whether to rough cut to length before running, or run enough to allow the development of enough specific lengths afterward. If we're buying out, we'll decide whether to order cut-to-length, or not.) If we stick with one number, and everyone on the team understands, much mischief is avoided. If an extra 10 or 15% were to be added by each of 2 or 3 well meaning folks, we could be furnishing much, much more than our Anticipated Cost had intended. True ... we may rip a bit extra, and we may run a bit extra in order to meet the shipping requirements, but it should be clear we're all working to the same number.

LUMBER WASTE FACTORS

Let's take a look at Hardwood Lumber, first and see why a 15% or 20% allowance for waste doesn't make it. Understand, all hardwood lumber is graded by rules that require interpreting. Hardwood lumber rules and graders are looking at the yield of their definition of "cuttings" which may have nothing whatsoever to do with what we intend to cut. Right or wrong, the rules have been in place a long time. Presumably they are working ... somehow balancing the needs of producers and distributors on to the various end users. Anyway, the recommendation is to understand and accommodate the rules rather than mount an effort to change them.

We purchase rough lumber, random width, and random length. Widths and lengths are not precise. We pay for "board measure". The measurement is taken with a "Board Rule" whose scales read board feet. The Board Rule has a hook on one end, and a handle on the other. The rule is hooked on the edge of the board to measure the width. Width is measured to the nearest half inch. The tallier judges the length, and reads board feet directly off the rule. "Even" feet lengths are one side of the scale, "odd" feet are on the other. Every woodworker should have the educational experience of watching this process. (Also, the grading process, for that matter.) Watching the process of a tallier deciding where to place the rule, interpret which side of the half-inch mark to read, and decide the length of the board … all at the same time … is instructive. If you admire precision, it may even be unsettling. But that's the way it is.

First off, the general rule allows a shipment to tally out 5% over or 5% under what is invoiced. Conventional wisdom says that the shipment is more likely to be under, than over. We just lost 2-3%. Next, it's possible we're buying a load that was tallied before it went into the kiln. We just lost another 5-7%.

Now, the highest grades available … firsts and seconds (FAS) … are expected to yield 91 2/3% and 83 1/3%, respectively. That averages 87 1/2%. On a good day, we just lost another 12 1/2%. We're already down 21% and we haven't talked about widths, lengths, or "cuttings"!

The book says FAS means 6" and wider and 8'-16' long. That means the board must be at least 8' … it does *not* mean they'll average 12'. (There are stipulations for percentages of lengths which vary by species … point is, developing widths and lengths isn't easy).

Now, about "cuttings". A "cutting" is a clear piece 4" x 60", or 3" x 84". Which puts a 7-0 door jamb on the endangered list. (We're still talking FAS, here … don't even think about getting it out of a No. 1 common board.)

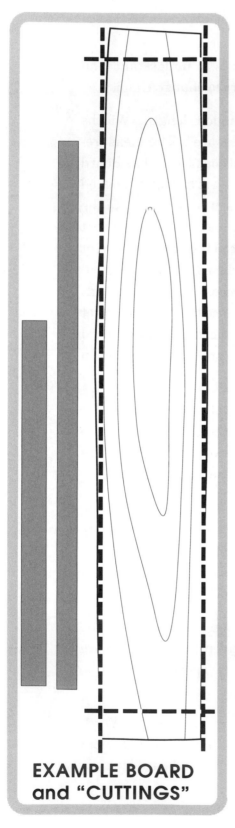

EXAMPLE BOARD and "CUTTINGS"

Take a look at our example board, nearby.

Let's say it scales 10" wide, and it is 10' long.

If it takes 1" to clean and straighten the edges, we lose 10%.

If we cut 6" off each end for end-checks (no defect if done in kiln), we lose another 10%.

Even if we use every bit of the rest of the board … we've lost 41%! And to have covered that 41% with a proper Waste Multiplier Factor, it would have to have been 1.69! (1.00 ÷ .59 = 1.69)

A word about the formula … its purpose is to answer the question:

If I lose 41% of what I buy, what must I buy to get 1.00?

If 1.00 represents 59% of what I buy —

1.00 divided by 59% equals the amount I must buy.

1.00 ÷ .59 = 1.69

1.69 is our Waste Multiplier Factor

It gets your attention, doesn't it? Many projects containing special widths and lengths will require ordering 2 times, or more, than what is needed. And we haven't allowed for those species who yield wide and long boards even more grudgingly. Point: Forget Waste Multiplier Factors of 1.3 or 1.4 in most hardwoods. Start with 1.5 and work upward. (And, of course, build our own history.)

Softwoods are not much better. If our needs can be met with 1 x 4's, 1 x 6's, etc., we *could* get better yield from a bunk of lumber. But, other times, we can't. Check it carefully!

This discussion is to instruct, not to alarm. We're saying that if we produce a broad range of custom wood products, it is better to buy the best (highest) commercial grade available, yet still expect our yield to be far less than we paid for. If we were to work in a narrow range of products, and use a narrow range of species, we could probably do better ... particularly if we were using small parts. Our "cuttings" may be even less demanding then the Hardwood Standards, and our yield could go up. The phrase "develop our own history" means to carefully monitor what we expected to buy, as compared to what we actually bought. The comparison can reflect several things, including:

1. Our product mix.

2. Our requirements for clear wide and long cuttings.

3. The grade we buy. (And receive.)

4. Our supplier's policies and performance.

5. Our efficiency in preparing (and combining) Cutting Lists.

6. Our manufacturing efficiency. (Including Waste Mgmt.)

7. The accuracy of our Anticipated Material Requirements.

8. Number of species we use.

Broadly, if we use a Waste Multiplier Factor of 1.65 for a certain species, and our stock keeps growing, we can cut back on the Factor. If, however we are using 1.65 and are continually ordering more, we must raise it. (We'll touch on this subject again in the *Manufacturing* Section.) One of the toughest questions ... the once-a-year exotic species. It's bound to be costly, either way. We don't want too much left over ... but how expensive is a reorder at the last minute? Observation: We will "go to school" and learn some lessons on these questions ... however, at some point, it's all right to let the customer help pay for the education. In other words, raise the price to cover unknowns.

PANEL GOODS MATERIAL REQUIREMENTS

We may have a bit more work to do on our Panel Material requirements. Wall Paneling should be easy. Paneling is pretty straightforward, if we've been thorough with wall lengths and heights. However, if our Listing tallied Shelving by Lineal Footage, and/or Cabinets simply by Elevations, or Rooms, we'll have some further converting to do. We need the Square Footage. For shelves, we'll have to convert those shown as 15", 16",18" deep, etc. ... still, no problem.

When it comes to Cabinets, a bit more work is involved. Broadly, we can pick up material requirements best from Elevations. Looking down from the Plan View we pick up requirements for Floors, Shelves, and possibly Tops. Front Elevations give us the Face Material, Backs, (and possibly face-frame material). Side Elevations give us Sides (or Uprights), Ends, or Finished Ends.   There are logical options for combining values here to expedite the Bidding. If we build modules (or "boxes"), we could develop a "standard" Material price per box (could also include an allowance for cleats and base material). The key is to work out a procedure, or policy, that:

1. Covers the Costs.

2. Everyone understands.

3. Everyone USES.

That way, we can follow it up ... Measure the results, and make the necessary Adjustments.

PANEL GOODS WASTE FACTORS

The various materials bought in panels, or sheets, have their own Waste considerations. It is a function of both the material itself, and the way it is used. Some materials are available in a wide range of sizes, so we can buy the size which gives us the best yield. Industrial particleboard is probably the best material for yield. It comes in many sizes, it has many uses, grain direction is not a factor, and it is not vulnerable to damage in the manufacturing process.

After particleboard, it gets more complicated. If we are buying hardwood veneered panels for paneling we may be able to get great yield. Unless we're to develop banded squares or rectangles to produce a certain pattern, when installed. (Or we're trying to simulate a sequence matched effect from warehouse sets.) Although, most high pressure laminate products are available in many sizes, some specials only come in 1 or 2 sizes.

COMPUTER HELP

One of the first "sophisticated" computer applications to consider after we have been up and running for a time is an "Optimizer". They start at about $1,000, but can be justified pretty quickly if we are bidding and buying lots of panels. The Optimizer application can quickly produce accurate yields from panels. We enter the list of sizes we need to develop, plus a list of panel sizes we can buy, and the application will show us exactly how many panels, which parts are cut from which panels, and the percentage of waste. Cutting sequence options are available (rip first, crosscut first, etc.), and grain direction is respected. Optimizers are useful in the Costing process, in buying material, and when we prepare to machine the material. They can even instruct our computerized panel saw. (Another example of how the "database" begun in the Listing can flow on through the whole job.)

The computer can assist even before we get our Optimizer. Using a modest drawing program, we can do some optimizing without the automatic part. We will have to draw the parts we wish to develop (to scale, of course) and also draw the panel sizes available. Then, it's a matter of moving our parts around to find the best combinations. It's not as fast as the Optimizer, but it's much faster than pencil and paper. A printout can become part of the Costing file for future reference.

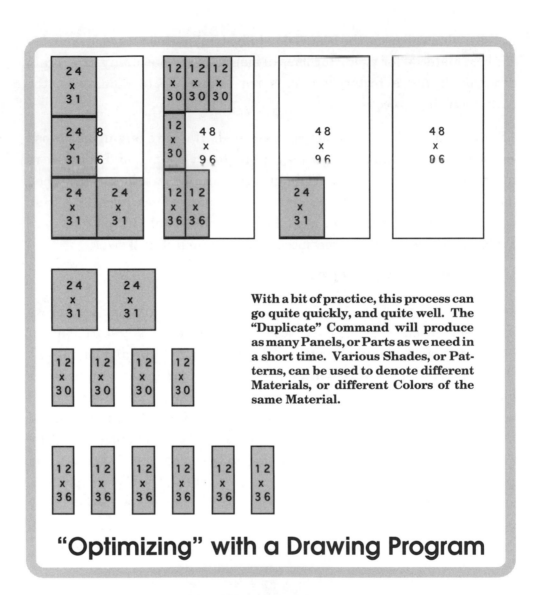

With a bit of practice, this process can go quite quickly, and quite well. The "Duplicate" Command will produce as many Panels, or Parts as we need in a short time. Various Shades, or Patterns, can be used to denote different Materials, or different Colors of the same Material.

"Optimizing" with a Drawing Program

Waste Multiplier Factors won't be as high for panel goods. A square foot is almost always a square foot. Sometimes, we even get a little extra material in the nominal size sheet, instead of shrinkage. Most Factors will fall between 1.2 and 1.3 . Here, again, we must develop our own history, plus apply good managing and manufacturing procedures. Poor Cutting Lists, poor purchasing, poor cutting in the plant can eat into Material Budgets quite rapidly.

FORMULAS FOR COMPUTING MATERIAL QUANTITIES AND PRICES

Here are the Steps required to follow through from the Takeoff List to the Selling Price of the Job:

1. Convert Lineal Feet to Board Feet.

2. Multiply by the Waste Multiplier Factor.

3. Enter the replacement Cost of the Material.

4. Multiply by the Material Overhead Factor.

5. Apply the Markup for Profit.

Let's review the *Board Foot Formula*, and apply it to an exercise concerning a certain molding.

A Board Foot = The cubic content of a Board 1" thick x 1' (12") wide x 1' long.

- Each linear foot of a 1" board 3" wide would be 3 ÷ 12 or 1/4 Board Foot.

- A 1" board 4" wide and 6' long will contain 1 x 4/12 x 6 = 2 Board Feet.

Suppose we needed to know how many board feet were needed to run 500 lineal feet of casing to a finished dimension of 3/4" x 2-3/4". We know that the 3/4" net thickness must be developed from 1", or 4/4 material. We also know to add 3/8" to the finished width to give us enough material to "rip and run". *(See earlier illustration.)* So our formula is 1 (thickness) x 3-1/8 (2-3/4 + 3/8 for width) divided by 12 (to convert inches to feet) x 500' (our length). Can be expressed as: 1 x 3.13 / 12 x 500 ... which computes to 130 Board Feet.

Would we order 130 Board Feet for this job? No, we haven't applied our Waste Factor, yet. Next we multiply the 130 by the Factor. If the Factor is 1.65, the Formula is 130 x 1.65 = 215. We would order 215 Board Feet.

REPLACEMENT COST

Now for the *replacement Cost of the Material*. First, why the phrase "replacement Cost"? For a good reason. If we *should* use some Material already on the premises, it's really not useful to try to find out how many different prices may have applied at the different times it was brought in. The only significant Price is the one which will apply when we replace it ... either right now, or when we buy for the Job. Develop a Company Policy on how the Price is to be determined. If the Item Price in question has been stable in recent months, we may simply use the latest quote. However, on a larger Job, we should not only get an update, but should also inquire about availability and trends. We may even request a formal quote ... even try to get the Price guaranteed for a time. The idea is to be sensible and thorough, but don't spend $100 worth of time on a question that wouldn't mean $5 to the Cost of the Job.

MATERIAL OVERHEAD FACTOR

The *Material Overhead Factor* is a Multiplier which properly assures us that the sale of this Material will contribute its fair share to the Cost of Operating our Business. We will introduce both the Concept and the Formula here, and then develop the concept further in the *Money* Section.

The Concept is one used by many Woodworkers, for many years. It is believed that every thing we sell, whether goods, or services, must pay its fair share of the Administrative Overhead. Everything should support the Base which, in turn, supports everything. Whether we use Material in Manufacture, or merely Resell it "as is" (without further processing), it should still make its contribution. Consequently, we calculate a Markup Factor to accomplish this, and apply it. The Factor and Formula shown on these pages is taken from our Example in the *Money* Section. It's sort of an "average of the averages" in Woodwork Manufacturing across a broad range of sizes and product mixes. The *Money* Section shows us more about how to calculate our own Factor.

The Multiplier Factor Shown is 1.338, which is the calculated Factor to be applied on everything we sell. This includes, Direct Labor, Plant-Processed

Material, Buyouts, Installation, plus any other goods or services we sell. As stated earlier, everything should pay its own way. If we begin to fudge and slip something through at a lesser Markup, who or what is going to make up the difference? I've discussed (argued?) this point for many years ... with myself, and with many others. I've heard all the reasons (excuses) and all the rationalization, but I stand firm ... don't cheat yourself. I've heard all the whining about "I can't sell (installation, finishing, doors, paneling, hard surface materials ...pick any or all), with that much Markup". My kindest response is this: You can't afford to sell it, then ... so stop selling it.

Just what does that 33.8 represent, anyway? Fact is, a 1.338 Markup Factor nets us 25.3% on that portion of the Sales Revenue, and that's what it takes to keep us going. It represents:

1. The cost of figuring enough Jobs to get one.

2. The cost of the paperwork to execute the Job.

3. The cost of Management required to execute the Job.

4. The cost of Collecting the Money.

5. The cost of Interest if the Money's late.

6. Everything else we've invested in to help us do our job.

Another thing ... how can we prove if it's the Markup on the whatever that makes our Bid high? Do some hotshots demand a breakdown, and then picked each line item apart. Are we to believe them? I think not. Point is, if we lower one portion of our bid, we MUST raise something else, or we lose money. Any messing around with these fundamentals just confuses the issue. If we can't make any money on it, why do it?

PROFIT

Applying the *Markup for Profit* is my favorite part. Everything about the Woodwork Business is fun, but it's a lot more fun if it includes Profit. And it doesn't just happen. We have to plan it, and insist on it. How much Profit? My strong recommendation is to Price for an expected Net, before tax, of

15%. Industry Averages are less, but that's not the measure. Don't forget, "Averages" include folks experiencing losses. I can tell you that many years of personal experience, plus many years of observing other successful Woodworkers shows that a 15% net is most certainly attainable, and sustainable. A few Woodwork Manufacturers don't make 15% because they haven't quite got their act together, yet. Far more, however could make 15% if only they would ask for it.

I'm saying, "Ask for it".

Too many Woodworkers only ask for 10%. And most don't even do that properly. They add 10% to the Anticipated Cost, which is not the same thing at all. If all went according to plan, the Net would be 9.1%, not 10%. Going for our Net of 15% is considered this way: Our Anticipated Cost = 85% of what? The Formula is Anticipated Cost divided by .85 = Selling Price.

Let's review the steps and examine the Formulas for each step.

> 1. Convert Lineal Feet to Board Feet.
>   1" x (2 3/4"+3/8") / 12 x 500' = <u>BF =130</u>
>
> 2. Multiply by the Waste Multiplier Factor.
>   1" x (2 3/4"+3/8") / 12 x 500' x <u>1.65</u>
>
> 3. Enter the replacement Cost of the Material.
>   1" x (2 3/4"+3/8") / 12 x 500' x 1.65 x <u>1.36</u>
>
> 4. Multiply by the Material Overhead Factor.
>   1" x (2 3/4"+3/8") / 12 x 500' x 1.65 x $1.36 x <u>1.338</u>
>
> 5. Apply the Markup for Profit.
>
> (1" x (2 3/4"+3/8") / 12 x 500' x 1.65 x $1.36 x 1.338)<u>/ .85 = $460</u>

That's quite a string of numbers. We will do well to try to combine some steps to uncomplicate things. Each step is an opportunity for error, so eliminating steps will eliminate errors. Perhaps this little demonstration will strengthen the recommendation to use a computer Spreadsheet.

	AD	AE	AF	AG	AH	AI
1			**LUMBER**			
2				OVERHEAD FACTOR		1.338
3				PROFIT MARGIN		15%
4	REF	WASTE	WOOD	REPLACE		**SELL**
5	NO	FACTOR	SPECIES	COST		**PRICE**
6	1	2.00	Walnut 4/4	2.80		**4.41**
7	2	2.00	Walnut 5/4	2.92		**4.60**
8	3	1.70	Cherry 4/4	2.60		**4.09**
9	4	1.70	Cherry 5/4	2.70		**4.25**
10	5	1.40	Poplar 4/4	1.36		**2.14**
11	6	1.40	Poplar 5/4	1.39		**2.19**
12	7	1.45	Poplar 6/4	1.42		**2.24**
13	8	1.60	Red Oak 4/4	2.22		**3.49**
14	9	1.75	White Oak 4/4	2.25		**3.54**
15	10	1.35	Pine 4/4	1.85		**2.91**
16	11					
17	12					

The nearby examples *are* actually produced on a Spreadsheet, although the principles are same. You can produce similar Tables with calculator or adding machine.

The Material Quantities Column has Calculated the Board Feet, *and* multiplied Board Feet by the Waste Multiplier Factor. This gives us the amount of Material to Purchase for the particular Item.

The Material Prices have been developed by adding both the Overhead Factor, and the Profit Margin Factor.

The recommendation is to use this procedure, whether with Spreadsheet, or not. It gives us the two things we need to know:

1. How much Material to order.

2. What price is to be Quoted (and eventually Invoiced).

The nearby Chart headed Moldings accomplishes this and also includes Direct Labor (which we will be discussing, shortly). Actually, it's on the same Spreadsheet used earlier for the Job Takeoff List. The Lumber table, also nearby, is on the same Spreadsheet, as well.

This gives us several options. We can enter the entire Takeoff into the Spreadsheet, and then sort for various parts of the Job and proceed with the calculations. The various moldings could be sorted, then entered into the Molding portion. All the moldings could be brought over at once, or other options could be used. Bring them over by Molding Number, by Species, by special shipping instructions … whatever.

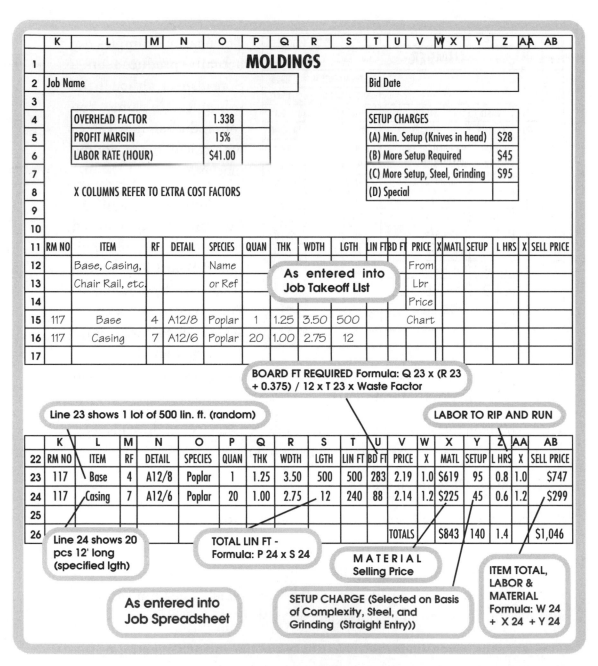

It might be useful to bring over all moldings of the same species, and then analyze for quantity (for purchasing considerations), or examine the lengths and widths (to see if we're applying the right Waste Factor). And, as mentioned earlier, if there should be a species change specified, we can easily recompute.

Something else ... note that the Molding Form is shown in 2 configurations. The Column Sequence is identical, but the Spacing has been changed to suit the purpose. Certain Columns have been expanded to make pencil entry easier in the top portion. The lower portion has been changed to grant better spacing for Data Entry. In other words, we can tailor it to suit the occasion. Print out Takeoff Forms in one position ... do the actual Entry in another.

There's still more. We could use the Lumber Table as a "Look Up" Table and speed the Entry and Calculating. We can enter the Species Number and then the instructions (which we will have entered previously) will cause the Correct Waste Factor, and the Correct Selling Price to be entered automatically. Speed AND accuracy.

We could actually ask the Spreadsheet to "look up" the Table in another Worksheet (or File). I choose not to. I like to tailor the Table to the current Job, and have it present on the current Worksheet. I want to be able to refer to Prices, Waste Factors, Overheads, and Markups anytime I want to. If it's in the same Worksheet, it's right in front of us.

COSTING / PRICING?

I think I heard someone say, "Why does he call it Costing / Pricing, and then throw them in together?" Glad you asked. We need to keep Anticipated Costing and Pricing separate in the discussion stage. They *are* different. Anticipated Cost is Fact. Price is Policy. We are now suggesting combining the arithmetic in the interest of Clarity, Consistency, and Accuracy. But it is imperative that all practitioners understand the separation, and also how the combining is then done. We must all understand the whole process, and we must understand what was done, how it was done, who did it, when, and why.

ANOTHER LISTING / COMPUTING FORM

Shown nearby is another example of a Spreadsheet type Form which can be used both for Listing, and Calculating. Again, the "design-your-own" approach is encouraged. This concept will work for any number of products.

Space for various materials, hardware, processes ... plus "checklists" of various kinds to remind of the urgency of certain information. Note that both Labor *and* Material are shown in close proximity. Just to remind wherever there's one, there's also the other. (Did we pick up both?) This type Form establishes the whole trail of what was done, what was considered (what was left out?) so when we resume after an interruption, we know where we are.

LOOK WHAT WE'VE ACCOMPLISHED

We have set out a method which can organize and consolidate a mass of information and put it in logical form. The information can be reviewed, checked, or modified as required. It is clear, it is consistent, it is legible ... and it is arranged for calculating, extending, and recapitulating. And, it can be Monitored all the way through the Job. It becomes a check on our performance ... at every stage, at every point.

It is the Cornerstone of a Successful Business.

LABOR HOURS AND THEIR COSTS

How long does it take? Biggest questions still involve Labor Hours. How long to Machine and Assemble? How long to Finish and Install? The question is asked again, and again. It's an elusive thing. We think we're moving closer at times, then some Labor Hours come back all wrong. Why is that? Let's look at a few of the reasons we're unsure about our Labor Hours.

1. At some plants actual times never get back to the people developing Anticipated Costs.

2. Some "raw" numbers appear on timecards, but they never translate to usable comparisons to our Budget figures.

3. We are inconsistent in the ways we produce things. Maybe we never do a thing the same way twice.

4. Maybe the methods are about the same, but we use different people. That may make a difference.

	AT	AU	AV	AW	AX	AY	AZ	BA	BB	BC	BD	BE
1		**SPECIAL CASEWORK TAKEOFF LIST**										
2		JOB NAME										
3		BID DATE					QUESTIONS/COMMENTS					
4		ITEM	Nurses' Station				DECISIONS:					
5							Ply, or part. bd?					
6		MATERIAL			Waste	Varies	Shipping joints					
7		COST			O'Hd	1.338	More support?					
8		CALCULATION			Profit	15%	Holes for wiring?					
9												
10												
11		MATERIAL	REP COST	UNIT	WASTE	PRICE						
12		Birch trim (for stain)	(From Mldgs cost sheet)									
13		Birch trim (for paint)	Same	L F								
14		P Lam	1.11	S F	1.30							
15		Substrate	0.58	S F	1.20							
16		Tack board		S F								
17		Task light	11.75	EA	1.00							
18		Drwr slides	etc.	PR								
19		Pulls		EA								
20												
21												
22												
23					MATL	MATL		LABOR		LABOR	LABOR & MATERIALS	
24		MATERIAL	QUANTITY	UNIT	PRICE	TOTAL	OPERATION	HOURS	RATE	TOTAL	TOTAL	
25		Framing mat.					Build frame					
26		Front panels plam.	230	sq ft			Apply plam.					
27		Front panels subst.	230	sq ft			Apply panels					
28		Drwr boxes	18	ea								
29		Drwr slides										
30		Drwr pulls										
31		Drwr Cabinets										
32												
33												
34												
35												
36												
37												
38					TOTALS							

NOTE:This brief example shows the possibilities of Spreadsheet use. Actual selling prices may be developed on each Item, reflecting waste factors, mark-ups, etc. Having a "Labor Hour" section across from the "Material" section provides a cross-check. A reviewer can quickly see whether the various components have been costed ... both the "M" and "L" portions. Various components could be pre-printed, and the Form becomes a checklist. The Form may be used as a Take-off tool, then the figures may be entered into the computer spreadsheet for calculation and extension.

5. We must also face the plain fact that some days things go better than others.

6. Some variables will be difficult to control. Job conditions for Installing can vary from day to day on the same Job. And how much time does it take to get a finish sample to the final approval?

7. How much should we allow for the added time of starts and stops and jumps from Job to Job because we don't know how to schedule?

8. How much longer does it take if someone insists on starting the Job before we have all the Material … or Approvals … or Colors … or other critical information?

Clearly we need to adopt Policies and Procedures which will help us do things more consistently. And then we must adopt good measurement techniques to monitor the Policies and Procedures. Measure and Monitor. Adjust and Refine. Then, Measure and Monitor some more. We need to tighten up the way we Figure a Job, the way we prepare for Production, the way the Job hits the Floor, and the way we support it and follow up and follow through all the way to the end. (More on this in the *Managing* and *Manufacturing* Sections coming up.)

METHODS OF FIGURING LABOR HOURS

An excellent method of analyzing Labor Hours is the "Operational Method". Which means examining each part, or piece, which goes into the product we're manufacturing and then studying all the Operations performed on that part. The fundamentals can apply to most any manufactured wood product. However, a breakdown with that much detail is extremely difficult to Measure and Monitor. Figuring the Operational Costs on each part of every Item on the Job can be tedious and time consuming. Therefore, we need better methods to actually Bid our Jobs. The best compromise is to combine Operations as quickly as possible wherever we're satisfied it won't sacrifice accuracy.

Example: Operations on Cabinet Side:

1 - cut to size w/panel saw
2 - apply edgeband
3 - line bore
4 - joint bore
5 - groove

Most of the time, all those Operations occur on every Side. So we could establish a category called "Machine Cabinet Side for Assembly" and establish a value of .4 Hours (or whatever it really is). Also, the Sides are usually paired, so we can say "Sides". But, why stop there. The Operations just listed suggest we're preparing to produce a "modular" cabinet (which is a "box" ... and an excellent way to build cabinets, by the way).

Why not call it a Box and figure it as a Box and assign the number of hours it takes us to build a Box. Isn't that the way we really Figure a Job? Count the Boxes (or box-equivalents ... 1-1/2 or 2 boxes if it's an outsize one), then count the Doors, then count the Drawers, finished ends, inserts, etc. With each set of cabinets, we can establish a "value" for each step. The "Box" value will vary if we have to apply surface material instead of using a prefinished material. Doors will vary if "nonstandard" hinges, banding, pulls, etc. are required. Same with Drawers ... special slides, construction, or pulls must be considered. But we *can* establish values for each, and we must. If we don't build "Boxes", we can substitute Bays. Find a "unit" that can be counted and checked during the Bid process, and then tracked through Production.

WHAT ARE WE TRYING TO DO?

We're trying to establish certain "units", or parts of what we do, that make it easy and logical to Bid; and, at the same time, make sure we can measure the outcomes. If we bid by the Box and track Boxes ... if we bid by the Door, then track Doors, we'll begin to get a handle on the situation. Let's set our methods so we can see how we're doing. Start with the easiest unit to use while Bidding, and see if we can't logically Measure the unit through

Production. If we need to adjust, we will know what to adjust, and how much. Of course, we must continue to strike a balance ... be thorough and accurate, but not strain at gnats.

Have we abandoned the Operational concept? Not at all. The recognition and examination of Operations will always be important. Analysis of Operations is particularly important when something changes. An Operation is added. An Operation is dropped. We change methods on one or more Operations. (New machine ... new technique.) Such changes must be carefully evaluated. But, then let's make sure we hand our Bidders some workable new values to use for the "units". It is impractical to re-engineer each Item as we Bid it.

THE MEASURING

Timecards are key to the Measuring Process. Proper design can provide what we need to know, but not be a burden to fill out. Some basics:

1. The most useful information comes from timecards filled out and collected Daily.

2. Cards should be checked (at least on a spot basis) by the Lead person in the Area to head off misunderstandings concerning Job No., etc. ... particularly when the cards are new, or when the woodworker is new.

3. After Date, Name, and Job No., a Job Item No. is useful. That tells us whether the work was performed on a Cabinet, of Shelf, or Trim, etc.

4. Use tenths of an hour. .1 = 6 min., .2 = 12 min., etc.

5. More information on the Operations can be added later, IF and as the system can sort it and use it.

5. ABOVE ALL ... KEEP IT SIMPLE. If it's too complex it won't be accurately filled out. And, even it is, the system can't assimilate it and/or show it in useful form.

But, try a few things. We don't have to design the perfect system the first time. If we are clear about what information we need and what we're going to do with it, someone on the premises will figure out how to get it. Computers are helping with this, as well as the rest of Job Costing. In fact computers are the key. They're getting better ... so must we.

THE STOPWATCH

There's another way to Measure. Try using a timer or a stopwatch, sometime. Ease into it. Let the folks know what's going on, so they won't feel intimidated. Prediction: You'll learn a lot ... but not necessarily what you expected to learn. Some revelations:

1. Things will speed up. (Everyone moves faster in the presence of a stopwatch and clipboard.)

2. You will be amazed at how few seconds some Operations take.

3. Exceeded only by the next amazement when you discover that ones-of-a-kind (sometimes two or three) take 4 times the Operation time to GET to the next Operation.

4. Often we double the Operation time getting the part up from the cart, and back on the cart.

5. Ten or more parts blows the whole thing because there's no place to stack that many on the nearby horizontal surfaces. (Have you looked near your bandsaw, or drill press, lately?)

A stopwatch or timer *can* help develop useful values for Bidding. But, it's more valuable when studying the way work flows through the Plant. (Maybe you'll get rid of some carts and let parts move on conveyors.) Don't forget, the timer/stopwatch approach eventually has to correlate with the Timecard. Although some Operational times can be measured, they must eventually be translated to time paid for. That is, we must account for ALL hours paid the craftsmen. Unless you let the timer run during breaks, drinks of water, walking around, head scratching, etc. ... the Operational values WILL NOT MATCH what appears on the paycheck.

The method has great value in evaluating new machines, new methods, and new materials. And the process will be a revelation. You will be pleasantly surprised at what can REALLY happen out there when good people, good machines, good methods, good materials, and good instructions all get there at the same time ... AND NOTHING IMPEDES THE FLOW.

THEN WHAT?

The Measuring will be an integral part of Job Costing. (Job Costing will be further discussed in the *Money* section.) Foremost is the determination of which Jobs make money, and which ones lose money. Next we'll seek to know which PARTS of the Job made money. Then the why. After the Measuring comes the Adjustments. There should be no surprise ... if any item takes longer (costs more) ... something has to give. Either we change the way we build the article, or we change the way we Bid it. It's our ongoing responsibility to search for the answer to: "How long does it take?"

It is important for those involved in the Bidding Process ... Listing, Entering, Costing, Pricing ... to understand and be interested in the Measuring and Monitoring process we've been discussing. However, it is not a license to meddle and muddle in the Manufacturing Operation. I'll guarantee it ... you won't save a dumb bid by harassing people in the plant. Another point: It is seldom useful to ask plant technicians how long it takes to build something. They're not really in a position to time the whole operation. It can be useful, however, to discuss *how* an Item might be built. If we know the Operations involved, we can better assign values. We agree that there must be a structured communication and dialog between ALL team members concerning these things. The operative word is "structured". Various aspects of this topic should be discussed at frequent, regularly scheduled meetings. (This will be further discussed in both the *Operations* and *Manufacturing* sections.)

PRICING THE LABOR HOUR

There are several components in the Price of a Direct Labor Hour. The woodworker in the Plant is first concerned with the agreed-on Wage Rate.

No. of Weeks	48		% of
Hours per Week	40	HOURS	Pay
Hours Worked		1920	
6 Paid Holidays		48	2.5%
1 Week Vacation		40	2.1%
2 Week Vacation		80	4.2%
Personal Days (ea)		8	0.4%

Paying for 6 Holidays, 2 weeks Vacation, and 4 Personal Leave Days adds 70 cents an hour to a $10/hr Wage. That's not bad, but it surely can't be ignored.

This little Table (part of a Spreadsheet, of course) demonstrates 2 things. First, it reveals how paid Holidays and vacations can add to Costs. Second it shows how to setup the Table and try as many "what-if's" as it takes to answer questions.

Of considerable interest is the Profit Margin. In between are several others … more than most folks realize. Let's take a look:

1. Agreed-on Wage.

2. Taxes and Benefits
   Social Security contribution.
   Worker's Compensation.
   Worker's Unemployment Compensation — State.
   Worker's Unemployment Compensation — Federal.
   Company Medical Plan.
   Company Retirement Plan.
   Paid Holidays and Personal Days.
   Paid Vacations.
   Plus any other benefits or privileges granted which cost money. All of these things count up. They often amount to 30% of the agreed-on wage, sometimes even more.

3. Administrative Overhead

4. Plant Overhead

5. Profit

We've already talked about the Administrative Overhead, and agreed that everything (including Labor) must make its contribution. Then there's Plant Overhead ... the space, the machines, the power, the supplies, the supervision, the maintenance, etc. The Plant Overhead will be recovered by placing its Factor onto Labor. Together, they amount to a Labor Factor of 2.052. (.338 for Administrative Overhead, plus .714 for Plant Overhead.)

WHAT'S GOING ON?

Here's the sense of it. We're keeping costs where they occur. The reason we have Plant Overhead is because we have a Plant. We have a Plant because we must provide everything our craftsmen need to Manufacture Products. When we sell a Labor Hour it pays for the Wage, for the Benefits, for the Plant, and also contributes its share to the Administrative Overhead plus Profit. That is also why we keep the Taxes and Benefits in with Direct Labor. Someone is hired, we immediately start paying Wages, Taxes, and Benefits. Someone leaves, everything leaves.

Next question: a Factor of 2.052 applied to what? The Factor is applied to the Average Wage for experienced Craftswomen and Craftsmen ... plus Taxes and Benefits. (Take the average of the top 3 Wages.) If the Average is $13.00, and the Taxes and Benefits run 30%, ($3.90) we have a Direct Labor figure of $16.90. Applying the Factor: $16.90 x 2.052 = $34.68. That's Cost. Selling will be: $34.68 ÷ .85 = $40.80

Selling Price for each Labor Hour is $40.80. This is for the example ... it's not yours. We'll learn how to calculate our own in the *Money* Section. Yours will not be much different, however.

BUILDING OUR OWN BOOK

So, where are we? And where do we start to make our Bids better? Start from where we are. Begin to build on what we know, plus other realistic values, and start the Measuring and Monitoring process to confirm the values. We can proceed along these lines:

1. Start a loose-leaf notebook entitled Labor Hours.

2. List our products, and the Operations required to build them.

3. Establish sensible Units of Operational groups which are logical to Bid, and logical to Track.

4. Focus on any Items which are uncertain, or erratic, and Measure them first.

Yes, it will take a bit of time, but not as much as you think. And the time saved down the road, plus the accuracy improvement and the increased confidence of the Bidding Team, will make it one of the biggest bargains you'll find this year ... or any other year.

"SETUP" AND "MAKE READY" TIMES

How much time do we save when we get to build 2 of a kind, instead of 1? Or 3, or 6, or 10? The key is the "setup" time, or "make ready" time. It will vary from Item to Item. Machine setups, jigs and fixtures, complicated layouts, (complex, confusing, or incomplete instructions?), can all consume lots of time before the first Item gets built. The only accurate hours come from careful timing of actual events. (Again, developing our own history.) Most Items follow a similar "curve". *(See nearby Table and Charts.)* The first Item takes the most time ... the second, somewhat less ... the third, still less, etc. After a time the "curve" flattens out, and all successive Items will require about the same hours. Our Managing and Manufacturing goals will focus on reducing all hours, of course, but particularly on "start up" times. If we are able to leave some machines setup for certain operations, the setup may only be start up and involve flipping a switch. Apparatus for gluing and clamping ... a press, or glue wheel, for example ... easels for applying adhesives to panel goods, etc., can speed the time for the first Item, too.

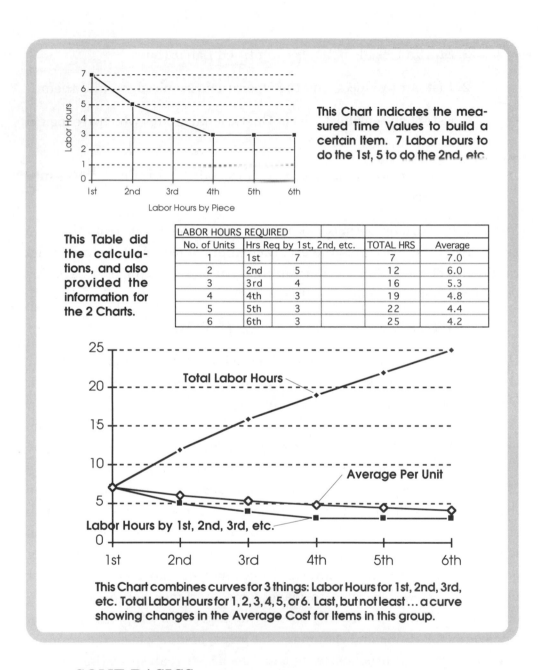

This Chart indicates the measured Time Values to build a certain Item. 7 Labor Hours to do the 1st, 5 to do the 2nd, etc.

This Table did the calculations, and also provided the information for the 2 Charts.

LABOR HOURS REQUIRED				TOTAL HRS	Average
No. of Units	Hrs Req by 1st, 2nd, etc.				
1	1st	7		7	7.0
2	2nd	5		12	6.0
3	3rd	4		16	5.3
4	4th	3		19	4.8
5	5th	3		22	4.4
6	6th	3		25	4.2

This Chart combines curves for 3 things: Labor Hours for 1st, 2nd, 3rd, etc. Total Labor Hours for 1, 2, 3, 4, 5, or 6. Last, but not least ... a curve showing changes in the Average Cost for Items in this group.

SOME BASICS

Here are a few basic Items to consider. We've touched on Moldings (any solid wood milled to continuous profile), and also "Box" Casework. Of course, breaking down Lumber, and also breaking down Panels is basic to any establishment of Labor Hour values for Anticipated Costs. Your product mix will establish priorities of additional values for Items, such as:

1. Edgebanding. Big difference in hand applied and automatic machine. Depending on Material, and method of application, develop Price either by lin. ft. or piece. Then combine with piece price, if possible.

2. Sanding. Tremendously important to quality ... also tremendously expensive to do. Another place where machines and automation can improve times *and* quality. Track this one closely ... it's costing us more than you think.

3. Special Casework. Desks, Credenzas, Tellers Lines, Reception Desks, Nurses Stations, Traders Desks, Conference Tables ... the list goes on. If we do a good amount of any of these, establish a "range". List the fastest time we ever had and the slowest, then judge where the "current subject" falls on the range.

4. Special Millwork. Door Frames, Window Frames, Windows, Doors, etc. As in all these products, solid wood parts begin by "milled to continuous profile" values. Next considerations include: number of joints (both in main members and applied stops, casings, or other trim), time to machine the joints, then time to assemble. Sometimes we need to figure on some "Prefit" work, even though final assembly will be done later.

5. Installation. One of the toughest Bid challenges. Start by figuring times after we're: in the building ... on the right floor ... in the space ... setup and ready to go. Then go back and calculate: How much time to deliver and distribute? How long (each day) to get Installers into the space and plugged in, ready to go? How many days do we do this? How much can we leave overnight? Are you sure? How about communications with home base? (Phone on-site? How many floors away? Across the street?) Supervision? And so on. It's not easy, but you can do it.

6. Finishing. Can fool us in several ways. The cost of Approved Samples can be startling. (Possible control: Stipulate 2 or 3 samples included in Bid ... more samples charged at $100 each.) Next fooler: we tend to think of applying spray applications, plus maybe some wiping and a little rubbing between coats. We forget how many times the product moves into, and out of the booth, and how much time it takes. Last fooler: touch-up. Be sure to allow for all of these.

KEEP WORKING AT IT

That's what I mean about the ongoing search for "how long does it take?" I realize we'll see Items we've never built before and probably will not build ever again. But there will be similar (if not the same) Operations. And our history will include enough similar Items, to give guidelines. Some of us have the advantage of experience in the plant. This can be useful as we apply what we learned in Machining and Assembly Operations, but there is a danger. The danger is this … we kept getting better. That's right. It used to take us 12 hours to build a certain Item. After 2 years in the Office, we can do it in 10. It's amazing … and dangerous. Go ahead and believe you're better if it makes you feel good, but DON'T BID IT THAT WAY.

MARKUPS THAT WORK

The 2 Markup System works because it keep us as competitive as possible, yet always covers the Costs. That's the heart of the Bidding Process … Price to get the Job, yet still make the Profit. The reason for separate Markups for Materials and Labor is this: In Custom Woodwork the mix, or ratio, of Material and Labor change with every Job. Sometimes the change is slight, but at times it can be drastic. What to do about it? The consensus among successful woodworkers is to use the system which always adjusts and accommodates the variations. Which is the system described, here. As we've shown in this Section, setting up the system is straightforward and uncomplicated. And once in place, it's easy and fun to work. I'm not saying the whole Bidding Process is easy … just the system. But there are enough concerns involved in the details of Takeoff, Costing Material, and Costing Labor. Why add the concern of changing Pricing systems on a Job-to-Job basis?

COMPLETING THE BID PACKAGE

We now have good numbers for Labor and Material. And, if we've used Selling Prices, we're getting close to the final figure. After the Buyouts and Installation are added in, we only need one more category. We need a category for Special Considerations. This is for anticipated extra costs for engineering, shop drawings, field measurements, delivery ... any of the items which are normally included, but for this particular job are not quite enough. Most people include shop drawings and delivery as part of normal overhead. However, some jobs are unique enough to require an extra. We can establish policies to cover this. Just make sure we all know the rules, and follow them.

Bids should be checked. By a supervisor, or by a colleague. That doesn't shift the responsibility, it's just one more look which will often reduce errors. After we've looked at the same pages for a time, we may not see things so clearly. A fresh look can spot inconsistencies and save us all some embarrassment.

A FORM TO PUT IT TOGETHER

Develop a Form for Recapping (Recapitulating) all the facts and figures we've been developing. The nearby example is a good starting point. Using the same Form means everyone is familiar with it and can find whatever information they may need, and find it quickly. The Form is consistent with the theme concept we've been following. Which is:

1. Gather the information.
2. Display it in logical fashion.
3. Arrange it so the calculations can be completed.
4. Show the calculations in a manner that can be reviewed and checked.
5. Have all the information displayed in the format most useful for all the next folks who will be using it, too.

In other words, as we build up to the Proposal, we should save each scrap of information (and each scrap of paper) but systematically consolidate the facts and figures. Each consolidation, or recap, should be clear and consistent to all who may need the information ... not just while it is being created, but to all that follows.

Include as much specific detail as you wish. Recommendation: Move toward more, rather than less. But keep the essentials set apart clearly. If we don't need all the detail every time, so be it. But when we do need it, everyone will know where to find it.

KEEP LEARNING

Learning to put a good Bid together is a challenging and stimulating exercise. Best of all it's fun. Approach it with enthusiasm, and with a cautiously optimistic stance. There will be some hard decisions. Occasionally some boldness is required in going for the "prize". We will make a few mistakes, but we won't make them again, and we learn from each one. We learn from them by admitting them, then by shrugging them off and moving forward. Try not to miss any Items completely. That's why we work so diligently in the Listing process. We can survive an error on Labor Hours ... even on Material ... but if we miss an Item completely, that's tough.

Now that we know how to put a good Bid together, let's go make that Sale.

BID RECAP SHEET
Whatever Woodwork, Inc.

Job Name: _____   Bid Date: _____

Architect: _____   Bid Time: _____

Job Address _____   Plan No: _____

Approlimate Time Frame: _____   Spec Book No: _____

	ITEM	MATERIAL	LABOR	INSTALL	TOTAL
1					
2					
3					
4					
5					
6					
7					
8					
9					
10					
11					
12					
13					
14					

SUB-TOTALS: _____ _____ _____ _____

INSTALLATION: _____

EXTRA SHIPPING: _____

OTHER EXTRAS: _____

SPECIAL: _____

GRAND TOTAL: _____

BID TO:	PHONE NO:	PRICE:	OUR COMPETITION:
_____	_____	_____	_____
_____	_____	_____	_____
_____	_____	_____	_____
_____	_____	_____	_____

6

Close the Sale

We have created a Jewel. Now, we must place it in the proper Setting. We carefully sorted through the possibilities and selected the best candidate to Bid. Then we meticulously Listed every Item, and scrupulously computed the Anticipated Cost and the proper Selling Price. Now, it's time to prepare a convincing Presentation.

> • *CLOSE — Prepare and submit the Proposal. Follow up. Negotiate as appropriate. Close the Sale and bring back the Order.*

THE PROPOSAL

A good Proposal should clearly and concisely spell out what we suggest should happen. It should state Who is going to do What, When they're going to do It, and Why. We propose to do and provide certain things for the Client, who, in turn, is to do and provide certain things for Us. As stated previously, there are 4 significant points, which are:

1. What is going to happen? (Scope)

2. When will it happen? (Schedule)

3. When will we get paid? (Terms)

4. How much will it cost? (Price)

When we have agreement on those four, we have a contract.

SCOPE

It is correct to state Inclusions and Exclusions. We must never underestimate people's ability to misinterpret things. Assumptions are made in the more formal bidding processes that the phrase "Per Plans and Specifications" says it all. It does not. It may come close if certain customs of our trade area are widely understood and applied. Due respect is in order for those established customs. That is, if certain Items are generally expected to be included in a Proposal for Architectural Millwork (for example), we should be prepared to furnish those Items. If we have good and sufficient reason to not include the Items, that is our right. But we should advise one and all clearly and specifically. In all communications, people deserve facts, not riddles. If we are Proposing to furnish woodwork described in a certain Section, we will be expected to furnish it as described. If we Propose to furnish products listed in other Sections, we must be clear about that, as well.

Some restraint is advised in the description of the Scope. We don't have to call out every cabinet, and every stick of trim, but we can make a thorough List with minimum detail. Gray areas appear when we Install. Not all Specifications are clear on who furnishes and installs backing and blocking. Factory Finishing can raise questions, too. I've read Specifications inviting us to Finish, while instructing the painting contractor in that area, as well. Part of the Service we offer includes clarification on these questions. We want our clients to view us as part of the solution, not as part of the problem.

THE SCHEDULE

It is not our place to Schedule the Job, at this point. However, it's not too soon to establish a flow of events concerning our Proposal. We certainly can, and must stipulate the *life* of the Proposal. 30 days is fairly standard, but if part of the package is an early completion date, and a "fast-track" schedule, 15 days might be appropriate. Our words and actions should demonstrate that we understand and respect schedules. We can also indicate our expectation to do business with people who *also* respect schedules … "We know how to do our part, if you know how to do your part". We're not pushy, just professional. We stand ready to serve and deliver. We do not enjoy waiting while they fiddle and faddle. We don't say it like that (necessarily) but that's what our Proposal should convey. We should stress again and again: We are selling a Time Slot, and things are really going to move. Production will be flowing, and Money will be flowing.

THE TERMS

Here we state our Terms and what our Policies are. Again, we should respect customs of the area, but not absolutely. I recommend pushing the limit all the time, here. Fair is fair. They can't have it all, and neither can we. Too many times, though, we give too much. We won't always get all we ask for, but we surely will never get *more* than we ask. In other words, ASK! We can ask for money up front. We must with many kinds of clients … homeowners, interior designers, any private party.

40 to 50% up front is fine. Then, 50 or 40% more on delivery, and the remaining 10% upon completion of installation. Most general contractors aren't accustomed to paying money up front, but they should. Ask for a 10% "Mobilization" fee to get the Job started. They get it … why shouldn't we? We should always get prompt monthly progress payments, too. Not just for work delivered … for work produced, and also materials purchased. (Different rules govern, but generally, if we offer a Bill of Sale, along with a Certificate of Insurance, there should be no legal hangup for anyone.) Shop Drawings will be billed when completed, too. Contractors may not understand … Architects surely do. Clauses about halting shipments for lack of payment should stay in. You'll get whimpering about "delay of Job" and crap like that. Don't be intimidated. Some characters out there are slow to grasp the simple truth: We are trading Woodwork for Money. We deliver the Woodwork, as stipulated, and they deliver the Money, as stipulated. What's so difficult to understand?

THE PRICE

Our Selling Price has been carefully computed. It can now be clearly and boldly stated. It probably won't include sales taxes, so clearly exclude them.

One lump Sum is best. Avoid long "laundry lists" of individually priced Items. If they didn't want them all ... why did they ask for the Quote? If they want to buy some here, and some across the street, then it's a whole new ball game. We are always willing to help solve budget constraints, and can do so when we are assured of the Job and are wrapping up the details. But it's foolish to try to negotiate down to budget while the Bidding is still going on. A long list of priced Items that they can shop around does us no good whatsoever, and doesn't really help them in the long run. Try not to do it. Same for "Unit" prices, and Alternates. We should stipulate time limits on the quotes, and in the case of "Unit" prices we can set minimum quantities along with time limits. Who needs an order for 1 Item 2 years after the Job is over?

We can adopt as many Policies as it takes to communicate and enforce Terms, or Pricing. We can do so with the intent to enforce them all, or merely use them for negotiating purposes. Nor are we naive enough to believe that our rules will never be broken by our clients. There are very few absolutes. Point is, we not only have a right, we have a duty to inform people what we want and need in the way of terms. Then, at least, they can't say, "You never told us that". Remember, all those points are a part of the Price. If they must have $100 shaved off the Price, they'll have to change the Scope, or improve the Terms, or something.

We don't have to offer the same Price to everybody. If we're bidding 4 contractors, we can have 4 different Prices, if we want to. Someone has suggested the Federal Trade Commission might not like this. They have rules about pricing when it comes to manufactured products. I'm convinced we're home free on this one, however. What we're selling is actually a different product to each contractor. When you consider all the exchanges concerning perfecting the Contract, handling the Submittals and Approvals, working out the Schedule, coordinating the Field Measurements, and scheduling Deliveries (and/or Installation), there can be a vastly different experience with each Client. Then there are the submittals for payments, the payments, the punch lists, etc. at close out. All of these exchanges can range from wretched to sublime. Who do you suppose has earned the better

Price? Well, if they've earned it, why not give it to them? Sometimes the up-charge for being a dork is called a "turkey tax". Unfortunately, sometimes the "turkey tax" must be applied to general contractors, other customers, even a few design professionals.

GETTING THE CONTRACT

For many Jobs, getting to a Contract is not so tedious. If we're doing a few cabinets for a homeowner, we won't have many pages of plans, specifications, or scope. The key, here is to make sure the expectations are correct. Many of these good folks would be thoroughly confused by Drawings and other documents. Show them with renderings or photographs they can comprehend. When we can show samples of the finish, the species, the style, and the hardware, we should be in good shape. They don't need surprises … neither do we.

Our Proposal can become the Contract. As the nearby Example Proposal shows, we can have a place for the client to signify acceptance. Other times a client may come back with an entirely different document. They may not even refer to our document. A very prominent contract lawyer told us at a seminar that our proposal terms are still valid and enforceable if our Proposal was *the* communication in the transaction. In other words if our Proposal is the *only* way they could have received the Quote, then by accepting the Quote, the Client is accepting the Proposal in its entirety. I'm no lawyer, and I'm not giving legal advice, but it makes sense to me. Again, we have something to talk about. If they accept it, they can hardly deny seeing it.   And if they saw it they shouldn't be surprised about the Conditions outlined. If they have serious problems with any of the Terms or Conditions, they should inquire before they proceed. If they come back with entirely different Terms and Conditions, some extremely serious discussions must be held before anything is signed.

A PROFESSIONAL PROPOSAL ALL THE WAY

Get the Proposal there on time. A Proposal received after the fact may not (probably shouldn't) be considered. Help direct it to the right place. Note

PROPOSAL

Whatever Woodwork, Inc.

Date

TO: _____   Architect _____

_____

_____   _____

JOB: _____

_____

All quotation and agreements contingent upon fires, strikes, priorities and other causes beyond our control.

Greetings:

We propose to furnish the "Woodwork" in accordance to the plans and specifications, for the Project described above, Plan Set No._____ including Addenda_____ and as listed below, subject to conditions shown on reverse side of this sheet, excluding sales tax, tailgate delivered to the job.

Base Price $_____

INCLUDED:

Exclusions: Bucks, grounds, furring, screens, flooring, siding, painting, priming, stairwork, metal or composition, metal doors, sash, frames, glass, chalk or tackboard, fabric, wood folding doors, finish hardware, installation, weatherstripping. Liquidated damages. (See also reverse side.)

Terms and Conditions:

1. Proposal good for 30 days.
2. If this contract is not installed by us, we are to be considered material suppliers and must be paid in full in 30 days. No retainage allowed.
3. Carrying charges will be billed at 1-1/2 % per month.
4. Liquidated damages will not be allowed.
5. Work in progress cannot be changed without a written change order.
6. No backcharges will be allowed without our written consent.
7. Clerical errors subject to correction.
8. Delivery dates shall be according to written Schedule and contingent upon contractor/owner/architect activities occurring by critical dates. Should job be unable to take delivery at scheduled time, we shall be entitled to payment for such materials upon presentation of proper certification and insurance.

Respectfully submitted,

_____   Accepted_____

By_____   By_____

Title_____   Title_____Date_____

READ REVERSE SIDE!

(A) The term "WOODWORK" as used herein includes all the finish woodwork--both interior and exterior-exposed to view after the building is completed, except the items excluded in Article (B), and this proposal is based on furnishing such Woodwork unless specifically mentioned as being omitted, it being understood that installation is not a part of this Contract.

(B) IMPORTANT: THE FOLLOWING ITEMS ARE NOT CONSIDERED 'ARCHITECTURAL WOODWORK' AND DO NOT FORM A PART OF THIS PROPOSAL UNLESS SPECIFICALLY NOTED ON THE REVERSE SIDE.

1. Cabinets, brand named or kitchen
2. Chalk, cork or bulletin boards (except wood trim, furnished loose, unmitered)
3. Compositions, except caps for columns and items to be shop fastened to millwork items.
4. Fabrics, felt or soft plastics
5. Fencing materials
6. Flooring, duck boards and catwalks
7. Folding or sliding brand name doors
8. Frames and pocket doors for folding and overhead doors
9. Glass, glazing or mirrors
10. Hardware. (nor the preparation for installation)
11. Insulation, cement or asbestos materials
12. Labor at job site
13. Laminated trusses, arches, rafters or beams
14. Metal items of any kind
15. Metal louvers, grilles, or their installation
16. Metal molding used with materials supplied by others
17. Overhead doors or their jambs
18. Plastic items other than laminated plastics
19. Priming, back-painting, finishing or preservative treatment
20. Repairs or alterations to existing materials
21. Roof decking, exposed
22. Shop notching or cutting on shelving and battens furnished loose.
23. Stair horses
24. Temporary millwork
25. Weatherstripping
26. Wood shingles, shakes or siding
27. Wood, rough bucks, furring, and other materials not exposed to view.
28. X-Ray and refrigerator doors
29. Dock Bumper

(C) Flush plywood panelwork furnished in commercial size panels unless shop work is required on edges.

(D) Terms are net, due 30 days from date of Invoice. We reserve the right to stop delivery of materials if payments are not made when due us. Payments not made in full in 30 days will subject the balance to a finance charge of 1-1/2% per calendar month or fraction thereof until paid.

(E) This proposal expires 30 days from date, unless extended by agreement.

(F) Upon acceptance, as evidenced by signatures of the purchaser and an officer of our company, this proposal becomes a valid contract. If other contract forms are used, this proposal **automatically becomes a part of any contract into which we might enter for the work covered--**whether or not contract states that woodwork will be as defined in this quotation.

(G) All contracts are contingent upon strikes, breakdowns, fires, or other causes beyond our control, and are accepted subject to approved credit.

(H) Work once in progress cannot be changed except at the expense of the purchaser. We will price and obtain written approval of all changes prior to manufacture.

(I) No back charges will be allowed without our prior written consent, and will not be considered if not within the meaning of our guarantee.

(J) Clerical errors subject to correction.

GUARANTEE

ALL ARCHITECTURAL WOODWORK is guaranteed to be of good material and workmanship and free from defects which render it unserviceable for the use for which it was intended. Natural variations in the color or texture of the wood are not to be considered as defects. The quality of ARCHITECTURAL WOODWORK is safeguarded while it is in our possession. To be projected by our guarantee, our products MUST NOT be stored in damp warehouses or placed in moist or freshly plastered building. They MUST NOT be subjected to abnormal heat or dryness. Permanent type heat must be in operation a sufficient length of time to "cure" building before any woodwork or doors are delivered on the site. (Temporary type heat such as salamanders are not considered by us as "drying" type heat.) Woodwork must be inspected upon arrival and all claims or complaints must be filed before painters' finish is applied. ALL DOORS must be properly sealed on all surfaces, **including top and bottom edges,** to prevent absorption of moisture. We will not be responsible for defects resulting from neglect of these precautions.

We agree within a period of one year after delivery date, to repair or replace (in the white, unfinished), without charge any woodwork which is defective within the meaning of this guarantee. We do not agree to be responsible for any work which was not originally performed by us. We do not agree to pay charges for finishing or installing replaced woodwork. This guarantee is not effective if goods are repaired or replaced without first obtaining our written consent.

on the envelope what the Job is, and when it Bids. Direct it to the person in charge of the Bid. Follow up, if there's time, to make sure it arrived and there are no questions. And then follow up, all the way.

Treat Proposals as you do your teenagers out on the town. You want to know who they're with, what they're doing, and when they will be back. Network with all players possible to learn who's low, and the prognosis. (Which general contractor is apparent low, and is it within budget?) Then, regardless of final outcome, we need to know where we are. This may take some negotiating. Some folks don't want to take the time to help with this. Some even say it's against policy (which is silly). Remind our contractor friends that they always get to analyze and compare their efforts, and it improves their bidding performance. We need and deserve the same. On occasion, I've suggested that if they won't make an effort to assist, perhaps they don't need our Bids, either. This seems to get their attention. They always want all the Bids they can get … even if they don't know what to do with them. Develop good contacts for this, and take good care of them. Don't impose. If they're busy, call later. Assist them with information, as well. Do all this ethically. Don't ask for, or give, information that is out of line with proper conduct. This network, and these contacts, are all built on integrity. Don't lie and don't cheat … and don't do business with those who do. A big gap in information gathering: Most woodworkers are not diligent enough in finding out how much money we left on the table. In other words, how much too low were we? That's something we should want to know. My woodworker friends can go on and on about how we lost Bids by 2%, 3%, etc., but never seem to know when we were 5%, 10%, or whatever, low. Possible reasons: We don't really want to know. People won't tell us for fear we'll raise Prices. Both understandable … neither valid. Find out.

KEEP A LOG

Log all our efforts in Bidding (including Prospects coming up). A loose-leaf notebook works well. Once again, a Form produced with a Spreadsheet is recommended. If we pencil in information about who we bid to, who we bid against, how everybody did (as much as we can determine), then entry into the Spreadsheet can open the opportunity for useful statistics. Our percentage of success, for example. Both as to number of Proposals, and as to dollar amounts. Our success with certain prospects, with certain design professionals, against certain competitors. Many possible patterns can emerge. Certain people always steer work to their friends or relatives. They may even be using us as a pricing source, never intending to buy anything. It is useful to know those things. Types of Jobs might not be right for us. The reasons can vary. We may be out-machined, or out-manned, or certain companies have determined to gobble up all that type of work preparing to raise prices, later. Or they don't know how much it really costs them to build something. Or they can't add. Whatever the reason, we would be well advised to avoid those types of Jobs for a time until the climate changes.

Our knowledge of such things can improve out success percentage. What should the percentage be? Between 20% and 25% for all contacts, including everything from negotiated work to hard bid Jobs. If we get more, we're working too cheap. Any less, were looking at the wrong Jobs, or talking to the wrong people. The percentages assume reasonable management and production skills, and sufficient efficiency to provide quality and value to the customer. All of which can occur at many levels of sales volume, number of people, and number of machines. It is a function of diligence, prudence, and work.

A PROJECT OUT FOR BID

A further observation of the Bid market is in order. On any given day, there are many projects out for bid. We may be invited to bid, or the project may be listed in a trade publication or posted in a plan room. Which means many opportunities for us to get a piece of business and make some money. This would also appear to satisfy an earlier stipulation about "finding out what they want, and then going back and building it". A specifier makes documents available stipulating the items needed, along with quality requirements and other qualifications. The Woodworker says, "Sure, we can do that" and responds by studying the documents, figuring the cost, putting a price on it and forwarding the formal proposal. From a Marketing standpoint it's a good start, but we haven't quite closed the gap. The specifications are written on the basis of a *perception* of what woodworkers can do. It might even be more appropriate to say *a perception of what the average woodworker* can do. Throughout this whole Bidding Process, we must be alert to every opportunity to educate all the people involved

THE "LOW BIDDER" EFFECT

One reason the perception of the average is stilted (widening the gap even further) is the Low Bidder Effect. Each time (and it happens much too often) the Low Bidder turns in a shabby performance, the perception (and the expectation?) is lowered. Heavy sighs, along with mutterings, "You just can't get good woodwork, anymore" are heard.

We know better of course. You and I know better, because we hear the opposite. I would guess most readers have heard the happy gasp of a specifier or other client within the past few days. "I didn't know craftsmanship like this was possible any more. This is beautiful!" So we bask in this friendly aura of adulation and feel good. That is, until a sad realization dawns, "If people don't know craftsmanship is available, how much business are we losing, and how much is it costing us?"

Specifiers and Owners have all kinds of methods to prevent the delivery of sub-standard woodwork. If they're too lazy to apply those methods, they don't deserve much sympathy. What's to be done? The best way we can influence, and hopefully improve the situation is by continuing our education process. We can gently, but firmly, remind our specifier friends of the tools they possess. "Clearly specify what you want and expect (I tell them) … then accept nothing less … I mean NOTHING less."

(What we're thinking, but probably shouldn't say, "Don't send me gold-plated specifications when you and your client are willing to accept garbage. If you're willing to go "cheap" and accept anything … tell me up front so I won't waste my time bidding the job.")

"But," they say, "we had to open the building in three weeks. There was no time to reject it and start over. What could we do?"

(Actually they could do their job, is what they could do.) But stay calm, and suggest this: If the woodworker is new to you, check them out! It's best to check their plant, and their work, before a Purchase Order is offered. But if that opportunity is past, you still have time. Watch for the Shop Drawings. (Do they even show up?) Late Shop Drawings, or poorly executed Shop Drawings should raise a red warning flag. Do not, EVER, assume that specifications rule. I've known (so-called) woodworkers who don't bother to read the specifications. Go to the plant. See the work in process. See how they perform. There are many, many opportunities to find out what's happening before the product shows up on the job. In short: DO YOUR JOB!

Actual statements, I've heard from "supposed" woodworkers:

"The contractor asked me to bid the cabinets. He knows what kind of cabinets we build. Why should I bother to wade through all that paper? We just build cabinets."

"What do I care if the specs said rift white oak? It's too expensive, and besides we had a lot of plain red oak on hand. I said we were bidding plain red oak, so what's the problem?" (The problem in one instance, the owner said, "Gee, we could save some money", and the architect said, "Well, if that's what you want ..." and 5 other woodworkers totally wasted thousands of dollars worth of time and effort.)

We would probably note such conduct in our Bidding Log. We may not want to Bid with them at all ... either the Specifier, or the Owner.

It's not a totally dreary picture. These things can and do happen, but not often. I mention them merely to reduce dismay when they do occur. We should still approach each contact expecting good outcomes and a satisfactory performance all around. We must make sure we never cut corners and start the cheating process. Approach each situation as an opportunity to teach a little, and learn a little. This is Marketing. Develop a superior Product, and then tell folks about it. Tell, and Listen. Teach, and Learn.

BIDDING PROCESS SUMMARY

This, then is the Bidding Process.

1. Make contacts and keep in touch.

2. Hone that Evaluation process. Carefully "qualify" each Bidding opportunity, and each Prospect. Spend time where it will be Profitable. Gently insist that all Bidders can read Specifications. Let's all be Bidding the same Job.

3. List meticulously. Learn to do it right, and then speed it up. Develop as many "Forms" or other tools to improve speed, accuracy, and confidence.

4. Keep refining the Costing / Pricing function. Get that feedback from the Plant. Accumulate Material quantities for quantity discounts from vendors. Study Waste Factors. Check those Formulas, and keep checking all the arithmetic.

5. Present a professional Proposal which states the pertinent facts clearly and concisely. Then follow it up. Be available to help with the final decision. Don't waste time running down the competition. Just be the Best, and then keep reminding everybody.

6. Learn to negotiate. Bring back the Order.

Then, bask in the Joy of Accomplishment.

7

Managing

Manage, Managing, Manager, and Management are all familiar terms. Definitions, however, are elusive. Our knowledge of the Discipline of Management is gradually growing, but we still have a long way to go. We know that "Manager" means much more than "Boss", although many definitions still stop there. We also know that Management can shape a business and also cause events to be shaped. Good Management can make things happen. Management doesn't have to wait for things to happen.

Woodwork Managers manage People, Situations, and Events. At the Top, there should be 3 Managers.

> One has the Responsibility and the Authority for everything on the PLANT side of the Door.
> One has the Responsibility and the Authority for everything on the OFFICE side of the Door.
> The other one has the Responsibility and Authority for the whole Operation … and the final say.

DO WE NEED A BOSS? YES!

The Top Manager must have the authority to instruct: "You will do this. You will do it this way. You will do it now." Curiously, once the fact is established, he or she seldom has to issue instructions in that way. But everyone on the premises needs to understand … the authority *does* exist. This is not a function of owning the most stock. Stock ownership does not equate with Management know-how. This manager doesn't even have to own any stock. This Manager **knows what a woodwork business should be,** and has the determination to take us there, and keep us there. This structure is recommended because it works.

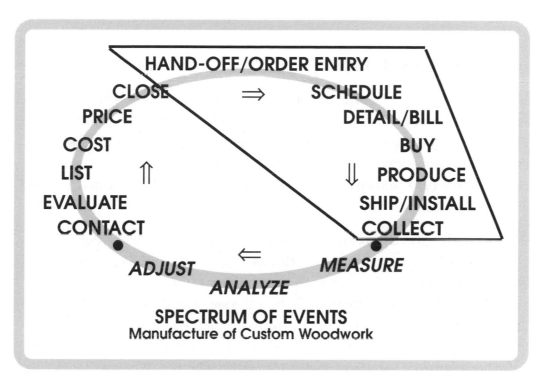

SPECTRUM OF EVENTS
Manufacture of Custom Woodwork

The primary responsibilities of top management, would include:
1. Define the Purpose of the Company.
2. Identify or Create Customers and Serve them Well.
3. Find and Maintain the proper balance of People, Plant, and Machines.
4. Innovate
5. Set Policies.
6. Follow Policies.
7. Pay Taxes.
8. Give Bonuses.

Actually, everything else that happens at our Plants is part of Management, and in fact can best be done by People who understand, and are capable of, Management.

The nearby recurrence of the Spectrum of Events reminds of all the Events involved in Managing the Project. Each deserves our study. Our Managers can learn from the Spectrum, as well. It reminds of the Tasks, and also demonstrates our interdependence on one another.

YOURSELF, FIRST

Woodworkers first learn to manage themselves. Next, they learn to manage others. Last, but not least, *some* woodworkers learn to manage the people who manage people. The last step is the toughest, and most often doesn't get done very well. I think our self-confidence, plus our ability to step up to a Task and do it, get in our way on this one. We can do it, so why do we need anyone else?

We misjudge the situation. We don't realize how many tasks there are to be done, or how their number continues to grow. And we don't realize how quickly we dead-end our growth possibilities by trying to do everything ourselves. This Book attempts to show the sense and the symmetry to the process of Delegating, and developing more competence and confidence on the premises. Who cares if we can do it all? Let's get off the ego trip. Plenty of others can do what we do, and many can do it better. When we learn this fundamental truth, we can begin to be top Managers.

LEADERS?

Managers are not necessarily Leaders. Leaders are not necessarily Managers. Leaders can generally be taught the skills of Management. We don't yet know how to teach Leadership. We're learning a few things about Leaders. They seem to have a special sense, or vision, about new concepts and new ideas. And they seem to possess a stronger ability to generate interest and enthusiasm … to engage other people in a new venture, or cause. Whereas Managers can do a superb job administrating policies and practices already established, a Leader might be more comfortable testing newer methods. We do know enough about management practices to assist managers in getting comfortable with the new and untried, to balance risks and gains. We can proceed quite well without establishing a quota for a certain number of Leaders. We can use them, all right, provided we can make Managers out of them.

And even if you and I don't possess the magic of Leadership, we can work with people by learning to Negotiate. Charismatic, or not, we can get the job done. Many times each day we need to deal with people. There is the need to establish (or re-establish) communication and a working relationship with someone. Whether we're selling, or buying … exchanging new information, or giving directions, we need to learn to do it well. And, that means talking a bit, listening a bit, and being aware of the other person's perceptions and reservations.

We will speak more on subject of Management in the *Operations* Section. This brief introduction and overview is designed to move us into the act of managing a Project through our Plant. The Business of guiding a Job to a successful conclusion involves Managing 3 Flows.

1. Flow of Information.
2. Flow of Materials.
3. Flow of Events.

We've already begun the Flow of Information, it began when we **Listed** the Job. The **Hand-off/Order Entry** function perfects and shapes the Information Flow. **Scheduling** provides the discernible plan for the 3 Flows. When we do the **Buying**, we stimulate the flow of Materials. Of course, **Detailing** (Drawings) and **Billing** (Material Bills) contribute to all 3 Flows. So it goes on through **Production** and **Delivery** (with or without **Installation. Collection** actually began at the Contact and Evaluation stage, but, of course, is enhanced all the way by our professional performance.

Hand-Off/Order Entry

WE GOT THE JOB! NOW, WHAT?

Among the joys and triumphs in the woodworking business, the receipt of a Purchase Order has to rank pretty high. But, as we celebrate the occasion, let's maintain our perspective. Go ahead … enjoy it. It's perfectly all right to bask in success, but then let's get to work. The preliminary bout has been won, but the main event is about to begin.

There is much to be done. The sooner we begin, the better. All the way through this process of managing a project, we need to anticipate. Anticipate every event, every task, everything which needs to be done, or could interrupt or delay. Again and again, we will face questions which have good options, today … fewer tomorrow … very few next week … virtually none in two weeks. **Let's make today count.**

THE HANDOFF

The Hand-off part of the Hand-off / Order Entry event refers to the conveying of all information from the Costing / Pricing / Closing function to the person who will manage the project. The receiver of the Hand-off will be guiding the flow of events on through to a successful conclusion. This should be the *responsibility* of one individual. The Scheduling, Detailing, Piece Billing, Purchasing, Production, Delivery and/or Installation, and the Collection should all be directed by one person. The person will have the Authority and the Responsibility to do so, and will be held Accountable.

The manager doesn't actually perform every task. The manager doesn't draw every line, or order every stick, or do the machining, etc. The manager directs, instructs, and also makes sure that everything gets done … correctly, and on time. The manager makes sure we deliver what we promised.

The Hand-off function ... or ritual, if you will ... is extremely important. It is necessary, even if the project will be managed by the same person who priced it. It's a shifting of focus, of emphasis, and of priorities. We must check every Item on the Scope sheet. Do we have everything? Are the quantities correct? Did we anticipate the Schedule properly? Huddle with the principal players who will be involved. Depending on the size of the Job it could be quite a huddle.

CHECK EVERYTHING

Any shift from the usual needs everyone's attention. New Materials, possible Supply problem, tight Schedule, unusual fabrication techniques ... whatever. It's a great time for everyone to walk all the way around the Job, looking at it closely from every angle. Are there ways to simplify, speed it up, purchase better, etc.? What about the Engineering? Are there inconsistencies ... ambiguities? Will we need a conference with Architects? Can we make partial Submittals? How will Change Requests and Change Orders be handled. Who will be authorized to approve them? (Includes our store and their store). Scrutinize that Schedule. If they sat on our Proposal for weeks, can we still Buy and Produce without stress? All in-puts are valuable, at this time. And, it gets everyone thinking and anticipating. Altogether, a useful exercise.

The next order of business is to "perfect" the Contract. Remember, we said to focus on the 4 principal parts ... Scope, Schedule, Terms, and Price.

1. Make sure they're ordering the same things we quoted.

2. Can we pin down the Schedule? Are there any surprises?

3. Do they understand and recognize our Terms?

4. Check to see if it's the same Price.

5. Examine every facet ... Warranties, Retainage, Final Payment, Punch Lists, Access to Premises, Lifts and Hoists, etc., check EVERYTHING!

Now is the time to do it. It is the very best time, because everybody's smiling. The sun is shining. We're all happy to have the Job. The mood is ideal. They WANT us to do the Job. We're low, or else we have the "best" bid because of our quality and service. Either way WE'RE THE ONE, and it's the perfect time to talk. It is the ONLY time to talk. They'll agree to Terms, today, that they won't even discuss down the road. On the other hand, when we accept, sign, and return a Purchase Order ... the options are gone. It's over. We don't have anything to talk about.

Policy Note: Purchase Orders should not be signed by just anyone. Establish ground rules. Who can sign? For what amount? Stick with it.

ORDER ENTRY

How is an Order Entered at your store? Where is it Entered? Who Enters it? Who all knows we have it, at all. It's an embarrassingly weak area for woodworkers. It may appear as the name of the Job, but without a reference to size, time-frame or anything else to indicate what sort of a commitment we have made. Sometimes I see a list of Jobs and their Prices, but no one can produce a list of Items which are to be furnished. What does it consist of? Is it Casework, Moldings, Buyouts, or what?

Strong recommendation: The same day we have acceptance of our Proposal (or our acceptance of their Purchase Order) the Job should show up in the Job Schedule Book, and on the Timeline Chart or Schedule Board. Of course there will be a File containing all the information, but the facts need to be on display for one and all to see at a glance. We can all take pride in securing the Order, and we can all be aware of the new responsibilities the Order entails.

MORE FORMS TO HELP US WORK SMARTER

Nearby are some Forms which can be useful for Order Entry. The Job Schedule and Timeline Form, along with its (reverse-side) companion the Job Supply Schedule, have been staples in my repertoire for lots of years. They are being replaced by some of my computer Forms, now, but they remain useful worksheets to assemble and display pertinent information.

JOB SCHEDULE and TIMELINE

Job Name:	Job No.:
Contract Acceptance Date:	Completion Date:
Job Address:	Their Job No.:
	Contact - Office:
Bill to:	Phone:
Attention:	Fax:
Address:	Contact - Job:
	Phone:
	Fax:
	Pager:

Detail/Bill *Red*   Finishing   *Black*
Production   *Blue*   Installation *Green*

Jan	Feb	Mar	Apr	May	Jun	Jul	Aug	Sep	Oct	Nov	Dec

	ITEM	MACHINE	ASSEMBLE	FINISH	INSTALL	SHIP
1						
2						
3						
4						
5						
6						
7						
8						
9						
0						
1						
2						
3						
4						
5						
6						
7						
8						
9						
0						

JOB SUPPLY SCHEDULE

ITEMS SHORT LEAD		QUANT	SUPPLIER	ORDER DATE	P O NO.	PROMISED	FOLLOW UP
1							
2							
3							
4							
5							
6							
7							
8							
9							
LONG LEAD							
0							
1							
2							
3							
4							
5							
6							
7							
8							
9							
0							

CHANGE LOG

Change Items	Received	Response	Expires	Accepted	Amount

SPECIAL ITEM CHECKLIST

FLUSH DOORS	FIRE RET PROD	SHEAVES	FABRIC
SPECIAL DOORS	PANELING	TRACK	LIGHTING
LUMBER	HINGES	LOCKS	SP ADHESIVES
PANEL GOODS	PULLS	CATCHES	SP HARDWARE
PLASTIC LAMINATE	SLIDES	GLASS	JOINT FASTENERS
MOLDINGS	SHLF STD	PLEX	K D FITTINGS
VENEERS	BRACKETS	LEXAN	
METALS	CLIPS		

And they're great if you're not computerized, yet. They're further evidence of the transition from pencil and paper, so they're good as stand alone pieces, or as part of the whole system. These Forms work great in a loose-leaf notebook. Instead of information buried in a file, somewhere, this puts it out where we can see what's going on. And we can make as many copies as needed. One notebook will contain all the Jobs. All managers have the Jobs they're running in *their* notebooks. Of course, they're responsible for keeping them up-to-date. Company policy spells out how copies are distributed, and to whom.

Make no mistake. **This procedure *saves* time.** It does not *take* time. The first one or two may require a bit of extra effort, but after that, we're on the plus side. We're only using information we must gather, anyway. The only difference is the method of display. Another mistake: Don't buy the notion that other team members need only be informed just as the Project moves into their particular area. They need to know about the Project as soon as it's signed. That way, they can exercise their "Anticipating" process. Let everybody get information sooner, not later.

We should start the Job Schedule and Timeline Chart the same day we receive notice we have the Job. We should have a pretty firm Timeline quickly, so we can perfect the Contract. (Timelines will be further discussed in the next Chapter: *Scheduling*.) Any discrepancies or apprehensions can be addressed immediately. (Anticipate, remember?) That means a Job Schedule will be all ready to go into the Book, plus we'll have a "near-final" Timeline to put up, too.

BUT, THERE MAY BE QUESTIONS

Don't make the mistake of holding up the Order Entry because a few points are unclear, or unknown. We may not have the "final" answers, or "complete" information until the Job is completed. We could almost say we produce this sort of document just so it *can* be changed. Reason: with each new update, more questions are raised. Don't dismay, it's all part of the process ... and part of our job.

The other part of Order Entry is to set up the Budgets for Materials, Labor, and Buyouts ("Buyouts" includes merchandise, Installation, or any Subcontract work). This is the start of Job Costing which will provide facts for review and analysis at the end of the Job. It can also provide Job Progress information. Material Purchase Orders will be deducted from the Material Budget. Payroll information will show how much to draw from the Labor Budget. Same, for Buyouts. This can be done with a Computer Database in a logical and straightforward manner. This information can be used for Progress Billing to invoice the customer, and also be available to any and all Managers. (More on Job Costing in the *Money* Section.)

9

Scheduling

Who does the Scheduling at your Store? The front office? The plant? The finishing room? Don't know for sure? Sad to say, in many woodwork companies, the immediate priorities are determined by an angry Customer. It's true. The ringing phone, plus the loudest voice, sets the schedule in an embarrassing number of companies. What do you suppose that does to efficiency ... and productivity ... and profitability?

All right, then, who *should* be doing the Scheduling? And when? Best answers: The Designated Project Manager (with a little help from the rest of the team) does the Scheduling ... and Scheduling begins as soon as we get the Order. I used the term "project manager", to identify the person of record charged with the responsibility to put the Job on track, and keep it there. Titles are not important. If you want to call it something else,

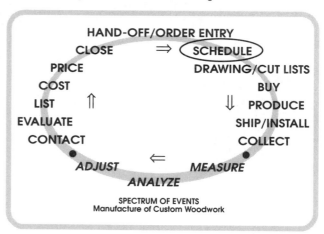

that's fine. Point is, guiding a Project through to a successful conclusion begins by setting the Schedule correctly and quickly.

THE STRUCTURE

Developing a Schedule is Management's chance to excel. It's a top-ranked challenge, but also a top-ranked opportunity. It requires a Structure. Everyone needs to understand *who* is going to do it, *when* they're going to do it, *how* they're going to do it, and *why* it is to be done a certain way. The way it is done must be a practical, sensible, discernible process that works.

And the fact that it works means that it can be believed. And if it works, and everyone believes it works, the customers will no longer override the system all the time.

Scheduling begins with the Timeline. Timelines have been around a long time, so we're not presenting a revolutionary idea. However, the Timeline concept here described has been adapted to woodworker's needs. The concept has also been tested and perfected with ongoing use by woodworkers.

A Timeline is a horizontal Line (representing the duration of the Project) superimposed over vertical lines representing time frames (weeks or months). Positioning on the vertical lines (really a calendar) can place the Timeline in "real" time. The Line begins when we get the Order. The Line ends when the Job is done. Say we receive an order today. The Line's length runs from today to the anticipated completion date. Don't agonize over the fact that the completion date may be adjusted ... plot the Line anyway. Since we are familiar with all aspects of the Job, we know precisely what events must occur, and pretty well what their sequence must be. Scheduling means determining WHEN all those events will occur.

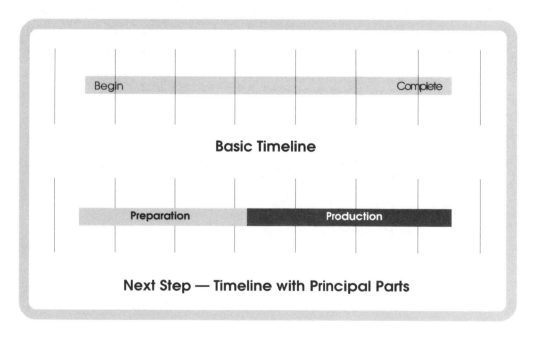

Basic Timeline

Next Step — Timeline with Principal Parts

THE PROJECT PERFORMANCE FORM

There is a useful Form (shown nearby) that can assist the development of our Timeline. It's useful enough, in its own right, for the information it sets out. Perhaps it is even more useful in establishing a document which is perfected, AND USED, by both Supplier (Woodworker) and Contractor (Client). It represents an early common endeavor in which we can mutually show our professionalism and our commitment to a successful project. Even if our client is unenthusiastic, at first, the Form's existence cannot be ignored. By requesting confirmation of the Dates, etc. as we see them, we quickly demonstrate 2 things. 1. We care about the Project and its execution. 2. We've thought it through and have a Plan. If the client fails to respond, and does not find reason to object, there is a reasonable assumption that the document has been accepted by default. Even if something should drift off-course later on, and the client denies acceptance of our Dates, at least we have shut off the whine, "You never told us".

Our purpose is not to put anyone on the spot, however. We earnestly want to elicit the correct information and expectations as early as possible so we can do our job well. In many cases, we could carry the Form to the client and fill it out, together. We could clear up any doubts about its use and purpose, and get better acquainted at the same time. The idea is to establish tentative Dates we can agree on, plus open the communication lines for updates as new information is discovered. This process validates our Timeline.

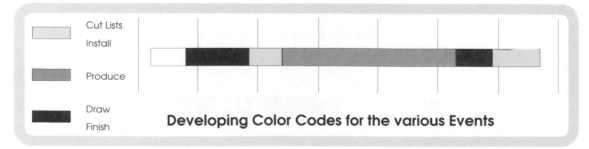

Developing Color Codes for the various Events

If we decide to set apart some of the Events (more than "Preparation" and "Production"), we can use colors, or shadings. The nearby Example uses 3

INFORMATION FOR SUCCESSFUL PROJECT PERFORMANCE
Confirming critical Dates and People, plus General Information.
Whatever Woodwork, Inc.

PLEASE Review and Confirm by: _____ **PLUS update as Required. Thank You.**

Project Name: _____   Address: _____

Contractor: _____   Address: _____

Key Dates: ## Special Notes:

Completion Date: _____   _____

Drawings, etc.Submitted: _____   _____

Approval Required by: _____   _____

Field Dimensions Taken: _____   _____

First Delivery: _____   _____

Second Delivery: _____   _____

Third Delivery: _____   _____

Contractor's Key People:

Project Manager: _____   Phone: _____ Fax: _____ Mobile: _____

Job Superintendent: _____   Phone: _____ Fax: _____ Mobile: _____

Accounts Payable: _____   Phone: _____ Fax: _____ Mobile: _____

Other: _____   Phone: _____ Fax: _____ Mobile: _____

Supplier's Key People:

Project Manager: _____   Phone: _____ Fax: _____ Mobile: _____

Accounts Receivable: _____   Phone: _____ Fax: _____ Mobile: _____

Other: _____   Phone: _____ Fax: _____ Mobile: _____

General Information   ## Special Notes:

Progress Billing Invoices must be received by: _____   _____

Contractor's Bonding Agent: _____   _____

Supplier's Bonding Agent: _____   _____

AFFIRMATION AND APPROVAL

Supplier   ### Contractor

Approved by: _____   Approved by: _____

as (Title): _____   as (Title): _____

Company: _____   Company: _____

Date: _____   Date: _____

colors (or shades) to denote the principal parts. That would seem to be enough to show clearly where one Event ends and another begins. Our ultimate choice will be determined by the way we produce the Lines, and the way we place them on the Chart. During the preliminaries, however, pens or pencils of 3 colors can get us started.

A word about the amount of detail. As always, we counsel beginning with an uncomplicated approach, then adding features to increase the usefulness. Our job is not to produce charts. Our job is to successfully manage Projects. The Charts are tools to assist. The Rule: Any Chart, or other tool we develop MUST be working for us. **We are not working for it.** Actual users of the Charts will add useful ideas as we go along.

With the next Timeline Example (this page) we're getting close to the ideal Timeline. We're showing Principal Events, plus a few Key Dates, but we have avoided clutter. However, the possibilities remain virtually unlimited. The next Timeline Example (also nearby) demonstrates further

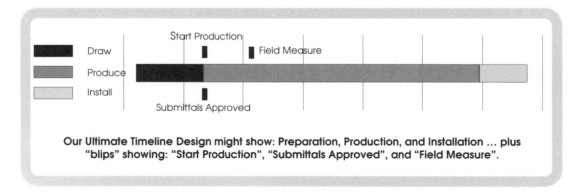

Our Ultimate Timeline Design might show: Preparation, Production, and Installation ... plus "blips" showing: "Start Production", "Submittals Approved", and "Field Measure".

possibilities. For example: We've set out Drawing, Cut Lists, Finishing, and Installation as separate Events. Many woodworkers do this because they seem to be areas of extra concern. Sometimes, they are "trouble" or "bottleneck" Events. Sometimes, they are partially (or entirely) done by others, therefore introducing another management aspect. As for Finishing and Installation ... if we do not even *do* one (or both) of these operations, they become a non-subject. Also, if the same people do the Manufacturing *and* the Finishing, then it's all Production.

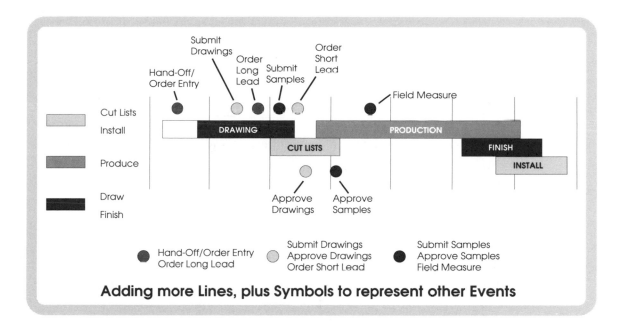

Adding more Lines, plus Symbols to represent other Events

It's best to leave Installation as an item if we're responsible for it. The recommendation holds true, even if some of the same Production people will do the Installing. We need to be alerted to the probable Time Slot, plus (if we're using the same people) be alerted to the loss of Production capability during that period. As for Drawing and producing Cut Lists, those Events vary quite a bit from place to place. Once again, if those Events are done by the same people, they probably don't need separation. We may be able to use the simplest Timeline: Preparation, and Production. That's fine.

WHEN TO DO WHAT?

A Key element in developing our Timeline is to "Count Back". Our keen powers of deductive reasoning lead to the discovery that if it takes 2 weeks to do something, we should start it 2 weeks before its completion date. The same superior intellect concludes that if it takes 2 weeks to get delivery on some hardware, we must order it 2 weeks before we have to have it. To those of you with a smirk on your face: If you think it's that obvious, why is it you have so much difficulty getting the work out the door on time? Sarcasm aside, there is a reason we struggle with Scheduling. It's because we forget how many things are going on simultaneously. We forget how many "trigger points" there are (specific moments when certain actions must be taken). We think we can keep track, but we forget how many distractions and interruptions there will be.

And we forget how many times we "assume" that since we ordered an item, it is *really* on its way to our Plant. We forget even the most *plausible* assumptions must be checked and followed up. Therefore, we need a mechanism in place which will give us an assist. Therefore, Timelines and Timeline Charts.

If we're Finishing and Installing, they'll be at the end. If it's "tailgate delivery", the delivery becomes the final step. The "count-back" for each Event gives us a **"Must-Start-Date".** That's what all our team members are looking for. Some Events can overlap ... some cannot. In other words, some Installation *could* possibly begin before the last pieces came out of the Finish Room. And the Finishing *could* begin before all pieces are out of Production. Other times either or both would be impractical. Job size could dictate. There's no point to mixing up special stain twice, when one mix could do. And if the Job is some distance away, we wouldn't want more travel time (and setup time) if one trip would do. So, in those instances ... no overlap.

Count-back from Complete Date for Installation's "must-start" date. Count back from Installation's "must-start" for Production's "must-start", etc. No Fudging, here. (That comes later.) Next calculations (and/or judgment calls) have to do with how much Production can be accomplished: before Field Measurements, before arrival of Long Lead items, before color selections, etc. Best: Try not to begin with less than complete Information and Materials. *Only in rare instances should we begin at all,* ***unless every piece of information and every scrap of material is in house!***

Yes, it *is* possible in this exercise to discover we should have started last week. (Don't ask how I know ... just take my word for it.) But, that possibility should be the very last thing to deter us from completing the exercise. So what if we discover some uncomfortable squeezes? Isn't it better to know sooner, than later? There are nearly always ways around all the surprises. But the options melt all too quickly. Today's options are better than tomorrow's.

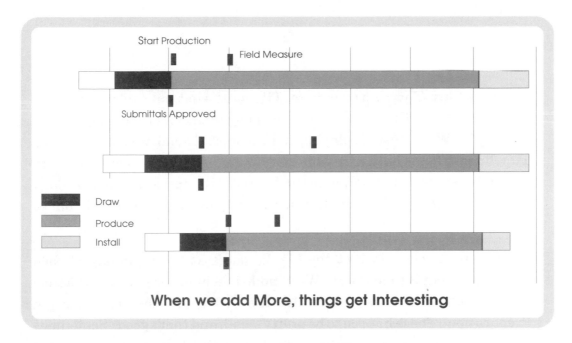

When we add More, things get Interesting

WHAT ABOUT THE OTHER JOBS?

Aha. Good question. Most of us project manager types can handle 1 Project at a time, even on our worst day. But, what about 3, or 5, or 10? As the nearby graphic suggests, "things get interesting". Also, we begin to see more value in the Timeline Chart. This modest start reveals a few things. With only 3 Jobs shown, we see things we could never see by looking at each Job separately.

We can begin to appreciate the build-up of workloads in certain areas. Drafters will be into No. 2, and even No. 3, before No. 1 has been completed. Although No. 3 Job is the last to come in, it must be completed first. Although Production starts are staggered, Production on all 3 Jobs must complete about the same time. Finishing Rooms start to get squeezed in this situation.

This graphic presentation surely must be the *most* effective way to demonstrate the influence of a new Job on all the rest. Even if all 3 of the Jobs were assigned to the same project manager, it may not be possible to grasp the whole picture. And, what if these 3 were all assigned to different managers. How would anybody truly understand all of the events which must occur this week … and the next … and their effect on one another? Sure, it's all in the files. But, who goes through each and every file every day?

All in the files. There's a point here. I'll repeat what was said in the *Hand-Off/Order Entry* Chapter: "We're only using information we must gather, anyway". We're just displaying it in a more useful way. Displaying Timelines creates only a tiny bit more work ... and the time saved with better decisions more than makes up for that. If our project managers don't "have time" to set up Timelines, it can only mean we're already out of control.

Please take a close look at the blank spaces at the beginning of each Timeline on our 3 Line Chart. We've added them to demonstrate the time period between the Day we receive the Order, and the Day we begin Preparation. These happen to be pretty small, and that's good. Sometimes they stretch out to ridiculous lengths. Generally, they are proportional to the length of the overall Job. That is: the more time we have, the more time we waste.

DON'T WASTE OUR BEST OPPORTUNITY

This particular time slot is one we shouldn't waste. We probably have more control of this space than any other. Most of us could pick up anywhere from 2 to 20 days, right here. Remember that struggle last month? We had to extend our best effort, but still shipped 1 day late. We weren't 1 day late because of what happened during the last week. We were 1 day late because we started late. In fact, virtually every Job has embarrassing amounts of wasted time up front. We can not only gain the 1, 3, or 10 days of actual earlier starting, we also improve our other options. Remember, with the benefit of the "option factor" we have many more opportunities. Jobs will go smoother, and be more profitable when we anticipate. Every management textbook talks about it: Act ... don't just React. The Timeline Chart is our chance to Act.

THE WHOLE YEAR ON THE WALL?

The Timeline concept has all kinds of flexibility. We can make the Charts any size we wish, and we can make as many as we wish. I urge you to install a large Master up on a wall. Make it prominent ... for all to see, use, and appreciate. In the Conference Room would be fine. A wide Hallway is all

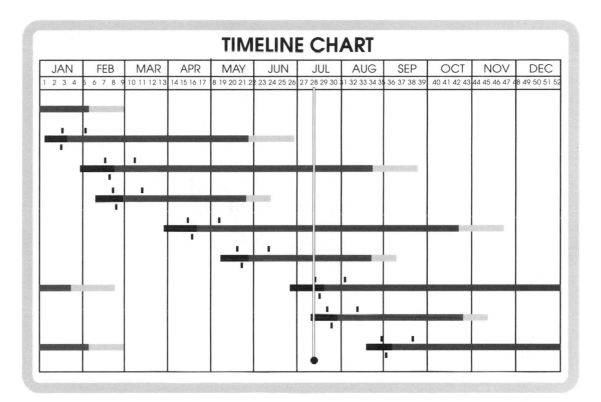

right, too. We will want the opportunity to hold meetings in front of the Chart, but they can be "mini-meetings". A "mini-meeting" where we don't even sit down can be most appropriate. We talk it over, make the necessary decisions, and then get back to work. No chatting ... no lounging ... all business. Distributing a number of small copies can be helpful, also. If we update the Chart on the computer each week, then various size copies will be accurate, yet easy to reproduce. We can omit the Job Names to maintain privacy. Each Timeline will be identified with the Job Number. The color of the Number can identify the project manager. Our prominent display can impress visitors without their knowing our business secrets.

The nearby Timeline Chart is an example of what a Wall Chart will look like. It shows some of the strengths in having a big Chart with complete up-to-date information. This Chart has all 12 months, and even the numbered weeks. This places all of our commitments into "real" time, including their relationships to one another. New Timelines are placed on the Chart as they come in. The Job Timeline is removed when all Work is complete, and all Payments received. The "Today Line" (a weighted rod, or cord moved to the right either weekly, or daily) clearly shows what should have happened. Everything to the left of the Today Line should have been accomplished.

The Today Line is another of the Chart's strengths. It's a priority setter. A glance tells us immediately what needs our attention. It boldly proclaims which managers are on top of their Jobs, and which ones aren't. If we are doing our Job, it's right out there for all the world to see. (Best way to show everyone how good we are.)

HOW MUCH TIME DO WE ALLOW?

It's time to talk about Timeline lengths. How do we determine the length of the Production (and other) segments of the Timeline? Each Timeline example we've shown has allocated a certain amount of time for Preparation, for Production, and for Installation. Some have shown allotments for Drawing, Cut Lists, and Finishing, as well. We need to examine proper methods for establishing those allocations. But first we need to look at some other things.

In order to keep the Timeline Concept sensible and workable, we need to understand the limitations. We also need to be clear on what we expect to accomplish. The first limitation is on Accuracy. When we begin to consider all the variables, we can drown in their complexity. Don't drown. Stay calm. When a new Project is getting under way, we're going to have to compromise with "would, should and could". We cannot stipulate what "will" be. The Timeline is NOT Production Planning. It is the preliminary to Production Planning. Production Planning will be discussed shortly.

But, managing a project means setting forth reasonable "would, should, could" parameters, and then systematically nudging them into reality. The evidence clearly shows that Scheduling and Planning can get us close. Drifting, and waiting to see what happens will not. The Timeline establishes quite clearly the total timeframe available. Our management skills will make the best use of the available time. But, we must not get bogged down in all the many details. We must focus on the essentials.

Timelines direct the Planning and Preparation on the Office Side of the Door. Although they alert the whole Organization to the extent of our commitments, and must be prepared as carefully as current information allows, they particularly direct office activities. At this stage in the process, we're arranging Events along each Timeline, plus fitting all Timelines into the whole scheme of things. Timelines must plan the Preparation sequences. Production Planning will plan the Production sequences.

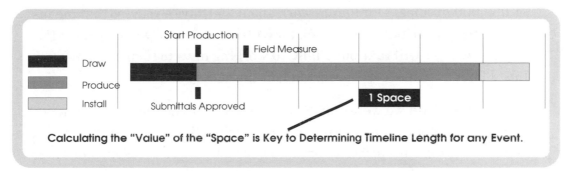

Calculating the "Value" of the "Space" is Key to Determining Timeline Length for any Event.

DETERMINING THE VALUE OF A "SPACE"

"A Space" refers to the distance between vertical Lines on our Timeline Chart. (The "calendar" portion.) First considerations: What percentage of the theoretical do we allocate, and how much of the allocation do we assign an individual Project? Since Timeline Charts do not plan Production, we shouldn't try to pack the Chart full. On the contrary since we are arranging many Events out into the future, it is prudent to be somewhat cautious about how full we pack things. Only carefully kept History can tell us precisely how full we should pack. My strong recommendation to newer users: Don't schedule more than 80%, at first. (Some woodworkers only Schedule 50%.) A flow of other small jobs, project changes, re-work of flawed products, vacations, holidays, flu epidemics … all sorts of surprises lurk out there to disrupt our plans. The theoretical Production Capability is seldom real.

Allocation for the individual Line depends on how many Projects we process at the same time. Our Example Wall Chart suggests 4 Projects under way at once. That will be a good place to start. We don't put all the small Jobs on the Chart. Actually, every Job follows a Timeline, no matter how small.

Practically, however, they don't need a Timeline on the board. Small Jobs can be Scheduled with the Production Planning Board. (Note: Small Jobs are another drain on the "Theoretical" capability.)

PRODUCTION

Try this: Let's say we have 10 people contributing Direct Labor to Production. National Industry Averages say 10 Crafters contribute the production for $1,000,000 in sales. Our Plants work about 250 days a year, so that means 10 Crafters contribute production for $4,000 sales each working day. Put another way, it will take our Plant 10 working days to turn out a $40,000 Job. (That's with everyone working on the same Job.)

However, we said we were only Scheduling 80% of the theoretical, and we were going to divide that allotment into four Timelines. Or, we can say we'll assign 2 Crafters to each of 4 Jobs and keep 2 Crafters in reserve for other contingencies. Re-stating the requirements for the $40,000 Job, with 2 People assigned, it will take 50 working days instead of 10. (10 weeks, instead of 2.)

Keep in mind: We're establishing broad approximate allotments. It is critical to good Scheduling, not because we must indicate what each Person is doing each day. It is critical to good Scheduling, because **it will keep us from allocating more than there is.** We're not saying that 2 People, and only 2 People, will work on this Project each and every day. We're saying the allotment must be made and respected. The allotment will be re-arranged for expediency and efficiency as the Job progresses. But, we don't promise what we can't deliver.

Result: A "Space" on the Production portion of the Timeline will equal $4,000 in Sales if the Space represents a Week, or about $17,000 in Sales if the Space represents a Month. And, when we have allocated a "stack" of 4 Spaces (same Time Slot on 4 different Jobs) we're "Sold Out" for that Time Period. (Which means if more Jobs come in, we'll begin to adjust, and make other arrangements … Overtime, Temporary Help, Sub-Contract, or whatever it takes.) And, again, the sooner we see this, the more options we have.

DRAWING AND CUT LISTS

That establishes the Space Value for the Production Line, but what about Drawing and Cutting Lists? Drawing on Industry Statistics, once again, we find that for 10 Crafters, we require the equivalent of 1 Person doing Drawing and Cutting Lists. If 1 Person is doing this for 10 Crafters, then this 1 Person is performing that part of the process for $4,000 worth of Sales each Day. (Remember, the Production for $4,000 worth of Sales is what 10 Crafters perform, each day.) But, since each of our Timelines Production is for $800 a day, we need 1 day of Drawing/Cut Lists for every 5 days of Production. The "Space Value" for Drawing/Cut Lists is: $4,000 per Day, $20,000 per Week, and about $85,000 per Month. Stated another way, on each Timeline allow 1 Day of Drawing for 5 Days of Production.

Call this a "Practical Presumption". The Presumption comes from the fact that we have 10 Crafters and 1 Drafter. If they all work the whole year, then they do the Drawing and the Producing for Sales of $1,000,000. Over a year's time, the ratio of 10:1 is valid. Will it be valid on each Job? We should all be astonished if it were true. But when we're starting from scratch, so to speak, it is certainly a "Practical Presumption".

As the project manager draws the first Timeline during the Hand-off/Order Entry Event, Drawing is considered. If we know a particular Job will require more, or less, Drawing ... show it on the first Timeline. Same with Installation. If we know that Installation is more, or less, in proportion to the size of the Sale ... indicate it on the first Timeline.

INSTALLATION

Applying the Statistical approach to Installation, let's also use the Ratio 10:1. Actually, the average company has slightly more than 1 Installer for each 10 Crafters. But we're entering a never-never land with so many variables, it is not useful to struggle with 1.2, or 1.3, etc. as we're getting our Timelines started. Even though we may hire part, or all, of the Installing done, it's still a good starting reference point. (I suspect the statistic number does, in fact indicate a Key "nucleus" crew which is augmented as required.) This Timeline allotment is probably the most "Theoretical" of all anyway. The other Events at least deal with stable numbers of People and Plant Capability. In Installation, the Job conditions may dictate a narrow Time Slot which we must meet. The Job may require 16 Man-days, which can be distributed all the way from 1 Man for 16 days, to 16 Men for 1 Day. In other words, the Job conditions may dictate our rounding up 6 or 8 People for a short stint. Point is, that's extremely difficult to Chart at the beginning. But, don't you see, if we *do* Chart it, we think about it. And as we think about those possibilities, we begin to see ways to manage the situation. And, at the beginning, we have options.

So, for Installation, our "Practical Presumption" is pretty far out. What the Ratio really says: Of those jobs which we *do* install in a year, this is the Person we retain to do it. It tells us little about individual Jobs. Still we are better off putting in something. Applying the 10:1 Ratio, the "Practical Presumption" says for a $40,000 Job the Timeline should allocate 10 Days for Installation.

SOMETHING ELSE

Note carefully: We have *not* applied the 80% rule for either Drawing/Cut Lists or Installation. Neither have we distributed the available capabilities over 4 Projects. We have bypassed them merely to keep our exercise simple. Analyze it like this: Neither our Drafter, nor our Installer is going to be working on more than 1 Job at a time. Why pretend otherwise? What we need to know for each Timeline is: How many days are required for our Drafter, and for our Installer? There will be no adding of "stacks" of 4. If one "Space" is full … we're "sold out" for that Time Slot. We'll have to create our own "slack", or "breathing room", as we refine our Timelines. We remain true to the purpose, however. We are presenting a "Practical Presumption" for study, and for further refining as we go along. With experience, with better History, with familiarity with our own product mix, and knowledge of our Team's capabilities, we can tailor our Timelines to become more accurate, and more useful. Any other Category we want to set out (in addition to Production, etc.) can be calculated and displayed in the same way.

OTHER KEY EVENTS TO SHOW

Other Key Events should be shown along the Timelines. Start with at least 3: "Start Production", "Submittals Approved", and "Field Measure". Of course, Submittals can only be approved if they are first made, so "Submittals" would be a good one, too. If I'm the CEO, I want to see a lot of Key Events and the Dates they're supposed to happen. I'd love to know at a glance whether things have been: Ordered, Submitted, Measured, Received, etc. I don't want to wait and hear about it in a meeting, and I surely don't want to hear about it when Production has halted. However, if I'm a Project Manager, I want to keep the list of posted Events to the minimum. We'll have to find a balance.

"Start Production" is mentioned first, because it's Key. It will first be pushed back toward the beginning of the Timeline in order to provide enough Production time. That's not bad, because we may want it back there for another reason: We may need something to do. But then it gets pushed forward by lack of Approvals, or wait for a Long-Lead Supply item. It is responding to many pressures, and some of those pressures had better be coming from an alert project manager nudging it in the right direction.

"Submittals Approved" may coincide with "Start Production", but not always. On a hot, short-fused Job, we sometimes can use partial Submittals, and partial Approvals. We always prefer to have ALL Approvals, and all Materials before we commence, but sometimes it doesn't work. It can go both ways. Sometimes it's to meet the Client's deadlines … sometimes it helps get us something to do. Either situation begs for alert management.

"Field Measurements" is an important Event. How soon can we get onto the Job and get "real" measurements? Can we get them all at once or will it mean more trips? How far can we proceed with Production without Field Measurements? Again, pick a tentative date (the Would be, Could be, Should be date) and then make it stick, or know the reason why. Things don't "just happen" we *make* them happen. And we can't do that if we don't even know what *needs* to happen.

WHAT WILL A TIMELINE CHART DO?

Let's review the reasons we are going to set out our Timelines in a dramatic graphic display, and some of the benefits we can expect.

1. It establishes the sequence of Events leading to a successful contract completion.

2. It establishes specific times of performance of those Events.

3. It establishes priorities. A glance at the Board will advise which action is most urgent.

4. It provides outstanding progress monitoring.

5. It is an information center. All changes immediately alert and advise entire team. Lessens need for further communication.

6. It focuses everyone's efforts ... from sales people filling it up ... to shipping and collections people clearing it out.

7. It establishes the tempo ... a rhythm ... and encourages everyone to pick up the pace.

8. It provides advance notice ... increases anticipation ... allowing action, instead of re-action ... increasing options for cost reduction during purchasing and all other phases of manufacturing.

9. It graphically reminds all team members of interdependence. Reduces chance of one member being overloaded ... or feeling overloaded.

10. It enhances team members' sense of accomplishment ... extra effort shows up on the chart, stimulating urge to do more.

11. It generates the phenomenon of extraordinary team effort that meets deadlines and keeps things "on track" ... something we are all capable of, and do quite naturally ... if and when we become convinced that it's really necessary. And it's even more fun when we can all clearly see the results.

12. It can even become a sales tool. On a selective basis, it could be used as "convincer" to prove that we are, indeed, adept at maintaining schedules.

13. Top management now has a gauge of People, Procedures and Machines ... the whole Process.

14. Chart aids definition of Tasks and Responsibilities ... leading to better specifics for Recruiting and Training.

15. Information is no longer buried in the files ... it's out where it can be seen and graphically dramatized.

Everybody knows what's going on!

THE PRODUCTION PLANNING BOARD

We have progressed from the *Job Schedule and Timeline Chart* in the Hand-Off/Order Entry stage. We've moved the Timelines onto the big *Timeline Chart*. What's next? We're now ready for the *Production Planning Board*.

We used the earlier steps to establish each new Project's place in the context of overall Events. Everyone in the Plant has had knowledge of each Projects existence, and more specifics have been available to all interested parties. The Timeline Chart has directed the Preparation activities ... making sure that when our Work Orders hit the Plant floor, everything is ready. No gaps, no confusion, no shortages ... it's full speed ahead.

When a Job enters the Plant, it enters a high-pressure, high-speed, high-intensity atmosphere. We can't afford stops for questions. We can't afford hesitation. We cannot allow any blurred or incomplete information. And, the People who direct this Process Flow need clear and consistent instructions.

We need one more step in which to review the "NOW" Schedule ... what's actually happening at this moment, what's happening next week, and the next, etc. We do this at a session with the Production Planning Board.

PRODUCTION PLANNING BOARD

WK 1	WK 2	WK 3	WK 4-7	WK 8-11	WK 12-15	WK 16-19

Slips or Cards about 1 1/2 x 2 represent Work Orders ready to Process. They include Job No., Job Item No(s)., Shipping Date, and Labor Hours Required.

Different Colors can denote Special Activities: Finishing, Installation, Moldings, etc.

JOB NUMBER
JOB ITEM NO(S).
SHIPPING DATE
LABOR HOURS REQ.

The Production Planning Board (shown nearby) can be any smooth surfaced, light colored board. Try a size about 3' x 4' to start. Again, don't agonize over doing it "perfect", just do it. The Board is the "domain" of the Plant Supervisor, and will reside in the Supervisor's office. However, portability is important. The Board will make a weekly trip to the Conference Room (for close proximity with the Timeline Chart, of course) for the Weekly Planning Session.

Thursday is a good day for this Weekly Session. Everyone needs a clear understanding of Next Week's activity before the week begins. Somehow, things seem to distract us on Friday, and this Session demands our full attention. This is the time when all project managers confess promises made to clients, and plead their case for us to abandon all other Projects in favor of theirs. Each manager is imploring the Plant Supervisor to listen to them and ignore the others.

At this point we need the services of the CEO as moderator, or mediator (referee?), so things don't get out of hand. A heated discussion is fine, but all questions must be resolved at this Session. Everyone must understand that when we leave the table, the next week's Production priorities are set. No sneaking out early Tuesday morning and harassing the Plant People to do it differently.

The small slips, or cards, shown in the nearby Board example contain information representing actual Work Orders. The little 1 1/2" x 2" notes with the adhesive on the back are about right, although sometimes they need some more assertive adhesive. Cards in slots, work. Magnetic card holders work (don't let the magnets get close to our computer disks). The slips, or cards, denote the Key facts from the Work Order.

    1. Job Number
    2. Job Item Number
    3. Shipping Date
    4. Labor Hours Required

The idea is to have a slip for each Work Order, and be able to move the slips about until they fall into the proper week's Production. As the Slips are entered into "WK 1" column, someone adds up the Labor Hours so we know when the week is full. A separate row beneath the main body of slips might contain some Orders which could move into "WK 2" if necessary. Also important will be a few Work Orders to be designated "ready-to-start-Production-if-needed. Equally important: Cram the week full to get the best use of the Plant facility, but make sure we're working the Jobs with the highest Priority.

Sometimes we struggle to find Jobs which can be postponed. Other times, we need to reach ahead and pull back some Items which can fill up "WK 1".

This is: Where it happens, When it happens, and How it happens. And it works! Project managers may leave the Session to plead with clients for more time ... or they may be making calls to speed things up to get us more work. Either way, everyone understands what needs to be done ... in the Plant, in the Office, and in the Field. And, it should require an extremely serious emergency to change anything that has been established during the Session.

Other slips in varied colors are suggested to represent other areas, such as Moldings, Finishing, or Installation. We are creating another "Know-what's-happening-at-a-glance" graphic display. Use it to the fullest advantage.

Columns to the right of WK 1, WK 2, and WK 3 can receive some different information along with the regular slips. Some "bulk" quantities of Labor Hours can be posted, even though the Work Orders have not been written. We can thereby inform that certain quantities of Labor Hours *have been committed* during that time period. This information can stimulate action on the part of the managers who *should* be preparing those Work Orders. Once again, we have a visual reference concerning what has been done, and what needs to be done.

Our project managers will retain much more than just a casual interest in their Jobs, even after they have made their way to the Production Planning Board and on into the Plant. However, it is inappropriate for project managers to wander about the Plant, distracting and harassing the People. If the proper job has been done in preparation, all required information will be in the right hands. If the preparation hasn't been done, it's surely a sorry spectacle to try to furnish it piece-meal on a day-to-day basis. We should not allow it.

10

Purchasing

ANTICIPATE

Purchasing follows the same concepts we've been laying down throughout the project management process. Anticipate: Study the situation and know the gray areas (for cost and delivery) and get the jump. Don't wait too long to start placing orders, but don't order too soon and tie up both Plant space and Working Capital.

Work with whomever is entering the Jobs into the Job Costing computer data base. If we've been tracking the Job from the first Takeoff Listing, we may have a nearly complete picture of Job Material requirements. After the requirements are completed and perfected, we can start combining like Materials with other Jobs. We can study the advantages of combining for quantity discounts, but also be aware of the "Flows", both Material Flow and Cashflow.

The object is to balance the whole picture. We need the Material in time to check it out (right product, right color, right quantity, right quality, etc.) but not so soon that it's in the way. A word of caution, here: When the product *does* arrive, check it quickly. Don't leave that special order of plywood in the crate till the moment it is needed. The moment it is needed is a lousy time to find out "plain sliced" was shipped, instead of "rift cut".

NOT ALWAYS PRICE, ONLY

Be prudent, but not stingy. Running out of something is far worse than having it in house a week too soon. And having quality goods which can be manufactured without aggravation is far better than saving 15 cents. In the area of Shop Supplies, buy what People know and trust. There can be subtle differences in adhesives, sand paper, cleaners, etc. which can make the day much nicer for the user. These subtle differences are seldom understood by purchasing agents ... always denied by contending sales people ... and *never* worth the few pennies saved.

Generally, it is better to have fewer, rather than more, People involved in Purchasing. We look more professional if we don't drive vendors crazy by having three people call with small orders on the same day. Help 1 or 2 people develop a flair for asking the right questions and being persistent in getting better prices and better delivery dates. It helps us because one Purchaser knows to combine like Materials for quantity discounts, and can also get to know vendors and how to get the best deals. The bad news is that the process just described can backfire. As vendor and purchaser get better acquainted, sometimes the question of who is getting the best deal from whom begins to blur. As with all activities, this one should be closely monitored by top management. We can control gifts and lunches with clear policy, and thereby keep a balance.

But, building good relations with vendors is important. We do not impress vendors if we spread our purchases out amongst many in the hope of saving a few pennies. Although it is not advisable to lock onto only one supplier of a particular product, 4 or 5 is probably too many. It's easier to negotiate for better prices and service when we buy enough to be noticed. If we keep spreading it around, we *won't* get noticed. Cultivate the suppliers who have good products, prices and service ... and then give them enough business to get their best efforts. Work with vendors who will accept a larger order, with attendant lower price, and then hold for spaced deliveries and billings. Discount as often as possible, and pay on time. Treat vendors fairly, then we're in a position to insist on fair treatment in return.

MANAGING PAPERWORK

It is seldom necessary to issue formal Purchase Orders for each purchase. We probably should, if the item is fairly sophisticated and we must be narrowly specific. Occasionally, we get an exotic item which requires a formal quote from the supplier (concerning price, terms and delivery). In such a case, our formal Purchase Order accompanied by a copy of their formal quote would be in order. For most other regular purchasing, an "internal" purchase order will do. Internal, meaning that our own People are notified that the order has been placed. The receiving Area should know what's coming, and when. The bookkeeping Area needs something to match with an invoice, etc. Notification can be a piece of paper, or merely availability on-screen. Use a P.O. number if you wish, but far more important is getting the Job Number placed with the order. Often, we can substitute the Job Number for the P. O. number.

HELP FROM THE COMPUTER

I've seen a handy recap sheet of all issued purchase orders produced on a computer spreadsheet. It is updated daily, and clearly shows deliveries, back orders, etc. Receiving areas love it because one piece of paper does the work of many. Such a recap sheet can be produced by the same spreadsheet, or data base, which produces the complete purchase order. We just set up a different form, and ask the program to show the data in a different way. It can even be arranged so that when the purchase order is produced, it debits the Job Material Budget and contributes to the automatic updating of the Job Cost Analysis. Another feature of the recap sheet: If it is available on a computer screen somewhere near the Receiving Area, "sorts" could be made to narrow the information scope. We can arrange P. O's. by Number, by Job, by Date, by Vendor, or by Material Item. It can be quite useful.

Items stocked regularly, whether Shop Supplies, or Manufacturing Material, should be ordered once a month. Each storage bin (or rack, or whatever) can be marked with a re-order point. The orders should be placed on the first day of the new monthly billing period. That way, we get the best use of our Working Capital.

The object is simple. We want the best merchandise at the best price. We want to never run out of anything. We want the right goods at the right time. We want to order just what is needed, process it quickly, and send out an Invoice for our work on the same day the vendor invoices us. Work on it.

11

Drawings/Cut Lists

There is a curious phenomenon in the Woodwork business. Nobody does Shop Drawings the same way. Everybody does them different. No matter how many times you ask the question, the answers come back with almost identical response

"How do you do Shop Drawings? What size Drawings? What size Details?"

"Well, see, we have a different situation. We do things a little differently."

Trying to determine: Different from what? How different? Why different? Leads one round and round a never ending circle. I've seen Drafting Room Manuals from several types of manufacturers. I've never seen one on the premises of a Woodwork manufacturer. It seems to be left up to the Drafters to determine what our style, and our standards, should be. Not necessarily the current group. They may be from long ago. (The old, "We've-always-done-it-this-way" syndrome.)

Maybe people don't like to think or talk about Shop Drawings because they really don't like them. Or don't really understand them. Or resent them because they always seem to be holding up the works. As with many other events occurring in our Plants, here's one which can make lots of money … or lose lots of money. It should be a helpful tool for everyone. In many Plants it's considered a nuisance. What do you think?

Your impressions may be revealed by answers to the following Quiz. The Purpose of Shops Drawings is to:

____	Inform
____	Translate
____	Answer Questions
____	Speed Production
____	Please the Architect

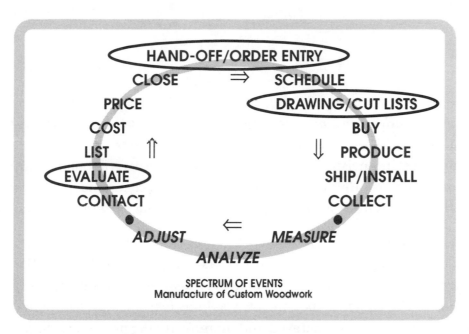

SPECTRUM OF EVENTS
Manufacture of Custom Woodwork

___   Please the Project Manager
___   Just get something Approved so we can start Production.
___   All of the Above

If you would hesitate to select the 3 most important points from the Quiz questions, and put them in order of importance, you're a member of a large club. The Industry agrees on very little in this regard.

Custom Woodwork Manufacturers have the most difficulty. Other manufacturers seem to be able to come to terms with the situation and produce consistent Drawings. Custom Woodworkers can't seem to agree on anything. Primary Purpose, Drawing size, Scales... any kind of "standard" is elusive. And now we're trying to approach these mysteries with Computer Assisted Drafting. Confusion increases exponentially.

Let's take a look at the situation. No matter how satisfied, or dissatisfied, we are with the situation; a close look is helpful. Going back to examine the basics is a healthy process.

INFORM

The Purpose of Shop Drawings is to Inform. Shop Drawings become a part of the contract documents. They assure other parties interested in the outcome of the Project that we do, indeed, understand the Specifications. We have already indicated with our Proposal that we understand the Project requirements, and stand ready to perform. Shop Drawings re-affirm.

Avoid misunderstandings with architects. Begin at the *Evaluation* stage of the Bid process. (See nearby *Spectrum of/Events*) Call attention to ambiguities, inconsistencies, and unworkable fabrication details or improper use of materials. Reinforce the point by calling a conference quickly after the *Hand-Off/Order Entry* stage of Events if some parts remain unclear.

Tact and Diplomacy are paramount. We're the good guys. We want a job we can all be proud of. We want to make all parties look good. We will always be part of the solution, not part of the problem. We must assure all parties to the contract they we are the knowledgeable professionals who understand the use of material and manufacturing procedures best.

We have no intention of changing the specifiers intent whatsoever. But, we know best how to deliver the quality and the correct performance of all woodwork. We must be extremely gentle as we explain how new techniques have replaced their outmoded, hackneyed (dreadful) details. Politely, but firmly, we must insist that their use of the Bid Process establishes that they wanted the best value (the best deal). Therefore, they *will* accept our joinery methods which take advantage of the latest equipment and methods, and in which our craftsmen are thoroughly trained ... and are assuring them the "best deal."

We are supplying information to:
>   Client and Representatives
>   Contractor
>   Architect/Designer
>   Other Subcontractors/Suppliers (Dr. Hdw. - Hollow Metal - Glass -
>   Marble - Etc.)

THE TRANSLATION FOR OUR PEOPLE

Shop Drawings also Inform our team members about their part in the flow of events. With the Shop Drawings, we translate our commitment to the client (and to the Project) into Shop Language. This Language must explain, with Consistency and Clarity, what each of us is to do. Machinists,

Assemblers, Finishers and Installers on one side of the office door. Project Managers, Purchasers, Cut List Billers, and others on the opposite side of the office door. Those involved in the Shipping, the Receiving ... even the Accounting Process, must rely on the integrity of these most important documents. This Informing/Translating process breaks the Contract into Specific Steps. It removes questions concerning:

    Scope
    Quality
    Materials
    Joinery
    Finishes
    Special Conditions (Methods of delivery - Phases, Floors, Bldgs)

THE PRIORITY

You may be asking, "Which is it?" Are we drawing for our Plant, or for the Architect?

Answer: We're drawing for our Plant. But let's try to eliminate the "either - or" aspect of the question. The preliminary discussions with the architect (mentioned earlier) can do much to clear the air. Find out which parts of the project cause the most concern. Assure the architect that we understand the intent. Hand him a sketch on the spot (if possible) to demonstrate how the intent will be fulfilled. If it's our first dealing with the architectural firm, bring samples of our drawings. If she murmurs that our style isn't the same as hers and might have to change, we might respond: "Ma'am, you and your staff have produced a fine set of drawings. There is little to be gained by duplicating your efforts. What we will draw, instead, is a clear set of manufacturing instructions whose style is dictated by the needs of our people and by our manufacturing methods. They will clearly inform that the design intent has been met." When presented quietly and confidently, a statement such as this usually closes the subject.

WHAT IS A GOOD DRAWING?

A good drawing answers all Production Questions in the first Package.

How do we do that? Start by putting ourselves in the shoes of manufacturing people. Their questions will probably include:

What is it?
What shape?
What size?
What material?
How many?
All at once?

If it's too tough anticipating their questions, just keep a log for a while. It will quickly tell us where our blind spots are. *And the answers must be where they can find them.* The phrase, "Well, it's all there on the drawing" doesn't cut it! If they can't find it, it isn't much good. Like it or not, we must draw to the level of comprehension. Of course we should try to raise that level, and we can … gradually. But raising the level of frustration, first, won't do it. *The cost of doubt, uncertainty, and frustration is enormous. Many, if not most of the manufacturing mistakes begin right here.*

PRODUCTION OF THE DRAWINGS
THE "AT-A-GLANCE" APPROACH

With a good drawing, there should be an almost instantaneous comprehension of what it's about. If anyone has to study the sheet to even know what the item is, things are off to a bad start. "Instant" recognition, followed by a clear path to the specifics is what we want. There are several things we can do to help.

1. Reduce clutter. And this may have to do with the size of the Drawing. If there's too much Drawing, where do we begin? If we're an Assembler, and we're looking at a carrier containing parts for a "What's-it", and we open a big drawing with pictures of 3 different "What's-its", is that going to make us feel confident?

2. Use consistent page layouts. Put dimensions in the same place. Place Notes about finishes, p.lam, hardware, etc. in the same place. Think about Title Block placement. One along the right-hand side works well. *(See nearby examples of bottom placement and right-hand placement.)* Consideration: How much folding and unfolding must be done to find the information? Job Numbers and Item Numbers must be prominent and easy to locate. In fact, they can (should?) be the Drawing Number, with the Job Number, first, followed by the Item Number as a "dash" Number. Example: 1234-17.

3. Consistent Scales. (And this may work back to our Drawing Size.) I like a smaller Drawing (would love to hold it to 17 x 22), but sometimes we bump into inconsistencies. Example: it would be grand if we always used the

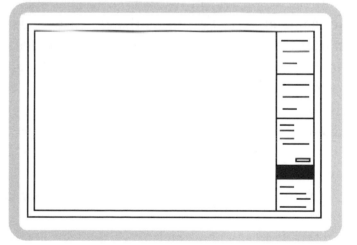

same Scale for Elevations, the same Scale for Plan Views, etc. Then we get a complicated raised panel wall detail that meanders all over a huge lobby. We have to compromise, somewhere. Most of the time the situation can be accommodated by doing the "whole layout" in a much smaller Scale, then breaking the "whole layout" into sensible "bite size" Drawings which focus on parts with specific features, or orientation. Or maybe we announce a policy change for this one situation, then use the same Scales throughout the project. We must achieve some consistency, somewhere.

4. Have a Book of Standard Details. Drawing clutter can be reduced by referring to the Standards. First of all, build one (the Book) ... then we can decide where all, when and how to use it. It's a given that we'll have a Library in our computer drawing system, whatever it might be. Whether we send along a Book with our Submittal Process, send selected pages, use the Book and/or selected pages within the Plant, only. Those things can be thought through and decided, later.

BUILD IT AS IT'S DRAWN, OR BUILD IT LIKE WE ALWAYS DO?

We should be able to narrow the gap considerably on this question. We should be able to both "draw it as it's built ... and build it as it's drawn." As mentioned earlier, we must negotiate with the architect to use our "usual" methods. (If there's any variation.) And then the Project should be drawn that way. What can our excuse be for drafters not knowing what our "usual" methods are? My travels reveal amazing differences concerning the merging of "way-it's-drawn" and "way-it's-built". Sometimes an awkward antagonism persists. It's as though each side will do it differently, no matter what. In such cases gather the parties for some serious counseling. *And if the condition persists they have earned a "good luck on your new job" notice.* Repeat: THERE IS TOO MUCH MONEY MADE ... OR LOST ... HERE TO BE CONTROLLED BY A BUNCH OF CLOWNS. The other amazing aspect of this subject is the difference in Plant requirements. Some Plants can produce woodwork from a sketch on the back of an envelope. Some "prima-donna" Plants wait for some "Leonardo" to draw everything perfectly before beginning. ("Leonardo" is usually working for the guys who would love to get an envelope.) (Murphy probably had something to say about that.)

Now that it's come up, let's address the "artistic" question. No doubt better looking drawings are produced by those with an eye for design and a sense of composition and page layout. And, no doubt, eye-hand coordination is a plus when it comes to getting the lines (and the information) on the paper. But let's keep it in the proper context. Our shop drawings are *not* end products. They do not achieve excellence by their form. They achieve excellence by their function. They are a critical contribution to the end result, but they are not the main attraction. We must find the logical balance.

HOW MUCH INFORMATION?

One of the tough questions. I dislike being stingy with information. I disdain the "need to know" game some like to play. I like to see team members receive as much information as they can accommodate ... not what some manager feels they "need". Sometimes, a Key Plan will show the special condition which explains why a particular assembly needs extra scribe on one end. Or it may explain why the shipping joints are located as they are. Good communication includes a clear *overview,* as well as clear *specifics.* I'd much rather have team members who want to know more about what's going on ... want to see the whole picture.

However, the concern begins when the mass of information becomes clutter, *or* our team member's interest becomes an obsession. If the team member begins to try to absorb all sorts of information regardless of relevancy (loading up their "gee-whiz" file), something has to change. Possibility: Plan it so that only minimum information accompanies the package (and the parts carrier), but have the rest of the story readily available in the Plant office. The eager craftsman (whom we sincerely want to encourage) will come looking, but the whole sequence can be managed. Maybe it occurs on the craftsman's own time, or maybe there *is* need for more relevant background. Either way, we can better direct this and future events.

DETAIL BOOK/DRAWING MANUAL

Follow through on the Detail Book idea. An 8 1/2 x 11 book of details has many possibilities.

- It may be used as part of the submittal process.

- It can be used on the Plant floor.

- It can be used as a Training Manual.

The training part is appropriate on both sides of the office door. New Drafters can begin to learn our ways, and have a reference resource, too. Shop People can begin to correlate what happens in the Plant with what it looks like on paper. It gets even better if we state our Drawing Procedures in the front, as well. A few pages outlining our approach to producing Drawings can have enormous value. It will be appreciated by current (even long-time) employees, as well as newcomers. Who does not see the value of uniformity and consistency? Achieving uniformity within the industry is a formidable task, but surely we can achieve it within our own store. When do we use *which* size drawing? Where are Title Blocks (and how do we fill them in)? Lettering, dimensioning, scales, number of drawings per Sheet, number of scales allowed per Sheet, etc. Spell it out.

THE "ENGINEERING" ASPECT

We need more "Engineering". Both the use of the term and actual Engineering. We should always be exploring better ways to do things. We must grasp every opportunity to figure out how to perform an operation better and faster. Don't be confused. The Engineering of which we speak is hard-headed application of sound machining, assembly and finishing techniques. (Also could extend to Installation.) It is the application of established principles involving best use of our Machines and our People skills. Engineering is not "Design" or "Inventing". Beware of Drafters who are frustrated designers or inventors. They don't think like Engineers. We often speak of a "Huddle" with key People as part of the Hand-Off/Order Entry. Engineering possibilities should be identified and the engineering begun at that point.

PLANNING THE DRAWINGS

First of all ... ***get right to it.*** No aging time is required. If we have the Order, we've had the "huddle", and we have a Timeline, we're ready to proceed.

Start with our commitments. When have we promised Product? When have we promised Submittals? Work from that. If we're installing, maybe we consider Key Plans (locations within the building space), first. Installing or not, look to shipping sequences. It is extremely helpful to consider what goes on the first truck, then the next, etc. This approach coincides with the aforementioned "Overview, then Specifics". Start with the sequence of Installer's needs, and the pattern of Production emerges. Know the pattern of Production, and the Drawing sequence emerges.

Work out a schedule for Key Plans (or "In-Place" Drawings). When the Product can be visualized "in-place" ... the logical set of assemblies, sub-assemblies and components becomes apparent. Whoever is managing the Project must be involved, here. We don't want to build more than was promised. We must not engineer in more features than were requested, or were bid. But applying this logic usually makes it easier to produce, and ship. Sometimes modest sub-assembly helps us keep track of all parts. It can assure a complete shipment, plus avoid confusion to the receiver. In other words, a tiny bit extra can save much down the road. (Remember, we're selling Quality and Service ... not Price. Service means well-drawn, well-produced, and well-shipped.)

As we determine shipping requirements and "in-place" considerations, we'll be thinking about scales. Some extremely small scales may be used to present the proper "Overview". (All the locations of some complicated stile-and-rail paneling, for example.) Then, after we've shown the whole "lump", we can break it down into sensible "bites". (Here, consider the way the Plant Supervisor and various Lead People will be viewing the Project. Example: Where do we start to make sure all components complete at the proper time? We can run stiles, rails, and moldings, but should we be gluing up some panels, first? And which moldings can be random and which cut-to-size?) Also, what is "safe" to build "ahead" if we need something to do?

Draw to meet those questions. The Overview, the Elevations, then the appropriate Sections and Details must clearly show the sum total, but also the individual parts. I'm not suggesting we start making those decisions in the office. Those are Plant decisions. I'm saying the Drawing process must assist the decision process. Just remember our purpose for Drawing.

CUTTING LISTS

Our Drawing requirements will surely be influenced by the way we produce Cutting Lists (Cutting Bills). Less detail is required on the Drawing if good Cutting Lists are used. In fact, use of Drawings throughout the Plant can be sharply reduced. ***This is not a small consideration.***

As we examine the methods and the purpose of Shop Drawings, we must look at the whole picture. And the whole picture includes what arrives at each work station. Think through each Package. What combination of Drawings and Lists does it take to start cutting Boards? To start cutting Panels? What sort of package will meet the needs at the next Operation … and the next … and so on.

CUTTING LIST/SKETCH

The nearby Cutting List is an interesting possibility for minimizing paperwork at certain stations. I've made the statement on occasion that I could build most items of woodwork without drawings, if I had a good Cutting List. No one's made me prove it, so I still use this one, with a Sketch included. I now leave more space at the top, and put more information near the bottom. (It was either that, or get the world to redesign clipboards.) It's also interesting in that it is printed from a CAD program, but it originates in a Spreadsheet. The left side is brought straight in from a Spreadsheet, using *Copy* and *Paste* commands. The Spreadsheet usually contains the whole Job, and is *Sorted* for whatever purpose. Quantities by species, thickness, sizes in diminishing order, etc., or Job Items called out like this one.

The Spreadsheet information is arranged, then Copied. It is then dropped into a Template waiting in the CAD program. Sketches are brought in from the "Library" as needed, notes and Job Identification information are added. The combination is then "Saved-as", with an appropriate name for the file, and printed out. Since the "Save-as" lifts everything out of the Template, it remains clear, ready to accept the next set. Imagine that sort of capability at your Store. Combinations of Lists and Sketches produced on a moment's notice to correctly inform whoever needs it.

CUTTING BILL

	PART NAME	QTY	THK	WTH	LGTH	MATL	SPECIAL INSTRUCTIONS
F	EDG BND	6	0.13	0.75	24.00	MAH	
F	EDG BND	12	0.13	0.75	26.00	MAH	
F	TRIM	2	0.75	3.00	24.00	MAH	
F	TRIM	2	0.75	1.50	24.00	MAH	
F	TRIM	4	0.75	1.25	75.50	MAH	
F	TRIM	4	0.75	1.25	35.50	MAH	
F	DR RAIL	8	0.75	1.50	35.50	MAH	
F	DR RAIL	8	0.75	1.50	7.00	MAH	
F	BACK	2	0.25	23.50	77.50	MAH PLY	
F	UPRIGHTS	4	0.75	11.75	80.00	MAH PLY	
F	SHLF	6	0.75	11.75	22.50	MAH PLY	
F	ADJ SHLF	6	0.75	10.63	22.38	MAH PLY	
F	DR	2	0.75	20.00	26.00	MAH PLY	

F

MAH BOOKSHELF
BUILD 2

CUTTING BILL		
DATE	PAGE	OF
PROJECT NAME		NO
PROJECT ITEM(S)		
ARCH REF		
NOTES:		

CHANGES

Do not treat changes casually! *Suggestion:* Re-draw, Re-print, Re-distribute by retrieving **_ALL_** old versions. **_ALL_** old versions should then be shredded. IMMEDIATELY. Marked-up, patched-up, screwed-up Drawings cost us much too much. Let's stop the foolishness.

OTHER CONSIDERATIONS

Who does the Drawing? (Best answer: experienced, knowledgeable Drafters supervised by Project Managers. And done with a CAD system.)

Precise scale, or proportional? (That's been a funny one for a long time. Most of us have always drawn to Scale, then added the note: "Do not Scale" because we didn't want to Re-draw the changes … merely change the dimensions. I say proportional is fine. Then, use a good Cutting List, cut the parts right, and build it!)

DECISIONS

Decide first:

We want to Inform (both our People, and others.)

We Translate (all Requirements, Commitments, and Specifications distilled into Shop Language for Production)

We draw for _Us,_ but don't ignore the Specifier (it needn't be "Them-or-Us")

GOOD DRAWINGS

Then go for GOOD Drawings. Drawings which answer ALL Production questions. And, answer questions the first time. And, answer them without the riddles. Not just "it's-all-there", but "it's-all-there-where-it-should-be-AND-YOU-CAN-FIND-IT." ("First-glance" recognition.)

Last, but certainly not least, the merging of *"the-way-it's-drawn"* with *"the-way-it's-built"* and the *"engineering"* part (which too often gets neglected). The "Merging" challenge is a great example of the "Perfection vs. Excellence" query. Go for Excellence.

Perfection is neither noticed nor appreciated … and it takes anywhere from three times as long, to *forever*.

COMPLETING THE PACKAGE

We need a Work Order to complete the Package that goes to the Plant floor. The information on a Work Order is very similar to that of a Delivery Ticket. In fact, one copy of the Work Order can be a Delivery Ticket. Principal parts include:

1. Job Identification (Job No., Customer Name, Address, etc.)
2. Items to be produced (Scope).
3. Completion Date and/or Shipping Date.
4. Labor Hours Required (Work Order, only. Conforms with Information on Production Planning Board).

The "Package" can be mounted on a clipboard and/or be enclosed in a plastic pouch for its journey through the Plant. Just make sure the Package stays together, is reasonably well protected, and can't get blown away with a gust of wind.

12

Manufacturing

One of the attributes truly successful woodworkers have in common is their love of Manufacturing. The love grows as understanding of Manufacturing's meaning grows. Today's woodworkers have the opportunity to build on a rich history, a heritage spanning generations of skilled artisans and craftsmen who shared this love. The dedication of all these people ... the ones who developed techniques for working with the material, plus the ones who developed the machines ... has provided an outstanding base for us. They've handed us the tools to produce excellent products.

Tallying up the efforts of the many skills and disciplines, and observing their culmination on our Plant floor has to impress even a casual observer. When you study the true origin of what we consider our "raw" materials, and all the experience, skill, and care involved in their journey to our Plants, you already have an amazing story. Think of all the steps from the forest to our door. Add in the engineering, the metallurgy, the circuitry involved in the development of our machines. Consider their power, their precision, the smooth clean cuts they produce. Then, consider the development of our own People. The art, the craft, the skill and knowledge required to comprehend all the properties of wood, the action of the cutting edge, head speeds, feed speeds ... the sensitive touch our technicians use to make it all happen.

Everything comes together on the Plant floor. The Manufacturing fulfils the Marketing effort, the Managing, the Planning and Scheduling. This is where we create the products of beauty, of quality, and of utility, which our Customers expect and appreciate..

I love to work in a woodworking Plant. I love to *be* in a woodworking Plant. I love it when everything is humming and things are happening. I love the sight of it, the sound of it ... even the smell of it. And, I even like to poke around when the Plant is quiet. I still hear the echo of the day's activity. The whine of the machines, the shouts of encouragement. *There is an incredible joy in the Manufacture of Woodwork.*

Some young woodworkers are reluctant to embrace the concept of Manufacturing. They correctly believe that creating beautiful woodwork is an Art ... and a Craft. Therefore, there is concern about methods. They are not sure if using machines is noble enough for true artists. Perhaps "Real Woodwork" demands generous use of hand tools. And what about teamwork? Shouldn't true Crafting be doing it yourself? They think doing it right means you pull the stock, machine every part, complete all sub-assembly and assembly ... and, in some cases, the finishing, as well (with as much hand work as possible).

THE REALITY

I understand such feelings, but I can't agree. And many other people, who are as true to the craft as can be, agree with me. The machine will always be an extension of the operator's skill ... never a replacement for it. The machine not only improves the quantity of production, it improves the quality, as well. Our machines remove much of the back-breaking drudgery of some operations, but they don't remove the need for our "touch", much less our knowledge and experience. The improved accuracy, the predictability, and the productivity, all combine to extend our abilities and increase our value, as well. This concept of Manufacturing enables us to make a good living, while still allowing more people to afford and enjoy our products.

And, the team concept ... where each of us applies our skill, knowledge, and experience to a narrower scope of the project ... performing our part with applied excellence, will produce far better results. The team can produce better quality, better consistency and predictability, and far greater quantity of product.

Manufacturing is the heart of the Business of Woodwork.

If you choose to stay with "Artistry" … if you would rather retain the "Craft" of your woodwork, I understand. I encourage you to follow your convictions and do your best.

But, that path is *not* the woodwork business. *The woodwork business is Manufacturing.* Manufacturing does not ignore the Art and the Craft. In manufacture we absolutely need Artistry. And we can't manufacture without knowing and applying the Craft of wood. But if we are to do well for ourselves, and for our families, we must learn to Manufacture. Fear not: Manufacturing Woodworkers are sincere, we are skilled, we are dedicated, we have knowledge … and we *are* noble.

THE DIVIDING LINE

Where is the Line? Where do we leave "Crafting" and begin Manufacturing? Probably Manufacturing begins when someone machines parts on one side of the room, and someone else assembles those parts on the other side of the room. If you can cut parts for someone else, or assemble parts cut by someone else, you're on your way to becoming a Manufacturer.

As Manufacturers, we will still encourage versatility and a well rounded learning experience. We still respect the craft, and will develop people who can excel at whatever task is required to do the job. A true craftsman can eventually become reasonably proficient at all of the operations, but to insist on performing all of them all of the time is totally impractical.

It is extremely important that we make the choice. The chances of any single individual being able to perform all manufacturing steps with the same excellence as those who specialize, is near zero. And keeping abreast of new materials and new methods would make it even more difficult. Our methods and procedures will be always changing. As our Marketing thrust shifts toward better markets, we will learn to manufacture new products, and constantly upgrade the old. We will learn about new materials, and we will add new machines. Our people can be constantly learning and growing. Team members skills and abilities will be every bit as good as "do-it-myself" crafters.

Becoming Manufacturers will change the way we recruit and train People, the way we buy Machines, the mix of People and Machines ... even the way we layout the Plant. If a Plant has more than 3 People producing products they should switch to Manufacturing.

Example: If we designate a team of 2 for Machining, we don't have to have a whole bunch of variety table saws (each equipped for lumber ripping, or panel processing). We can acquire a serious rip saw for lumber, and also a serious panel saw. Since a small team will move from machine to machine, our Plant Layout can have some overlap of in-feed and out-feed corridors. This arrangement will improve productivity and quality while conserving Plant space.

But there's more. This same team will service and maintain the machines, assuring sharp tooling changed on time ... not on a "someone-else-can-do-it-I'm-in-a-hurry" basis. Last, but not least, we achieve much better material management. If fewer People access the material stocks, we'll have much better control of waste factors ... plus a far neater material area.

Embracing the concept of Manufacturing, is embracing the quest for excellence. We can Market better ... Manage better ... and fulfil the total Customer satisfaction proposition much better.

13

Process Flow

When we're talking Manufacturing, we're talking "Process Flow". "Process", as in methods and procedures for performing Manufacturing steps or Operations. "Flow", as in continuous stream, with specific direction and appropriate velocity. It is important to consider both to "the Process", and "the Flow".

The manner we choose to perform Operations such as ripping, shaping, boring, edgebanding, assembling, etc., (Selection of machine, operator, sequences, etc.) defines our own unique Process.

It is appropriate to bring Process into focus from time to time. Too often our entire focus is on the Product. A finished Product is similar to a Bottom Line. You can't adjust the results. You have to adjust the events leading *to* the results. More often than we realize, the quality of the results is determined back in one of the early steps.

The idea of a "Flow" is important, too. Many woodwork manufacturing Plants have more spurts and sputters, than "flows". Rather than an ongoing stream of events we have lumps and clumps of orders, or parts of orders, each "on its own" as far as starts, stops, and momentum are concerned. How much better if Work Orders were to be drawn along by the force of the whole "Flow" rather than depend on an individual push or a shove.

Process Flow can actually describe the total area of managing a project. It includes structuring, guiding, and monitoring. And there are three "Flows."

    1. Flow of Information

    2. Flow of Material

3. Flow of Events

The Flow of Information actually begins with the listing or take-off part of the estimating process, and continues on until final payment.

The Flow of Material begins with off-loading the supplier's truck (perhaps even back when we place the order), and ends when the customer signs it off as delivered or properly installed.

The Flow of Events refers to the methods and the timing of the handling of Information and the handling of Materials.

Let's discuss the Flow of Events which occur in the Plant … from the time the job hits the floor, to the point where we have loaded the truck.

Flow of Events. The operative word is "FLOW." Flow, as in fluid ... as in a stream. That's what we want ... a stream of events. Each work station in the plant should have each new event happening hard on the heels of the last. No gaps. No pauses. No hesitation. Which means clear, consistent detail drawings along with clear, consistent cutting bills are flowing right along with the material. Beginning with the basic starter machines: The lumber rip saw, and the panel saw, and following all the way through. The "hoppers" should be full at each station. No one has to break the rhythm, to break stride. Every move can count. That's efficiency, and that's Manufacturing.

PRODUCTION LINE?

If you think this is beginning to sound like a "production line" you may be right. Please don't tense up. I'm aware the terms "Flow" and "production line", make folks think of an "assembly line", which woodworkers reject out-of-hand when applied to custom woodwork. "Can't be done", we say, "Can't have production methods, because everything we do is different."

I know all the verses to that one, and the chorus, too. I've sung it many times, myself. But, it's wrong. We *can* have a production line, we *can* have production methods, we *can* establish that flow *if we try*. We have allowed ourselves to be blinded to some basic truths.

There is no question ... our product mix is indeed diverse, and our end products *are* very different. Different sizes, different shapes, different species ... and on and on. But when we think it through, a light dawns. Though the end products are quite different, *the Operations are not.*

LOOK AT THE SIMILARITY

The operations on the parts remain the same. A Board is processed like a Board regardless of size or species. And there aren't that many different things we do to Boards. (In the early going ... i.e., selecting, facing, planing, ripping, defecting, running to continuous profile, etc.)

Same with Panels. Whether raw, prefinished, laminated, hardwood, softwood ... a Panel is a Panel. And it's treated like a Panel. And there aren't that many different things we do to a Panel.

You're right. As parts become more complex ... and are knit into sub-assemblies, then assemblies ... they begin to look and act quite differently. But we accommodate that in Assembly Areas, not in the Preliminary Manufacturing Area.

Test the idea for yourself. Start with the Rip Saw and follow a board through several steps. Start with the Panel Saw and follow a panel through several steps. There are not as many variations as we thought, are there? There can be logical sequences. There can be a flow.

MORE THAN ONE LAYER

Another point. There can be several layers in this stream ... several layers of events. And as each board or panel is cut into "parts", each "part" can flow according to its end use. The part will have certain operations performed and then become part of an assembly (or, perhaps a sub-assembly ... then a final assembly). Point is, each will flow on its unique course and probably at its own unique pace. Sometimes we hinder the flow by assuming that all parts pertaining to a job must flow together. Not necessarily.

Although a complete project has an identity, and its own size and shape, that needn't dictate the manner it flows through the plant. True, each job begins as one entity. True, it most certainly will be re-gathered into a complete group for shipment. But, in between, the various components may be separated into a number of events related not to a particular job but, rather to the various processes. A rip-saw operator shouldn't be ripping one job, only. When he's cutting 4/4 red oak, he should be cutting two or three lists ... maybe more. He's obliged not just to cut for job number 4204, he's obliged to make the best use of his and the machine's time (and the occupied space) while getting the best yield from the bunk of material. Those parts don't care if some of them become trim, others cabinet parts, and others table top surround. They don't care which layer they're flowing in.

Same with panel cutting. Like material and like parts are batched for best yield and best use of time. A single cabinet might float along with any number of similar units "flowing" its way. We thereby gain the economy of scale as though it were one of ten or twenty, rather than one-of-a-kind. Hold it! I didn't say to start bidding jobs that way. We do it whenever possible, but we don't start making wild assumptions.

USE THE COMPUTER

A computer on the Plant floor to sort combined Cut Lists can be a big help, here. If the "spreadsheet" technique has been used to produce the Lists ... combining them is easy and sensible. All the 4/4 red oak (from the previous example) on three Jobs can be combined. After combining, we can re-sort to put the widest and longest pieces at the top, again, for proper cutting. Of course, we'll have to stack by Job, but that's no big deal. And it doesn't diminish the value of this efficiency if one of the Jobs remains in the area for a time, either. If we can cut the 4/4 red oak for the whole week, why not do it?

Critical point: Yes, WE WILL KEEP TRACK OF TIME SPENT ON EACH JOB. As we cut from three lists we will log proportional time to each one. (Let's not strain on a gnat, here ... 6 minutes one way or the other won't hurt). (Reminder: Think sixes for timecards. Get rid of fives and tens ... they're invalid. Think, and write, tenths of an hour. .1 = 6 min. .2 = 12 min. .3 = 18 min. etc.)

MAINTAIN THE FLOW

But the essential thing, here, is to maintain that flow. The flexibility of this approach will show up in many ways. As we think this through and structure the flow properly, we will establish work stations where certain things happen. During peak production periods, each station could be manned and working. But as the workload ebbs and flows, several stations could also be covered by one craftsman. If we have lots of moldings to run, we'll move some of those good hands into that area. Next week, those willing hands may be on frames or casework. We want to give the plant supervisor the opportunity to get the best possible match-up he can between craftsman, process and job priority. His task is to mobilize the available resources each day and get the best results from those resources. He'll do it if he gets the procedures and the support.

We're saying that jobs can flow through the plant in an orderly fashion, in a predictable sequence and with a minimum of starting and stopping. And they won't get lost! Think about this: How many different things can happen to a board after it's ripped? How many different things can happen to a panel after it's cut? There aren't really that many options, are there? Even though our end products are quite diverse, the different operations performed on each part don't vary that much, do they?

THE PREMISE

If we will take time to study the sequence of events involved in manufacturing our products, some good things can happen. We can place machines where they're needed, and get them closer together. We can move material on roller conveyers (with and without carriers) and end lots of stooping and lifting. We can design the optional paths into the scheme of things and provide compact "parking" spots where parts may accumulate for the next operation. The consolidating will free up more assembly area and eliminate much clutter. We can modify the methods used in writing Cutting Bills and Work Orders to reduce hesitation and questioning. We'll start to spend more time producing woodwork and less on head scratching and walking around.

Norlin's Rule on Process Flow: *"The value of the product is not enhanced by the number of miles it travels through our plant ... nor is the value enhanced by the number of miles traveled by the People who produce it."*

THE SEQUENCES

Study the sequence of events. How best can we do that? Observation in the Plant is a must, but we can begin with the format of a "decision tree".

Example: To produce a Shelf. The panels were received and stored. They move to the Panel Saw, then the Edgebander, and then the Sander. They may, or may not go to Finishing before returning for shipment. The movements can be diagramed like this:

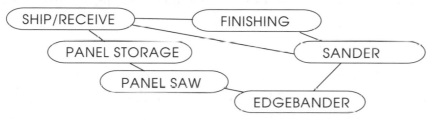

If the Shelf were to become part of a Cabinet, its path would be expanded:

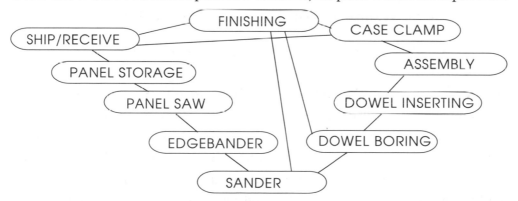

Exercises like this are quite useful. Use the computer to generate the "trees". It's much faster, and much easier to modify. Do a sequence, print it out, then study it for awhile. Put it up on a wall so you look it from time to time as you perform other duties. Let others observe and comment, too. You'll be pleasantly surprised at how this stimulates ideas. Of course, anyone can play ... Plant Supervisor and Lead Craftsmen, first. Then, Project Managers and the CEO should be involved, too.

FROM TREES TO LOOPS

Thinking through the Process Flows on various parts, sub-assemblies, and assemblies will verify what we've been saying about the production line. The processes don't vary that much, do they? And flow in certain directions and patterns begins to form. Build on this. Think in terms of "Loops", rather than straight lines. The nearby diagram indicates a more complex application of the techniques we've been discussing, and shows examples of Loops.

The lower portion shows the Panel Area. Included is a short Loop in which Panels are laid up. A somewhat longer loop involves Machining and Assembling Casework. The longest Loop includes Panel Parts becoming made into more involved Special Casework, with solid wood parts coming over from the Lumber Area.

The Lumber Area has its Loops, too. A short, tight one produces Moldings. A somewhat longer one could produce Sash and Doors. The longer Loops would be for more involved Millwork ... Circle work, complex Frames, etc. We must consider Gluing. Gluing for thickness ... Gluing for width, and then getting the resulting work pieces back into the Flow.

Custom Woodwork lends itself to production Loops as opposed to straight lines. Parts move better in Loops or S's ... winding around the Area but not getting too far away. This keeps the options open for the various changes in sequences, plus reducing the travel distances for both Parts and People. This particular diagram happens to show everything Flowing, or Looping, back to the "Shipping/Receiving" Area. This works well for small and medium Plants because the same material handling equipment can be used for both. Also, storage racks and areas may be used either for the staging of raw material or the storing of finished goods. Note, too, that the central location of the Finishing Area allows the option for preliminary staining and/or sealing of parts before final assembly.

In fact ... our thinking about, plus sketching, "trees" and "Loops" has been building into the subject of Plant Layout.

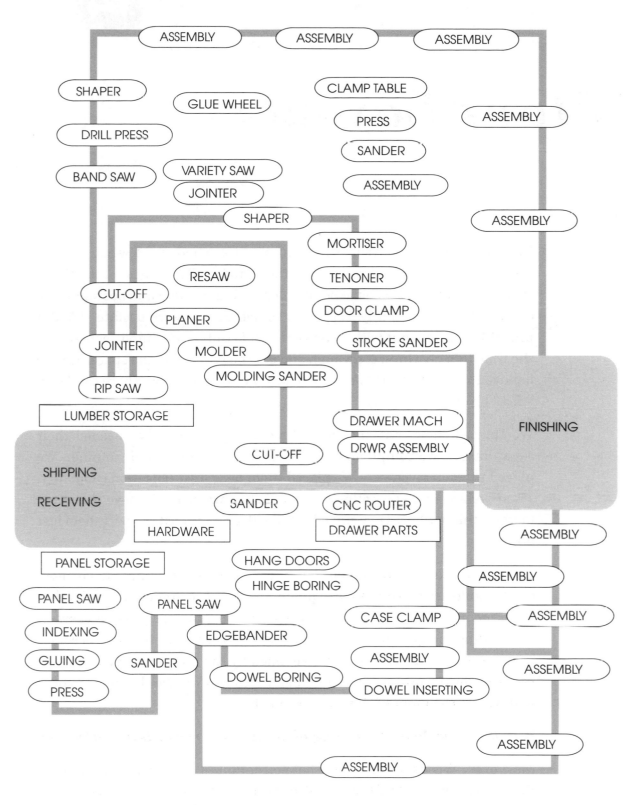

By the time we place all Operations in "Trees", then "Loops"
we will be well on the way toward revising our Plant Layout.

14

Plant Layout

Plant Layout is a tough subject. Many of us have had very few options. We just sort of accepted whatever was there and made the best of it. Every Plant was "laid out" at some point. Mostly, Plants were laid out similar to one in which we recently worked ... something we were used to. (And it probably was laid out with a similar lack of study.) We didn't seem to find the time to truly think it through and get the best use of the space. Or, we believed the myth that "since we're custom woodworking, there can be no 'ideal' layout, so why try?"

We "placed" new machines according to expediency. We needed their capability, so we compromised in order to get them up and running. We placed them near power. We placed them near dust collection capability. Their weight and size influenced us. When we couldn't move them any farther, that's where they stayed. Or the floor might not support them just anywhere.

Trying to plan the Layout is never easy. Most of us are much more comfortable acting than we are planning. And the arguments with other team members doesn't make it any easier. So, after the passing years ... and adding many more machines ... and getting by ... the task becomes even more difficult. We are overwhelmed by the seemingly endless steps required for the process of improving. When will we find the time? Where will we get the money? It's just too much.

But, it can be done. It is being done. And the rewards are fabulous.

Most every Woodworker agrees that better Plant Layout can make us more Productive, more Profitable, and more Predictable. But we don't fully appreciate the possible gains. If we did, we would figure out a way to get started. So, let's work on it.

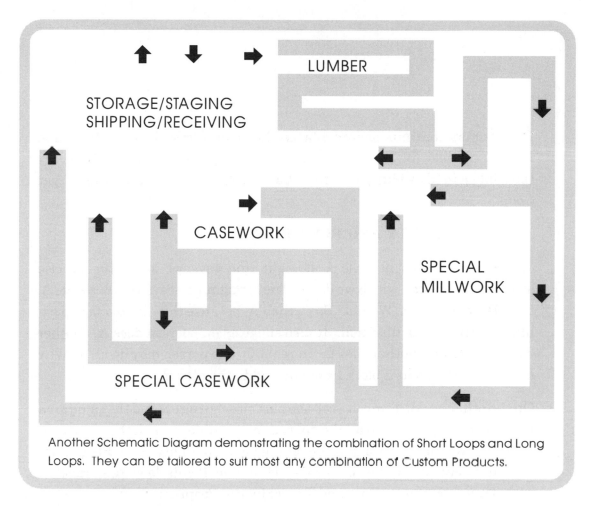

STORAGE/STAGING
SHIPPING/RECEIVING

LUMBER

CASEWORK

SPECIAL
MILLWORK

SPECIAL CASEWORK

Another Schematic Diagram demonstrating the combination of Short Loops and Long Loops. They can be tailored to suit most any combination of Custom Products.

When we think of the Flows ... Flow of Information, Flow of Material, and Flow of Events as we look out over the Plant floor, we can begin to visualize some improvements. And then we can think about Loops ... the paths the parts travel ... from raw material storage to finished product storage (or shipment). A Loop is not limited to a particular geometric shape. It's probably a series of S-curves or rounded rectangles. It may double back on itself, or make a little side Loop, and then return to the primary Flow. It may return to the proximity of its beginning (true to its name), and be staged for shipment. Or it may continue on into a larger Loop.

Moldings make a fairly tight Loop. (Select, Rip and Run, Tally and Bundle, then Ship.)

Uncomplicated Casework makes a fairly tight Loop, too. (Cut Panels, Edgeband, Groove, Bore, Dowel, Clamp; Install Doors, Drawers and Pulls.) Drawers come from their own Loop, and Doors from a Loop within the Loop (more passes through edgebander, then to hinge boring and insertion).

Boards may continue on into a larger Loop for Jambs, Frames, Sash and Doors. Panels may continue on to become parts of Special Casework (possibly joined by trim pieces from Lumber Area), entering another larger Loop.

PROXIMITY AND FLEXIBILITY

We counsel Loops because a straight line says we know the precise sequence of events, which we don't. The straight line says we always do A, then B, then C, etc. We can't do C, then A, because they are too far apart, plus it's the wrong direction. It also suggests one person does A, another does B, and yet another does C. In real life, one person may do all 3. Why have to move a half a block from one end to the other?

On the other hand, if we can keep the part circulating around the same area until we have performed all the operations possible ... in all the sequences possible, we have accomplished our goals: Proximity, and Flexibility. Proximity cuts down the distance, and the time. It cuts down the Travel ... both Travel by the Product and Travel by the People.

If we use a Jointer to straighten an edge before ripping, the Jointer should be next to the Saw ... not 30 feet away. If we use a Jointer for facing before planing, the Jointer should be close to the Planer ... not across the room. But if we keep the Jointer close to the saw, how can we keep it close to the Planer? By keeping the Planer in close proximity to the Saw.

Why do I mention it, when anyone can see the logic? *Because I encounter this blind spot in real life about once a month!*

The nearby Layout for processing BOARDS illustrates the point. In this basic Layout, many options are possible. Whether we decide to Rip first, Joint first, Face first, or Crosscut first ... the options are all there. Each successive Board may require a different sequence, but we're never locked out. And it's still convenient to perform the same 2 or 3 operations continuously to many boards. The Proximity of all machines, plus the table designs, give us the necessary options.

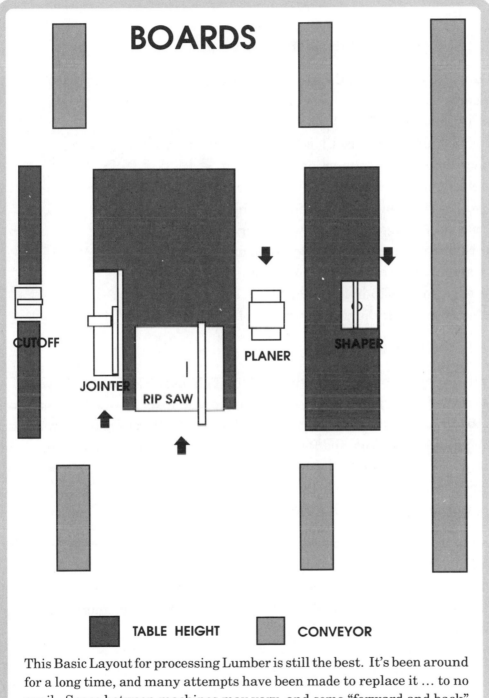

BOARDS

CUTOFF

JOINTER

RIP SAW

PLANER

SHAPER

TABLE HEIGHT   CONVEYOR

This Basic Layout for processing Lumber is still the best. It's been around for a long time, and many attempts have been made to replace it … to no avail. Space between machines may vary, and some "forward and back" movements may help the fit in your Plant, but the basic relationships should prevail. Start with "smooth-top" tables (waxed tempered hardboard works well). More sophisticated transfer tables can be added later.

PANELS / CASEWORK

The PANELS/CASEWORK Layout (nearby) continues the theme of Proximity and Flexibility. The close Proximity of the machines required for the various operations gives us the option of changing the sequence as required. Again, these layouts are not presented as "ideal". They are merely suggestions of what might work for you. In this area, we would use a Carrier which allows the Parts to stand on edge so that individual Parts can be selected without digging through a pile. *(See nearby illustration.)*

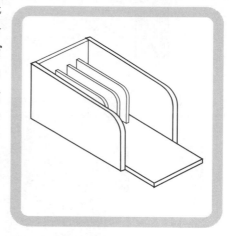

NO CARTS

You may have noticed something different about these example Layouts ... *no carts*. This indicates we're getting to the essence of a powerful possibility of the Process Flow. We can get rid of 95% of those dumb carts and redesign the plant for Product and People instead of carts. Using a combination of larger working-height tables, roller conveyors, and transfer tables at direction changes ... we find we can move material in carriers along appropriate paths much easier.

As we think through this Flow and understand the concept of Proximity and Flexibility, the importance of carts fades. We can provide logical paths, and we can also provide appropriate "pause stations" where certain parts may be "staged" for the next operation. This gives us even more Flexibility concerning our methods and sequencing.

Example: We can accumulate two wood species that receive the same profile. One "pauses" close at hand until the other arrives. So, too, with panels. We can machine cabinet sides and let them accumulate and "pause" until field dimensions, or other information, is received and we proceed with floors, backs and stretchers. We can groove sides as they come, or save up and do a larger batch all at once. All, without Carts getting in the way.

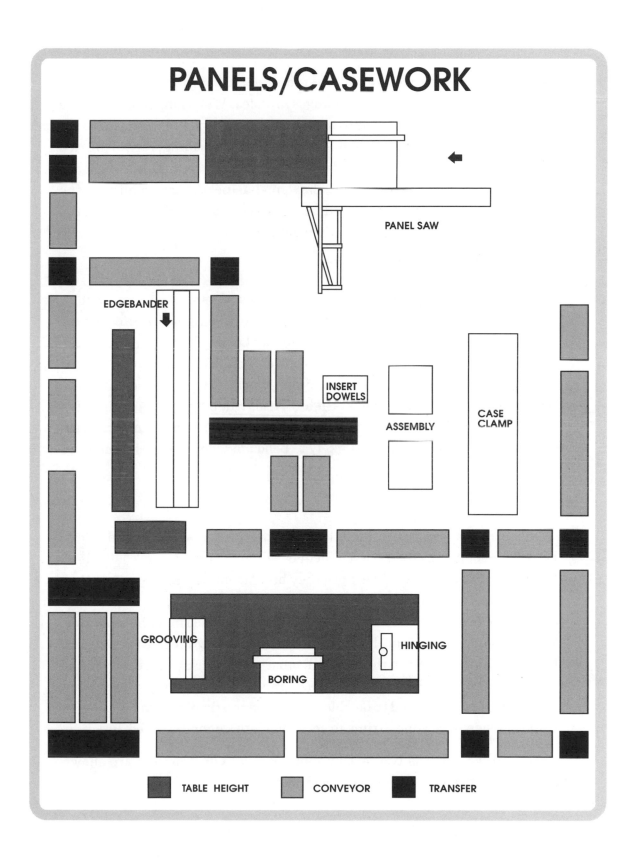

PANELS/CASEWORK

PANEL SAW

EDGEBANDER

INSERT DOWELS

ASSEMBLY

CASE CLAMP

GROOVING

BORING

HINGING

| ■ TABLE HEIGHT | ■ CONVEYOR | ■ TRANSFER |

One of the reasons we are able to group our Operations and place the Machines closer together is the changes in aisles. We no longer have to have wide aisles for carts. We only need aisles for people. Forget aisles for forklifts, too. Forklifts are great for on-loading, off-loading, retrieving raw materials from storage racks and placing it behind starter Machines at the beginning of a Loop. But forklifts have no business roaming all over the Plant ... bumping into things and hogging aisle space. Keep them in the Shipping/Receiving Area where they belong.

CARRIERS, INSTEAD

Instead of more and more carts (mostly about the same size and shape ... big and awkward) we can tailor Carriers to the right size and shape designed to do what is necessary within our Loops. Instead of losing our favorite cart when someone else appropriates it, loads it up, and moves it to the far end of the Plant. We'll have our favorite Carriers which circulate within our area ... never out of sight. Also, when we get our conveyors worked out, ANY Carrier will be accessible. It won't be parked behind six others. (Carriers are also less likely to be loaded with scrap rippings and parked for years.)

TOUGH TEST

The nearby Layout which includes a Molder presents the toughest test. Handling long lengths is a challenge. Other parts more easily lend themselves to the concept because they become manageable sized as they come off the starter machine. We must accommodate long lengths, yet deliver the boards to the most convenient point for each machine operator. We also need a Carrier at the most convenient point to receive the out-feed from the machine. Then the Carriers must move quickly and easily to the next operation, and so on. We must provide for "parking places" and "turnarounds". We need to be able to "reverse the field" and make a run to the other side from time to time to accommodate a change in feed direction.

Note that we surpass the cart in another way. Our Carriers are shown moving "sideways", as well as forward and back.

MOLDINGS

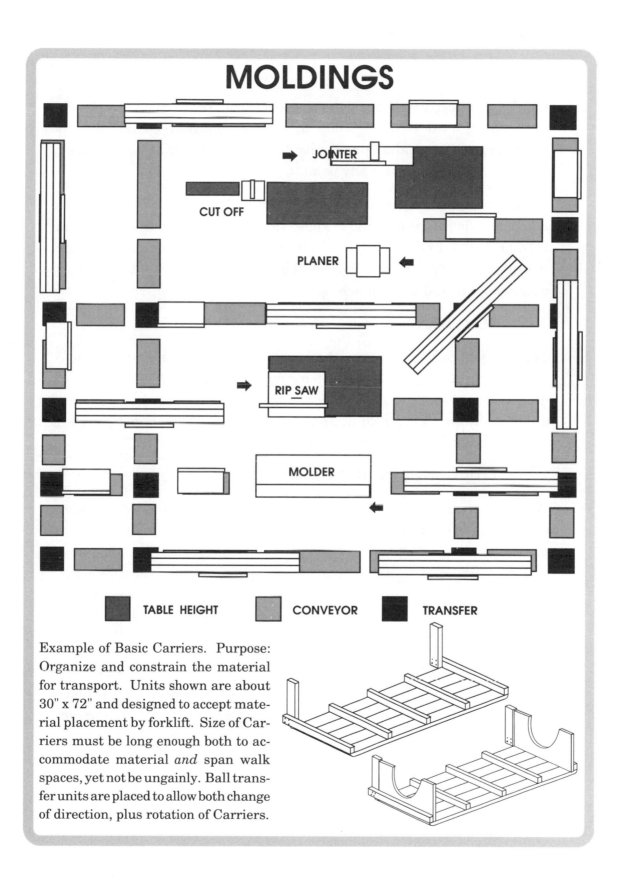

JOINTER

CUT OFF

PLANER

RIP SAW

MOLDER

TABLE HEIGHT   **CONVEYOR**   **TRANSFER**

Example of Basic Carriers. Purpose: Organize and constrain the material for transport. Units shown are about 30" x 72" and designed to accept material placement by forklift. Size of Carriers must be long enough both to accommodate material *and* span walk spaces, yet not be ungainly. Ball transfer units are placed to allow both change of direction, plus rotation of Carriers.

Our Layout pretty well meets the specifications. The perimeter conveyors can hold several Carriers while they await the next operation. The perimeter also provides opportunity to add raw material, or take away finished goods, from most any point.

Material would likely be placed and/or removed from one side, or from two adjacent sides of the rectangle. Those sides would be adjacent to material storage racks, and to shipping. From the other sides of the rectangle, material can flow to the rest of the Plant. The concept can easily accommodate additional Machines.

SORTING

The way you pick boards from the main stack will have a major influence on the system design. There are too many different preferences to design a universal system. But that doesn't mean it can't be done. Study and analyze the way People do it, and go from there. One possibility: Sort outside the perimeter while going from forklift to Carrier.

THE CONCEPT ISN'T RADICAL

We're not strangers to conveyors. We use them as returns for edgebanders (and other machines). We use them as approaches to panel saws and presses. Other industries are way ahead of us. (Someday, I'm going to try to get a picture of a Plant using conveyors as they manufacture carts.) Conveyors will provide a better working height, too. Carts are low, ostensibly to prevent tipping, creating a hazard for backs as we lift and turn.

Takes up too much space, you say? Only that part of the wide aisle we're reclaiming. Actually, we're saving space. We're making our primary manufacturing areas smaller, and we're freeing up more space for assembly. Consider that when next we need more space for a conference table, or a nurses' station.

OTHER ADVANTAGES

Shortening the distance between machines, plus providing logical paths and flexible sequences gives us more staffing options. It can make it easier for fewer People to staff an Area. Yet, it retains the option for using *more* craftsmen when there's a deadline crunch. It's easier on the Area Leader, too. The Leader can see the whole spectrum of Operations, and arrive at any of them with just a few steps.

WIRING/DUST COLLECTION/SOUND CONTROL

The logical grouping in this fashion also can simplify dust collection. Shorter runs, plus better organized drops are possible.

And it can make wiring easier. Shorter runs from the main box will save money. Stay flexible, though. Use twist-locks instead of disconnects whenever possible. As already established, we need to be able to make adjustments as product mix changes. Also the same options and flexibility will assist in the "change-over" when we begin. Even if some of our placements do become stabilized over time, being able to move a machine even a foot or two might make a big difference in a good Flow.

And it opens possibilities for sound control. When patterns of placement and Flow become stabilized, we can erect walls (whether partial, or full height) to shut in (or shut out) some of the more annoying noises.

THE BENCH AREA

By consolidating our Machining Areas, we will be freeing up more square footage for Assembly, plus shipment staging area. We can retain the Flexibility concept, but the Proximity becomes real tough. There are too many variations when it comes to sequences which include Bandsawing, Shaper work, use of Drill Press, etc. Throw in some CNC Router work ... well, you get the idea. A sound approach to the question, though, begins with the same concepts already outlined. If some of the machines in the Special Millwork area, or the Special Casework area can be located in close proximity with one another, so much the better. All the previously outlined advantages (conveyor transport, wiring, dust collection, etc.) are valid. If they can be placed "back-to-back" so to speak, the questions of infeed and outfeed shouldn't become problems. The logistics should be manageable even on the days when we must run them all at once.

Benches, and their uses, have changed over the years. But they are still needed, and still used. At one time, some of the Assembly took place on the Bench, along with final Machining of Parts, as well. Then, as parts came to the area with the Shaping, Routing, and Boring mostly complete, the Bench changed. The size and shape of the project had influence, too. You don't build a conference table on your Bench. So, in some cases, the Bench became a "back-bench". A repository for hand tools (powered, or not) and a place for special hardware used on the project ... and a sort of station, or home, or office for the individual Crafter. Which is good. All People on the Plant floor need a "home", or an "office" to call their own. The Bench makes a good one. Suggestion: Make the Benches easy to move. Their proximity to the task at hand can make things easier, and more efficient. Some days they may be back to back. Other times they may be side to side, or even arranged into a circle around a complex project requiring the skills of several People. The "home", or "office" concept remains intact even if it has wheels.

Assembly tables have their use, too, and we should retain that option. The problem there is their bulk. When not in use, they're an aggravating obstacle. And the sturdier they are, the more impossible the lump becomes. *(Benches and Assembly Tables will be discussed a bit more in the Chapter, "Machinery and Equipment".)*

STORAGE AREA

We've been examining the Flow of Material from the time it enters the Plant until the time it exits. We surely can't ignore the importance of a good Storage Area. Storage for both raw Material and finished product must be considered. Cantilever racks are more expensive, but ideal for Lumber storage. Conventional pallet racks work well for Panel goods, as well as many finished products. The nearby Illustrations suggest possible ar-

STORAGE

Lumber stored on Cantilever Racks. Arms about 30" on center seem to accommodate the various lengths well. Pallet-like platforms may be used, as well, to accept several small species amounts on one set of arms.

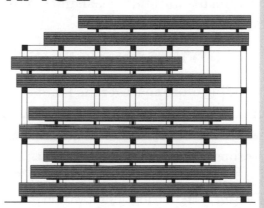

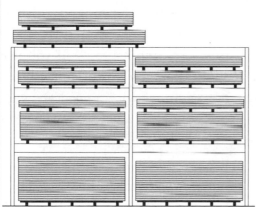

Panel goods stored on pallet racks. Most racks have moveable beams so spaces may be arranged to suit. Note longer lengths placed on top.

Pallet racks used for mixed storage. This flexibility helps us cope with change. Some months we need raw material storage... other times we need a place for finished goods.

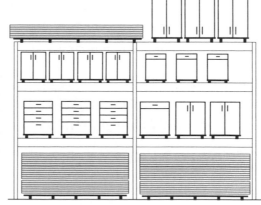

rangements. This is the Area where the forklift is at home. The forklift is at its best when off-loading trucks, on-loading trucks, placing lifts of material behind starter machines, or placing those lifts of material back in the racks.

OFFICES ON THE PLANT FLOOR?

Providing office space for the Plant Supervisor is a good idea. There will be times when good communication with Lead People will be much improved if we have an enclosed area with less noise and more privacy. Its size should be proportionate to the main Plant. If we have 25,000 square feet of Plant area, the office should be big enough for a computer and an assistant. The office for a 10,000 foot Plant would be more modest. A 100 square foot glass-enclosed space is a good start. Glass-enclosed so that everyone on both sides of the glass has a sense of togetherness, plus an awareness that things are happening. It's not a case of "Big Brother is watching you". If you need watching, we probably don't need you. Rather, it's a confidence factor. Whatever the question, the resource for assistance with a good answer is right there in sight.

A PERFECT LAYOUT?

There is no "Perfect" layout because each Woodworker has a different product mix as well as different method preferences. Plus, even if we found the "Perfect" layout today … it wouldn't necessarily be "Perfect" tomorrow. In fact, we shouldn't think in terms of "Perfect", or "Ideal". And we should NEVER conclude that we have "arrived" at the optimum Layout. We don't "arrive" … it's an ongoing journey.

As we move to find the best niche in the ever-changing Marketplace, our Products will change. And our Methods will change. In fact, our Methods should be constantly changing (improving) even if the Product mix is not.

HOW TO BEGIN

How do we approach the task of improving our Process Flow and Plant Layout? Start by observing. How do we do it, now? Track a board through a sequence. Track a panel, or two. Check the distances. Get your stop watch and check the time. With your Lead People, think through the various options for sequencing. Involve any and all People possible somewhere in the process. They'll come up with some good ideas.

Where do we park carts, now? Directly behind? ... a bit to the left? ... a bit to the right? That's where we should deliver a Carrier. Watch how parts travel from machine to machine. See a place where two operations can occur at one stop? Great! Go for it!

It doesn't have to happen all at once. Take it a step at a time. Expect some trial and error. First, try larger table-height surfaces. Design them to permit some sliding from place to place, plus a bit of "parking." Try different width conveyors. Try different heights. But, try!

BOTTOM LINE

The exercise of thinking through the Process Flow, and then laying out the Plant helps us to truly become MANUFACTURERS. These steps will help us by improving the Product. And, we can achieve enormous rewards by improving the *Process*.

Are we Craftsmen? Absolutely. Are we Artists? Yes indeed. But we're even more. We're MANUFACTURERS!

15

Plant Supervisor

My in-plant consulting takes me all across the country, and into many different plants. Each has a unique size and shape. Each has a different focus and a different product mix. However, there are threads of sameness which tie all woodworkers together.

One of the "constants" in the manufacture of woodwork is the need for a good Manager in the Plant. Curiously, this need doesn't always get the respect it deserves. Too often, the Supervisor is taken for granted and/or not included in the decision making process.

The Plant Supervisor isn't *always* the "forgotten one"… it's on a selective basis. The Supervisor is quite visible as the delivery date approaches and completion is in question. At that point, he is not only visible, he will be spoken to. Perhaps, often. And, perhaps loudly. But at other times, the Plant Supervisor is often ignored.

He may, or may not, be consulted when:

• Acquisition of new equipment is contemplated.

• The decision is made to bid a job much bigger than we've ever processed before.

• Large material orders are placed.

• Changes in drawing and/or cutting list procedures are considered.

• Other "management" type decisions are made.

JOB DESCRIPTION

Plant Supervisors are seldom given a definitive list of tasks and responsibilities. Written job descriptions are rare. *I've even known cases where the Supervisor didn't even know he was the Supervisor.*

Many young firms have real "hands-on" owners. One or more principals may work with the tools from time to time, as well as perform office functions. In such cases, I always inquire about who's in charge when those principals are away. Some of the answers have been astonishing. Example:

Q: "Who's in charge when you're away?"

A: (After long pause) "Oh, I guess Ed would be the one."

Q: "What do you mean, 'you guess'? And why the long pause?"

A: "Well, we're not too formal about things like that".

Q: "Is that fair to Ed, or the rest of the team, or to you? And by the way does the rest of the team know of this arrangement?

A: "Well he always answers the phone and signs the delivery tickets when we're gone, so they must know that we trust him."

The number of times we've had this particular conversation is an embarrassment to us all.

Too many times, the Plant Supervisor ... this key individual on whose shoulders rests an enormous part of our success ... is given woefully inadequate consideration. *As far as the craftsmen and leadmen are concerned ... he **is** management.* People in the plant assume his words and deeds represent official management policy. They assume that he is precisely in step with the powers that be.

But, it's extremely unlikely that our Supervisor sees it that way. Particularly on some days, he doesn't know whether he's management, or labor. He's the "man in the middle" ... with those enormous responsibilities ... but not necessarily with the proportional authority. And even when he does have the authority, he may not be well enough informed. He's trapped between unrealistic expectations on either side.

The hands-on craftsmen want a hassle-free job. The Office wants fantastic production at low cost.

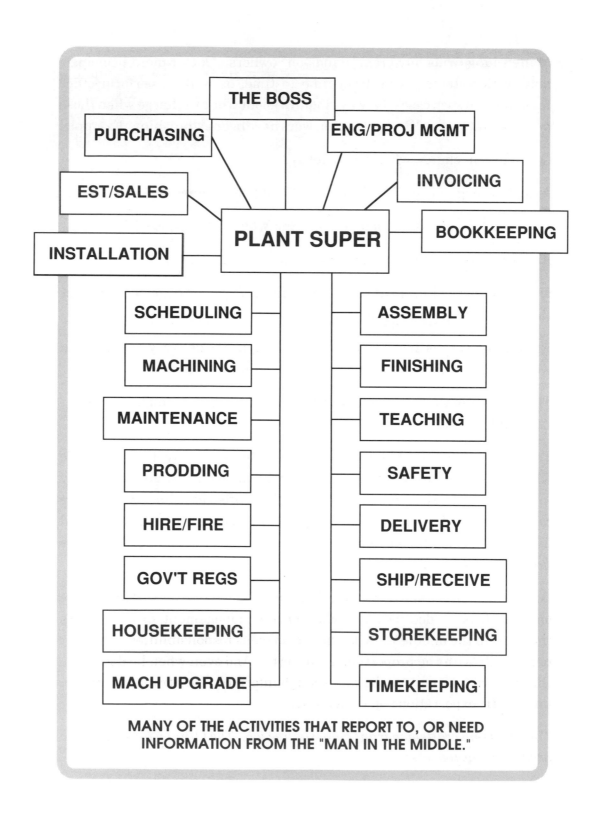

MANY OF THE ACTIVITIES THAT REPORT TO, OR NEED
INFORMATION FROM THE "MAN IN THE MIDDLE."

In some plants, there is even this subtle notion that unless you wear a three-piece suit, you aren't truly worthy to participate in the important decisions concerning the ongoing goals and objectives of the company. The way one Supervisor expressed it: *"They treat me just like a mushroom ... keep me in the dark and keep on shovelling the manure my way."*

INSTEAD

Let's talk about a better way to handle it.

As always, a good management decision begins with a clear definition.

A clear definition of anticipated results. What is it that we need ... and expect ... to happen? We must know *that* before we can properly choose the methods. Define the outcomes before we select and advise those who will produce those outcomes. If we don't know what we want, how can we expect anyone else to know? And what are the chances of anyone delivering?

Let's examine some of the things which we expect to happen on the plant side of the office door. The Plant Supervisor is to be our designated delegate to make sure that each and every one of these things gets done. Notice, we said "make sure that each and every one *gets* done!" *He doesn't* ***do*** *each one!* Such as:

- Job assignments

- Prodding

- Teaching

- Coordinating schedules

- Safe practices

- Conformance with gov't. regulations

- Recommend Machinery and Equipment

- Housekeeping

- Storekeeping

- Personnel decisions

- Timekeeping

- Maintenance

- Groundskeeping

You didn't realize there were so many, did you?

Point is: If we expect all of these things to get done, we should say so. Tell our Supervisor what is expected, and give the support needed to get the job done.

EXAMPLES:

- *Job assignments.*

Assigning the various tasks to the right people and in the right sequence takes some doing. We want to make sure that we're working on the right job (priority) and we want the job in the hands of the right people, who can do it correctly, and quickly.

As the Plant Supervisor understands this and develops a feel for it, he will make the best use of all resources. He'll get performance out of people, machines and even space. *Many decisions which achieve maximum performance must be made on the plant floor.* The decisions concerning priorities must be made by joint efforts of people from both sides of the office door, but many specifics be decided in the Plant.

Best method: using the Production Planning Board. The weekly meeting establishes the priorities, states the objectives for the coming week and puts it on a Board for all to see, and use.

Always give the Supervisor whatever is needed to do the job. Anticipate. Have the drawings, cutting bills, materials, color selections, etc. there in time for some planning. Just a day or two more notice affords a much greater opportunity for efficient resource mobilization.

- *Prodding*

Don't take it too literally. The dictionary says "prod: to jab, as with a pointed stick." If we really have folks who require that type of "prodding", we might consider wishing them good luck on their new job. The requirement is a "presence" on the floor which constantly reminds the urgency to keep things moving. Of course, that urgency, along with a brisk tempo has to be built into our methods and procedures (our Process Flow). No amount of bellowing and snorting is going to force good things to happen if we don't have a good system to begin with.

- *Teaching*

Our Supervisors must be Resources. Resources for upgrading the skill and knowledge of all our people. It's hard for most of us to accept the truth that we're running a school. But, if we expect to manufacture with quality and consistency we must be training people on an ongoing basis. Whether part of an organized program (union, or whatever) or entirely on our own, we *must* be involved in the recruiting and training.

From establishing entry level positions to the upgrade of experienced craftsmen, *we* must be doing it. And it all happens on the Plant Supervisor's turf.

- *Coordinating schedules*

Touched on during job assignments. But there's more. Completion date is the key, of course. But even if our labor hour budget is right on the money, that still won't tell us precisely which day each operation will commence. Different parts of the job will require different lead times. Then, there's the question of temporary overload in a certain area. All of a sudden, everything requires a special finish ... or we have all casework ... or moldings. It takes quite a maestro to conduct the symphony, some days.

And then there's grouping of product for long distance delivery, or servicing special needs for several installation crews at the same time. *And we haven't mentioned change orders.*

- *Safe practices*

An all day, every day job. It goes beyond vigilance. We need aggressive searching for any weakness in our methods.

- *Conformance with gov't. regulations*

Can be particularly frustrating, especially when rules are not clear. Often there are inconsistent interpretations. But the rules exist and we must respond. *And guess who's right out there in the middle of it?*

- *Recommend Machinery and Equipment*

It is extremely important to maintain ongoing dialog in this area. Owners are uncomfortable with surprises concerning a machine we "have to have" by next week to properly do a job. Plant Supervisors tire of hearing "we can't afford it". We will always be faced with items we can't afford, but can't afford to be without. Some advance planning, and clear understandings about budgets will make it easier. The responsibility of the Plant Supervisor is to advise of needs early, clearly, calmly, patiently, and persistently. *(More on this in the Chapter "Machinery and Equipment".)*

- *Housekeeping*

The task no one takes seriously enough. Somehow it gets done, but only under duress in some plants. There is an enormous amount of sawdust and offal developed in the course of a job. It can become a serious problem. If we don't take it seriously and manage it well, it will become quite an expense. The clutter wastes space, and people's time. And it can be a safety hazard. Decisions need to be made. Shall cleanup of an area be the task of an entry level person, or do we hire people just for that? Or should a benchman brush out his own area at the completion of a project? Should the cleanup specialists function during the workday, or after hours? A good case can be made for all of these suggestions.

- *Storekeeping*

Another one we tend to sort of "back into", rather than face it head-on. Procedures for reorder points on all supplies is a must. Adhesives, fasteners, sanding sheets and belts, drill bits, router bits ... none of these things (and there are many) are a grievous expense ... except when we run out! How much is a $15 router bit worth when we desperately need it, deadline is here, and the stores are closed?

Stock material items must be managed, too. Few even try to compute the dollar loss that comes from running out of something. *It can be staggering!*

- *Personnel decisions*

Who does the hiring and firing? When? Why? In some plants, the Super doesn't want to be involved in the interview. He may say "you hire 'em, I'll fire 'em." (Curiously, I've seen it work!) Others want to see the candidate face-to-face. Whatever works. The Supervisor will definitely be evolved in Evaluation process. *(More on this in the "Operations" Section.)*

- *Timekeeping*

Plant Supervision includes the monitoring of Timecards. Spot checks, at least, for the minimum. For larger Plants, some tabulation in the Plant office, too.

- *Maintenance*

Our recommendation: Quickly delegate machinery maintenance to the Lead People in an area, but it must be monitored. Overall Plant Maintenance schedules need to be established.

- *Groundskeeping*

Groundskeeping? Well, who else will assign chores such as snow shoveling, grass and weed cutting, etc.? Is it included in the Job Description?

And, we haven't yet discussed Working Supervisors. That's right ... in some places our Man is supposed to take care of all these things, *and still work with the tools!* Yes, it *can* work ... in a few cases. While we're still in a start-up phase ... and trying to get some momentum going, yet keep costs down ... it can work, and work well for a time. Don't cling to the arrangement too long. (And don't let the Super consider it, either.) Either, or both, may get too comfortable with the arrangement. It's a sure way to stunt our growth, and foul up a smooth Process Flow. There will be opportunities to utilize our Man's skills and experience in the Manufacturing process on a "spot" basis. But, better to have a reserve "pinch-hitter", than have a much overqualified player in the regular lineup.

SUMMARY

The "Man in the Middle" is a key team member. He deserves the full recognition and respect of everyone. We should clearly communicate our expectations, and work for a consensus on how best to accomplish the tasks and responsibilities. After the results and methods have been agreed upon, we should make sure that all resources are furnished. As we grow, more assistance for the Supervisor will be required. A "second-in-command" should be selected and trained ... whether for an ongoing presence, or merely to fill in for vacation, or other days away. A computer and printer make sense, somewhere along the line. A quick Drawing, combining several Cutting Lists into one, help with the Timecard information entry ... any one is sufficient reason. Together, they make the move mandatory.

The good news? It's getting better. More and more, the "Man in the Middle" *is* involved as he should be. If it isn't happening at your Plant, yet ... think about it. Then get started. You'll be glad you did.

16

Machines/Equipment

CAPABILITY

Capability is what we actually sell.

I know ... we think in terms of selling the products we load on the truck, but those change all the time. If we're in the custom business, the product mix changes almost daily. If we manufacture a line of Furniture, or a line of Cabinets, the change is not so frequent, but it's there. We're not building the same products as last year ... and next year will see change, too.

The constant is the Capability we have to Manufacture those Products.

Capability enables us to respond to the Market. Good Machines, with good People to operate them, good methods, (combined, of course, with an understanding of Process Flow and Plant Layout), enable us to offer new Products and Services as quickly as we perceive the need. That's good Business!

THE PLANT'S RESPONSIBILITY

The acquisition and upgrading of Machinery and Equipment is an extremely important subject. This Chapter examines the process, stressing the Plant's involvement. The topic will be addressed, again, in the *"Money" Section* ... with additional considerations of Valuation, Justification, Budgeting, and Financing. The whole process will proceed faster and smoother if People on each side of the office door will listen and comprehend one another's viewpoints.

THE CASE FOR HAVING GOOD MACHINES

Most of the reasons for buying machines are fairly obvious. If we need to do a certain operation, and don't have a machine to do it well, we buy that machine. If a machine is not performing well, we seek to upgrade it.

Maybe it's the down-time, or the repair bills. Maybe it takes too long to setup. Or maybe it doesn't hold a setup, and the last piece is different than the first. Perhaps it cuts best at 20 feet-a-minute, and we need 30 feet-a-minute. Those reasons are obvious, but there are others.

THE BUSINESS POSTURE

Having good machines is good business. When we're out at the leading edge of the available techniques, we send a message to our craftspeople that we want to help them do a good job. Morale improves. So does Productivity. (Both the People's efforts and the Machine's ability.) And the word gets around. If our plant has the best Machines … that's where the best People want to be. Recruiting (and Training) become easier. We are building and maintaining our Capability.

"Good Machines" means dependable, predictable Machines which turn out parts cleanly and accurately. "Good" doesn't necessarily mean brand-new. It doesn't mean fancy. It doesn't mean with lots of bells and whistles. It does mean sensible setup and setups which hold. It means putting out parts (or edging, or sanding, etc.) fast enough to keep up with the Flow. And "dependable" and "predictable" includes parts and service.

As we get to know about Machines, get to know dealers, too. There are some very good ones … but some are better. The right ones will help us acquire the right mix of new and used, and can help find the right one at the top of the priority list. Establish some teamwork which doesn't waste our time … or theirs.

ESTABLISHING PRIORITIES

The acquisition of new Machines is much too important to be left to chance. We must Plan better. Three considerations:

- Priority

- Timing

• Money

To start: WRITE A LIST OF ALL THE MACHINES NEEDED IN THE NEAR FUTURE. Work it up ... study it ... refine it till it's right. Consult your colleagues. (Possibly have each of them develop a list, then combine all lists to get started.) Each of us has ideas on Priorities. None is absolutely correct. Work on it together. Added benefit: The cooperation on the implementation will come much easier if there has been participation all along the way.

Often, the three items which work their way to the top of the list are almost equal in Priority. As the weeks of study and review go by, they may swap positions from time to time. So, it's best to focus on them and write out more detailed specifications.

THE CHECKLIST

The nearby Checklist is designed to assist in that most important step. Fill one out for each Machine under consideration. You'll find it a valuable Tool in the process of determining both Priority and Timing. The Checklist prompts us to look beyond the Machine itself, and examine all the peripheral items which must be considered.

Note the Specifications Section. It's important for the key People on the team to be on the same page on this one. Questions about size, number of spindles (or stations, etc.), horsepower, feed rate, new or used ... and all the rest. Usually, when we are clear on our specifications (size, speed, power, etc.) the number of manufacturers narrows down. Two or three names emerge for the "short list" and we can proceed to pin down both manufacturer and dealer. (Lower portion of Checklist.)

Then there's the effect on the rest of the Plant. That Section asks about Location, then prompts us to think about Support Machines, Tooling, Wiring, Dust collection, Material handling, and the rest. As those questions are answered, we can address the Time Requirements. Assign realistic lead Times for Ordering, Shipping, all the hook-ups, etc.

MACHINERY BUYING CHECKLIST

MACHINE:

SPECIFICATIONS:				PLANT REQUIREMENTS:	
(size, horsepower, amps required, spindles, spindle size, tilts, stations, etc.)				Location in plant	
				Support machines	
				Tooling	
				Wiring	
				Dust collection	
				Material handling	

TIME REQUIREMENTS:

Machine Order lead time		"UP-TO-SPEED" TIME	
Tooling Order lead time		Financing	
Material handling Order lead time		COMMENCE DATE:	
Shipping		MACHINE ARRIVE DATE:	
Wiring		COMPLETE SET-UP DATE:	
Dust collection run			
Set up/hook up Machine		**"UP-TO-SPEED" DATE:**	
Set up material handling			

PROS	CONS
MANUFACTURER ABC	
DEALER LMN	

Don't forget the "UP-TO-SPEED" time. Those Machines aren't very smart when they first arrive. It sometimes takes weeks, or even months, before they finally learn what we want done. If the "UP-TO-SPEED" Date is the critical one, all the other time components must be figured very carefully.

IDEAL PRIORITY AND TIMING

You may well ask: "What are the most appropriate conditions for Machinery Buying?" When should we buy a Machine? Try this List:

> Right Priority
>
> Right Machine
>
> Right Brand
>
> Right Time
>
> Right Price
>
> Right Jobs coming up
>
> Right Financing

If all those conditions were present, it would most certainly be great. But, when do we *really* buy that Machine?

> Breakdown
>
> Machinery Show excitement
>
> Bargain
>
> Smooth sales pitch

Are any of those times the best?

Some of us buy only when forced by a breakdown. Never mind that there are no bargains to be found at that time. Never mind that it occurs when we're already behind, and the down-time kills us. Never mind that we had plenty of warning from previous glitches.

Did you ever have a machine break down when there was Time to replace it?

... When you had already located the Right Replacement?
... and it was available at the Right Price?
... and you had the Money?

Nor is it ever likely to happen. So let's make our List, write Checklists for Machines moving toward the top, and get our Plan working.

We incorrectly apply the old cliche: "If it ain't broke, don't fix it." ... which totally misses the mark when applied to Machinery. Even the finest equipment begins to wear out ... and begins to become obsolete ... the moment it's placed in service! Years later, we may still be "getting by", but we're not necessarily getting full value. Unfortunately, in some plants a craftsman's skill is largely measured by his ability to "keep that 'ol clunker runnin' pretty good." Imagine what that ingenuity and resourcefulness could do if applied to getting product out the door with a *good* Machine. The saddest extreme ... and I've seen it happen several times ... is a company waiting so long to upgrade machinery that the expense is overwhelming and they go out of business, instead.

The recommendation is to Budget a serious amount of Money to be spent each year on Machinery and Equipment. Check back over the last few years and see what we have actually been spending. You will be astonished! *Lesson: We've been spending it, but not as part of a plan.* If a certain amount is stipulated, then planned for, much of the consternation is removed. We don't have to wonder *if* Money will be spent ... only when, and on which. Plant People know upgrades are coming. Our Banker is aware of the plan and is not surprised. Everybody gets more comfortable, and better decisions are made. We'll be far more apt to buy the Right Machine, at the Right Time, at the Right Price, and with the Right Financing. *(See "Machinery Purchase" in Money Section.)*

OTHER EQUIPMENT

We stress, again, the importance of good storage devices, and good material handling. The combination of proximity, plus accessibility, is worth far more than you realize. In some Plants, locating certain material is a big deal ... getting to it is another hassle ... than getting it to a saw is more trauma. Don't allow such confusion in your Plant. Don't stall on conveyors. There are bound to be corridors where material moves from one point to another on a regular basis. Start there. Use some rollers placed at a sensible height, and try it. Some powered rollers could be added in some instances. Plants who have tried conveyors can't understand why they waited so long.

THE BENCH AREA

The nearby illustration shows how the craftsman's "home" might appear. His/her special, personal station which includes all personal hand tools, plus company assigned portable power tools, clamps and other special apparatus. Our strong recommendation remains: All craftsmen should have drills, routers, sanders, spline cutters, etc. assigned to them, personally.

In other words, each craftsman has custody, and accountability, for practically all of the daily used small tools. Other craftsmen who may need to "borrow" a tool, or its bits, may do so only with permission from the "custodian." This works best, because the true craftsman likes his equipment maintained and adjusted "just so," and can work far more effectively (quality and quantity) if he doesn't have to deal with "community property."

Recommendation: Assign enough drills so that time isn't wasted looking for, and changing bits. Probably the minimum is 3. Apply the same concept with routers, trimmers and sanders. Our people will plan their work and accomplish tasks with a minimum of setups and changes if we give them the chance. But if we elect to short the team by getting chintzy with the equipment, we will pay dearly when people waste time running down a tool ... then a bit ... and sometimes end up with a tool with a defective switch.

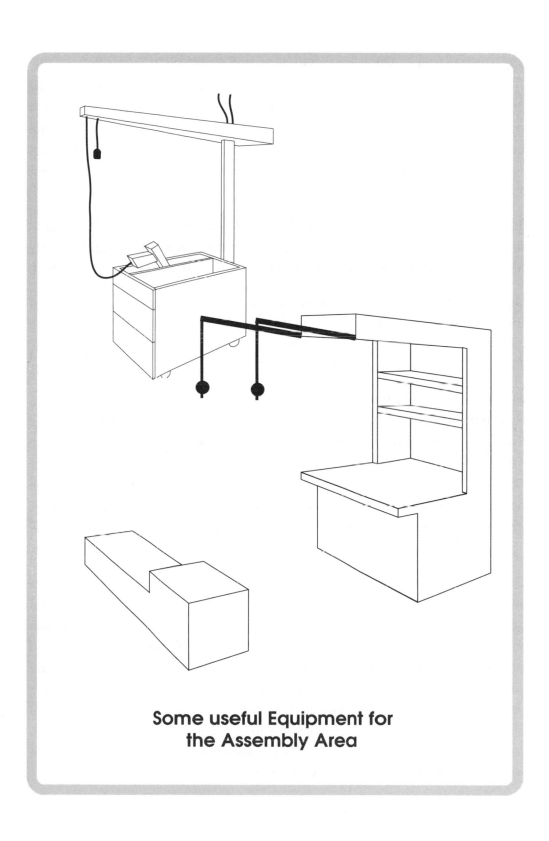

Some useful Equipment for the Assembly Area

The temptation to not report a faulty switch is always there with "community property". Human nature perceives very little incentive to take the responsibility to have it repaired. We'll save money by having enough equipment. The senior skilled people will probably end up with more equipment and a more "permanent" work station location. That's O K. Let it even become a status symbol. That gives the rookies something to shoot for.

There is very little agreement on the use of assembly benches. It seems to depend on how we were "brought up." I was brought up using assembly benches a lot, but grew to dislike them because of all the space they robbed.

Sensible compromise: use them as required, but restrict their size and insist they be movable. Worst mistake: Building an assembly bench big enough and sturdy enough to accommodate any project we can imagine. That big lump will ruin your life.

Study the requirement. We need a method to begin the process of knitting together all of the parts. When the sub-assembly is small, raising it off the floor with a bench or trestles or something makes a lot of sense. But as the unit grows, the comfortable working height may require a lower platform. To put it another way: joining the first two pieces together might best be done on a surface 30-36" off the floor. But as other pieces are added, the unit probably grows too big and awkward to remain at that height. Many items begin on a surface 30-36" off the floor and soon end up placed on the floor.

One effective way to assemble special casework is the two-level bench such as the one in the nearby illustration. "Level" is a key word, here. The initial preparation and assembly begins at the raised level, then is transferred to the lower level (actually leveled by floor levelers). Drawers and doors are then fit to the boxes, and since everything is level the installation is made simpler. Simply align the doors and drawer fronts all together, then secure the unit. When one part lines up, they all line up. Then as the unit grows bigger and bigger (such as a nurses station, teller line, reception desk, etc.), we need all the space we can find. We probably wish that the assembly table we used at the beginning could simply disappear for a few days.

A companion consideration to the assembly table is the access to air and power for fasteners and other operations required during assembly. First choice is air lines and power cords dropping down from above. Properly designed, they can give us the reach and the stretch we need. And there will be no hazards under foot. Our composite assembly station illustration, nearby, indicates drops with connectors in front of the back bench. Another variation is the roll-about cart. This basic configuration works for many combinations ... air, electricity, both ... holsters for air nailers, or drills, or routers, or trimmers, etc. Appropriate supplies are in drawers below the holsters. The cart, itself, is fed by drops from the ceiling. This type cart works well for adhesive spraying, too, and flood or spotlights can be added for excellent task lighting. (Believe it, or not, some plants have dark corners with less than optimum candlepower.)

A big assembly table is a necessity for sash, door and frame work. Of course a clamp table is ideal, but it's not always possible to justify one. Allow for clamps and fixtures for bending circle heads, etc. This means including capability to screw stops and jigs to the table surface. Driving and pulling nails is hard on the table. Screws work best in holding down the apparatus. Plywood is the preferred substrate, but another surface is suggested to prevent slivers under the fingernails.

DON'T CHEAT ON EQUIPMENT

Giving our key Manufacturing People anything less than they need to do the job is foolish ... and costly. Many times the cost is a direct transfer. Either we spend the dollar on Equipment, or we spend it on Payroll. And many times, we pay for the Equipment once, but pay the Payroll amount again and again.

17

Moving Day

There's an oft repeated, but much ignored good old rule:

"Plan your work, then work your Plan."

If you weren't convinced before, you'd better become a believer as we approach Moving Day.

An efficient, economical move *positively* must be planned. The lost production time *can* be kept to a minimum. The employee disorientation *can* be avoided. The confusion of "lost" parts, components, hardware, etc. *can be* virtually eliminated. But, only if every step is planned. *All the sequences and placements must be thought through, written down, and then meticulously followed.*

Some prominent myths and errors which keep recurring:

• *Myth 1: The object is to make the move as fast as possible.*

Wrong. The object is to do it smoothly and with minimum disruption of normal manufacturing events.

• *Myth 2: Move with the fewest loads possible.*

Wrong, again. Part of the first mentioned error. Proper sequencing is more important. Even half a load is O K if a critical machine is delivered in time to be placed and hooked up with electricity, air, and dust collection so some machining can begin. This will be a tough fight. There's a strange compulsion to grab anything within reach and throw it onto the truck. Of course, those odd items have no place to "go" upon arrival so they're dropped, ker-plunk, right in the doorway at the new plant. By mid-day it's impossible to maneuver around the doorway. And the assortment of odd boxes and barrels … whatever … have been stacked, restacked, pushed, pummeled and possibly severely damaged. Worst of all, no one knows what's where and critical items may be lost for weeks.

• *Myth 3: Palletizing, Lot numbering, and Lists are for sissies. Real he-men just throw everything onto the truck.*

Another critical example of the necessity for good planning and disciplined follow-through. Get some office people with clerical skills to help. As items are strapped to pallets, tape on a prominent Lot Number. Someone with clipboard duty can briefly list the items included under that number. Series of numbers can be assigned to different loops. Example: 1 thru 19 belong to hardware room. 20 thru 39 belong in special casework assembly. Items not boxed can be placed in "trash barrel" type containers with appropriate padding and similarly marked.

Palletizing will take much longer than the actual loading, hauling, and off-loading, so don't wait till Moving Day to start. Good news: some listing and palletizing can begin days, even weeks, before moving day.

Integrate everything into the regular production schedule. Moving is an event equal to any other on the Timeline Chart or the Production Planning Board. Working them together can show when to pack up and move the machines, which finished products can move directly to the jobsite, and when various raw materials flowing in can be directed to the new location.

• *Myth 4: The main thing is to get everything over to the new place. We can do the sorting, later.*

You can't believe how much this approach can cost. People stumbling all over the plant, pawing through one pile, then another. Things get shuffled in the process, too. Even if you think you remember where a certain item was … it's probably been moved by the time you get back.

PLANT LAYOUT

That's the place to start. Apply our Process Flow and Plant Layout methods to prepare for machine placement.

Build on the existing plan. Surely, the Flow has been modified and streamlined in the present facility. *If it hasn't, how do we know we need to move?*

The chance to finally get a good plant layout can outweigh all of the hard work of moving, and then some. Merely getting all the new extra space is not enough. If the space isn't used well, things will seem just as awkward as before. Don't make the mistake of taking this opportunity to put more space between each machine. *(One of Norlin's Laws states that a Woodworker will fill any space you put him in. But, you don't have to.)* That guarantees every part and every person traveling extra miles every day. The cost of that extra travel comes right out of your pocket.

And don't stretch everything out into a long line. The assembly line might work for cars, but not for custom woodwork. Instead, stick to the Loops. Keep each function tight enough so that a small sized crew can man the whole thing without ending up half a block from home. A good understanding of how many loops we need and their lengths will be the best guide to building selection. The right building will be quickly identified when we know what we're looking for.

There is a rule of thumb. Having about 1,000 square feet per craftsman works pretty well. So, if you're struggling with 10 or 12 craftsmen in 7,500 square feet, it's probably time to be looking around.

However, don't let that be the limit. Having more than 1,000 per person is not a crime. Having room to grow and having space to stage extra raw material (or finished goods, for that matter) can certainly make life easier. At $4.80 a square foot for rent, each 1,000 square feet costs $400 a month. An extra 1,000 or two may be a real bargain.

GETTING THE TEAM INVOLVED

Planning the Process Flow and the Plant Layout should involve the whole team. Hopefully, people have already been involved in the past. But, if not, we can start now. Don't get everyone involved if we're still at ground zero.

Start with the Plant Super and Lead People, instead. But bring everyone in as the thing evolves.

There are two excellent reasons. First, line people probably have some great ideas we can use. Second, if they know it's their plan, too, things will be implemented smoothly. If the whole team understands why certain things were decided, it can make a tremendous difference. ***Folks who believe in a plan will make it work.***

Have a theoretical plan and small models of the various pieces of equipment (all to scale) in the lunchroom. Much can be learned as everyone tries to design the "perfect" layout. It's extremely educational (even humbling) to discover how many compromises and trade-offs are necessary to make everything work.

If it's feasible, take people over to show them the new place. That, plus their work on Plant Layout, will help them visualize themselves working and moving about in the new space. The familiarization can begin well before Moving Day.

PEOPLE POWER

Recommendation is to keep the team involved with the move, too. Check with agencies who furnish temporary help. Temporaries can perform many of the routine chores. Regular team members will direct and assist those folks. Regulars know the items which belong together and will be alert to a bolt dropping out, etc., whereas the uninitiated would never see anything. Security is better with our folks right there, too.

Talk with professional machinery movers. They have all the neat tools and dollys, as well as the know-how. If our machines are not too heavy, or too sophisticated, we might try the do-it-yourself route. But, bolting machines to skids and lugging them around isn't great fun. I'm always concerned for the safety, too. Safety for the people and the machine, too.

FORKLIFTS

For moving day, only, we're going to set aside some very specific rules.

The Regular Rules:

> • *Forklifts are for vertical movements of goods. (Horizontal movements are handled by conveyors, pallet jacks, etc.)*

> • *Forklifts stay by the dock for loading and unloading. They don't wander around all over the plant. Wandering around the plant is forbidden because wide aisles waste floor space. And, with or without wide aisles, there's too much chance for smashing and crashing.*

In other words: *ordinarily,* forklifts are limited to off-loading a truck, placing the material in a bin (or behind a panel saw/rip saw); or, the corollary … taking finished goods out of the bin or off the floor and placing it on the delivery truck.

On Moving Day, only, we can allow forklifts to roam a bit farther. As we prepare items for shipment, we can begin shifting around to provide sufficient clearance, and forklifts can shuttle back and forth staging goods for loading.

HOW MANY TRUCKS AND HOW MANY FORKLIFTS?

Well, let's see what we can work out. Start with some carefully considered assumptions about:

• *How many truckloads will there be?*

Factors include: Will some machines be on Mover's trucks? Will we use only our own trucks, or will we rent? (Flat-beds are handy because you can on-load and off-load from more directions. Make sure we have enough tie-down straps and stabilizing braces … also tarps if weather is threatening.)

• *How long for a round trip?*

As with all activities, we like to see a brisk tempo. We like to "get on with the job" and see things happening. **But, remember, smooth, safe and**

certain are more important. We'll be into some activities we don't do every day. If we start pushing too much we'll cause problems. Allow for traffic delays if we attempt to span morning and/or evening rush hours.

• *How many doors will we use?*

Are we shipping out of one, or two? (Receiving must be the same.) Are we using drive-in doors, or docks?

Example: If we assumed 30 truckloads, total, and a two-hour round trip, and a ten-hour day ... we could probably do it with three trucks, using one door and one forklift at each end, and do it in two days. (It won't be quite that tidy, unless we've loaded at least one truck the night before, and possibly even have one truck at the new place ready to unload first thing. Which brings us back to whether we can drive in, or not. We don't want a loaded flat-bed sitting around out on the street.)

NEW MACHINES

This can be a great time to upgrade machinery. Theoretically, it's possible to have the upgrade machine running when the old one shuts down. However, it's tricky. We're introducing some new logistics which are pretty "iffy." Example: If we have established an even flow of trucks on the first moving day, having some other delivery truck butt in might not be the best. Or if we have counted heavily on a timely delivery that becomes delayed, there goes the schedule. If, on the other hand, the new equipment can be delivered a day or two early; it could work out great. Particularly if we have an "advance party" there, anyway.

ADVANCE PARTY

Advance Party work includes everything from marking the exact spot for each machine so wiring and dust collection hook-ups can begin, to standing by to tell the telephone installer where the phones go. Items to consider, as well: Check-out of burglar alarms, sprinkler system, other utilities.

Of course, several things should be settled before the lease is signed. There must be enough electrical service coming in. (Bringing in another 400

Amps can get expensive) Consider natural gas service capacity, too. Air make-up for the finishing room can absorb a lot of BTU's. Whether we're leasing or buying, considerations like these can have a drastic influence. This is the time to check smaller details, too. Electrical door openings are much better than manual. What about dock bumpers, weather canopies, or air curtains. Even security gates for when overhead doors are partially open for ventilation. Our landlord might know where he can get hold of some of these items much easier and cheaper than we can, and if the question is phrased properly, these little goodies might just be thrown in to close the deal.

Advance Party work could also include some office remodel. Even some partitioning. Our degree of involvement will depend on how busy we are at the time, plus the rapidity of unfolding events. Broadly, let others do as much as possible unless their quotes are outrageous. That shouldn't happen. We should have enough contacts with general contractors and other trades to get the right price *and* service.

DON'T FORGET! WE'RE IN THE MANUFACTURING BUSINESS, NOT THE MOVING BUSINESS OR REMODELING BUSINESS. While we're happily dabbling with odd chores here and there, demonstrating how clever and versatile we are ... PRODUCTION AND PROFITS WILL DISAPPEAR!

I'm not ruling out special volunteer teams to do these things evenings or weekends. That's terrific. In fact that sort of team spirit, with its excitement and enthusiasm might be one of the best parts of the move. Just don't burn out those good folks. Let's keep our priorities straight.

MATERIAL DELIVERIES

Delivery of material could also occur while some Advance Party folks are on the scene. Just be sure to have material handling equipment available, and know where to put stuff so it doesn't get in the way. Storage racks not required, at this point, but nice if we can have a couple there.

HAVE ELECTRICIAN STANDING BY

Depending on how big a wiring chore we have, the electrician could arrive a day or two ahead of Moving Day. He should be there to hook up machines as they are placed. Several should be running the same day they arrive.

DUST COLLECTION

Toughest problem is in Lumber area. Molders, Planers, etc. really can't be operated without waste collection. And the formulas for deciding how much of the old ductwork to move, and when, are tricky. Sometimes it's cheaper to re-run much of the duct-work than to dismantle and re-assemble. Unless our stuff is fairly new, the correct size and capacity, and has good machine hoods and sweeps, it might just be better to start over. In so doing, we gain the tremendous opportunity to have most of it installed before the machines arrive. Smaller machines, particularly the ones dispersed around the Special Millwork assembly area are best served by smaller collectors on the spot.

INSURANCE

Add a call to your insurance agent to our Moving Day Checklist. Make sure both locations are covered during the overlap period, and make sure everything is covered in transit.

FINISHING ROOM

Another set of tough questions. Similar to the trade-offs of the dust collection system. How much can we keep and when do we move it. The finishing question is probably more complicated because of delivery schedules, as well. It would be grand if we could get all caught up on finishing for two weeks, pack it all up, and move. Don't count on that. Many companies I work with, and other friends, as well, are expanding and upgrading finishing capabilities. Factor in the different equipment to handle chemicals designed to meet the new emission standards, and this becomes an area right for new apparatus.

SEQUENCES

Broadly, it's best to think of moving and setting up in the same sequence our woodwork is produced.

Example: Machine ahead to sustain two of three days of assembly. (Possibly some overtime involved) Then pack up the machine area, and move. Number 1 craftsman (or No. 2) proceeds to new facility to become part of the Advance Party. (Even *be* the Advance Party) He joins electrician and duct-work people in preparing for machine arrival. Equipped with rented forklift, is prepared to receive raw materials and/or new equipment. Soon joined by someone (possibly from office) to greet folks and direct traffic. Rest of machining team arrive in proportion to machine arrival … complete setup, and start machining. As new parts are machined, the assembly people and their benches will be arriving. They can get situated and reasonably settled, then begin assembly.

This is where the previous involvement and familiarization process pays off. Rather than strangers arriving in a forbidding place, they'll be entering something they've been looking forward to. Also, the new arrivals will have their lists, and will know where to find everything they need.

BUILD SPECIAL STORAGE BEFORE MOVING

If new racks, bins, shelves or whatever can't be bought and must be built, the strong recommendation is to build them at the old plant. Even with the best case situation for a super-smooth move, the efficiency at the new plant won't match the old for a while.

THROW OUT THE GARBAGE

An important part of preparation for Moving Day includes getting rid of all that stuff we've kept too long (or shouldn't have saved in the first place) Now is a great time to throw it out. Be ruthless! Particularly with those things you've already moved once before.

PLAN IT, WORK IT, AND HAVE A GOOD MOVE!

18

Considerations

This Chapter combines some very important Topics which need to be examined, but don't quite require Chapters of their own. Rather than bury them in some other Chapter, we wish to emphasize their importance by presenting them in this Chapter.

We recommend both the Finishing and the Installation of our manufactured products, because it provides far more assurance that the end result … in both Quality and Customer Satisfaction … will be up to our standards. But since customs and needs vary, we can't say it's a must for everyone. Each requires a sizable commitment, too, so we must consider the prospect very carefully.

FINISHING

Even if we're not presently Finishing, we should still be studying the subject and gaining knowledge. Our professional competence should include understanding the needs of the Finisher. By making Finishing easier, we will make more friends and get more business.

Pressures of regulation, time constraints and other factors have increased the need for Finishing before arrival at the jobsite. So, either we will be doing it in our Plant, or coordinating shipments so it can be done at a Finishers Plant. Working with a good Finisher is a good second choice to doing it ourselves. We can exercise some influence on Quality and Scheduling. And we can be observing and learning. I know of several instances when a Finishing subcontractor was induced to come in and manage a new in-plant facility because a mutual respect had been built over time.

When we decide to make the move, that's the sort of knowledge and experience we'll need. We will also need help from reliable suppliers concerning their finishing chemical's ability to meet regulatory standards. Same for the applying equipment. New finishes are being developed with new solvents. And new equipment is coming on line to accommodate those new finishes and put more finish onto our product, and less into the air. There will be serious space considerations, too. In addition to the spray-booth area, we need a larger, clean area for staging, rubbing, drying, etc. All these considerations are linked together. Starting with our best guess about our volume of work and the variety of finishes, the number of coats, time (and rubbing) between coats, whether some acceleration with heat would be beneficial ... it's a complex question which definitely involves the chemicals and their characteristics.

Our basics concerning Proximity and Flexibility are still operative. Actual spraying times may be a fraction of the time moving goods into, and out of, the spraying area. Did I mention conveyors? They'll help, here.

Some other business basics can be mentioned, too. Early on, adopt strict procedures for samples ... their production, and their cost. Make it clear that various pieces of wood will accept finish differently. Not every board or panel will have the identical appearance. Nor is it easy to do a match from a postage-stamp-sized sample (sometimes shown in a different species). It is appropriate somewhere in the contract stage to stipulate that there will be two samples produced (or more, perhaps, but certainly a specific number), after which the samples will be billed at a stipulated amount ($100 each is about right). The formulas for the samples should be kept in a notebook in the office. The approved samples (1 for the Project Manager's file, 1 for the Specifier, and sometimes 1 for the Owner) should have signatures of approval on the back, along with proper dates, and job identification. The samples should be produced precisely as they will be in production. No "sprucing up" to get approval, then delivering something else. Have clear understandings on touch up, and the furnishing of touch up materials.

INSTALLATION

There are some parallels between Finishing and Installation. Even if we're not yet Installing, we should be learning and getting ready. Also, the jobs should be engineered with Installation in mind. Shipping joints that make sense, sizes which fit on elevators and through doorways, scribe strips and/or closer strips to help the job go smoother and look better ... all are the mark of a professional woodworker. Also, there is the parallel of finding and working with a subcontractor. We will be able to make a proposal on those jobs which request Installation, and gain that measure of control. Don't shy away from the responsibility of Installing, and don't shy away from charging for it. They know they're going to pay somebody ... why not us?

We can ease into the Installation by first working with subcontractors. At some point, it might make sense to have an Installer or two on our payroll. They can handle part of the Installations, and supervise other parts ... supplementing the crews as required (possibly with the same subcontractors). All those folks understand the ebb and flow of Installation volume. I would counsel against using Plant People for Installation except in highly unusual circumstances. It's a different world. Different conditions, different tempo, different equipment to accommodate (not to mention possibly different pay scales and insurance rates). Biggest drawbacks of all: If our overhead rates are figured on a certain number of folks using the Plant, we'll have to add Plant Overhead onto their outside work. Plus, the Scheduling is in jeopardy, too. We can't maintain production that way.

Other Installation advice: If we do it, do it right. Equip a Van with the right equipment, enough fasteners, adhesives, etc. And, use extra care in loading out deliveries. Make sure it's all there.

SAFETY

Safety considerations are of top importance all of the time. Every operation, every procedure needs to be examined and re-examined on an ongoing basis. More so than past years, there is currently a strong focus on Plant Safety practices. On balance this is good, although some of the conflicting information and instructions tend toward bureaucratic nonsense. Nonsense, or not, we must take it very seriously. We need to be more formal about how we monitor and change practices. A permanent Safety Team should be formed in accordance with local and national laws. The Team must meet regularly, and record all actions. We should pull our own inspections on a regular basis, mimicking if we can, an outside inspection. All Lead People should be members of the Safety Team, and be accountable for safe practices in their area. They can rotate the task of pulling our in-house inspections. Each rotating "inspector" can pick the time for his surprise. All inspections can be documented, including what was found … and what was done about it. Every weakness, and ensuing correction, must be followed up. Even when there is ambiguity in the instructions (Feds say one thing, State says something, Insurance people say something else), our consistent good-faith efforts to comply should carry the day when there is a question. If we have done nothing, we're vulnerable … even to the mildest going over. And the mild ones will be rare. Do it because it's the right thing to do … **for the company and its People** … but do it by the book to avoid misunderstandings and conflicts.

PLANT MAINTENANCE

Who? And When? Who does it? Who reports the need? Reports to whom? Then who does the work? And When? Let's keep order in this important area. If we have people who are handy with repair and maintenance, consider them. Best, though, is to have a regular maintenance schedule with professionals. We have already suggested that the folks who *use* Machines and Equipment also maintain them. But Dust Collection, Compressors, Heating Equipment, etc. presents a different situation. And preventive maintenance is always best. You know by now that Heaters go out on the coldest day, and Air Conditioners go out on the hottest day if they are not maintained. Good Management, here means having clear policies about what happens when the need is first detected.

SECURITY

Another topic which sometimes drifts until we actually sustain an "incident". Get some local advice on what works, and doesn't cost too much in your area. There is *some* confidence in knowing the alarms are in place and ready to alert the authorities. That good feeling is diminished somewhat, after you've received a few phone calls at 3:00 in the morning. There is more to Security than nighttime alerts about fire or break-ins, however. Well lit parking areas, for example. The ability to see if someone is outside the door before you open it. Winter evenings, when it gets dark early, suggest certain habits to protect one another. When we can't all leave together, the last two might depart together ... each making sure the other reaches the car safely, then waiting until engines are running and headlamps are on before leaving the area.

Daylight hours are not immune. We must make certain to keep strangers from wandering in the back door. Such intrusions benefit no one. None of us likes to appear paranoid. And, we are embarrassed to over-react. However, we have a group of very important People to protect, and they deserve the best measures we can implement. The incidents, which are occurring regularly, are not likely to diminish ... particularly if we all look the other way.

19

Operations

Which would we rather have: an Organization, or a group of people doing something or other in the same building? Does our current group know what the company's goals and objectives are, or do they just do (more or less) what they're told and try to avoid the boss's wrath? Do we really have a team, or do we have a bunch of people in business for themselves, but using our address?

Why do some companies seem to have their act together, and some do not? What steps can we take to make the difference at our store?

By now, we know "the Organization" is the entity also referred to as the Business, or the Company, or the Team. This is the Group designed to process Transactions ... the Events of the Spectrum.

We now have a clearer picture of Tasks and Responsibilities required for successful Transactions. We now see how People and procedures combine to make things happen. What is not so clear is how to get all those activities working smoothly.

THE KEY

The significant key to smoothly operating teams is the understanding of Operations. It is the sense that specific acts are needed to produce desired outcomes. Best performance happens with players who know their own specific steps, and know what to expect from other players. How do they come to know this? One way is to learn it from years of experience (including lots of trial and error), but there is a better way. They can learn it from our Operations Manual. But first, we have to write one.

An Operations Manual is the document which says we know what we're doing, and we have put it onto pages. It is reference for new employees and current employees ... appropriate for full-time, part-time, or temporary

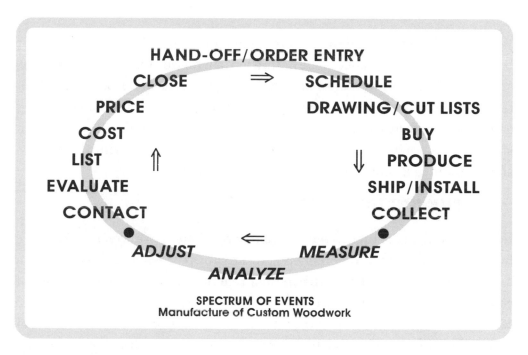

SPECTRUM OF EVENTS
Manufacture of Custom Woodwork

workers. It works for the Office side, and also the Plant side of the door. Operation descriptions become part of the Employee Manual, and also Job Descriptions. Operations can include everything from who answers the phone (and how) and who opens the mail, to how a sales call is made and how a proposal is presented.

Clear guidelines are appreciated by Employee and Employer alike. Guidelines can also head off intrusions from outside parties. Some outsiders who might try to gain from misunderstandings (real or imagined), might not be interested when everything is spelled out.

CODIFY WHAT WE'RE ALREADY DOING

The choice is whether we begin to write it down, or continue to make it up as we go along. We must still answer the same questions, and make the same decisions. But, if we don't start the Manual, we will be re-answering the same questions and re-making the same decisions again and again. Every decision we make is a contribution to what we perceive to be the needs of the company *at the time the decision is made*. But, the day-to-day approach is too fragmented. We need policies that carry over from one day to the next.

Writing an Operating Manual may seem a daunting chore, but it needn't be. It begins with that one-page definition of who we are, what we're doing, and why. The similar statement describing our reason for being ... which is also the basis for our Business Plan. From there on, we keep breaking down the broad outcomes we expect into specific steps, and define how each step will be performed. It will develop faster than you think. Anyone should do it in 6 months. You can probably do it in 3.

THE RELUCTANCE

I understand the reluctance to write down policies. We woodworkers are free spirits, and tend to fiercely resent any form of restraint. We want to be free to respond with an instinctive reaction, not according to a set of rules. Two things wrong with that: a) Even if we're all by ourselves, we need to develop more consistency than that. b) By the time we have 10 team members all responding with instinctive reactions, we have total chaos.

NO BUREAUCRACY

The other part of the reluctance is our appropriate refusal to become a bureaucracy. We see too much evidence of agencies operated strictly according to "regulations", and find much to dislike. Most of those agencies blindly enforce regulations without ever wondering if they make sense. And they don't seem to have anyone looking for ways to improve the system.

WE DO IT DIFFERENTLY

We don't have to be like that. Our policies set forth methods which work for us ... we don't work for them. And we look for improvements all the time. And we respond immediately when changes are beneficial. The advantage in writing the Manual, then refining it: there's always something in place ... we're never operating in a vacuum. We are never flying blind.

EVERYBODY HELPS

One person doesn't sit down and write an Operating Manual. Everyone should be involved. Most details can be spelled out by the People who do the job. The People who make the longer range commitments, and higher dollar commitments, will specify the broad goals and strategies (Markets, Products). Those People will then assist in the first "breaking-down" of those components (Staffing, Budgeting).

We have discussed the various Operations on a part during manufacture. There are steps to everything else, too. Steps to making Marketing contacts, putting a Bid together, preparing the Proposal. There are other Tasks and Responsibilities in addition to those required for the Events in the Spectrum. There is Bookkeeping, Corresponding, Invoicing, Telephone answering, and other important work to be done. Purchase Orders, Letters of Transmittal, etc. all must be done by correct methods. Why not spell it out?

WHAT IT DOES

The Operations Manual directs People, and an orderly Flow of Events. We establish clear consistent patterns for lines of authority, and lines of communication. The Manual provides Instruction, Direction, Guidelines, Support, Monitoring, Follow-up, and Follow-through. It establishes answers to the questions: What, When, Who, How, Where, and Why?

- **What** outcomes do we expect?

- **Where** will these events happen?

- **When** will they occur?

- **Who** has the responsibility?

- **How** will these things be accomplished?

- **How** will we measure the performance?

- Does everyone understand **Why** we are doing this?

(Get familiar with the series: What, When, Who, How, Where, and Why. In varying sequence and, perhaps, changing emphasis, they will be applied again and again. Whether giving and receiving instructions, setting policy ... virtually every question asked and answered should contain the What, When, Who, How, Where, and Why series.)

GETTING STARTED

Again, start the Operating Plan with that single sheet of paper. The Basics: company Name, Location, what Business we're in (Cabinets, Furniture, Architectural Woodwork, etc.). WHY we're in business (we discovered a lack of fine Solid Hardwood Storage Units). Revenue expectations (We expect Sales Revenue of $800,000 next year). Staffing (we have 8 People in the Plant and 4 in the Office). Profit expectations (We anticipate a Net Profit before taxes of $100,000). The Operations Manual goes on to describe the Who, the How, the When, and the Why of producing those outcomes.

Don't be afraid of being too detailed. Put down everything you can. Figure on writing, then rewriting. Goals and Policies are not forever. The goals may be refined and updated as needed. They're reasonable, flexible, and attainable ... or they get changed. And, it will eventually be slimmed down. The quality of the Operating Manual is measured by the number of good, clear, concise instructions. The fewer words, the better.

The Operating Plan should continue to expand into specific parts of all activities. Marketing strategies, Machinery Upgrades, Hiring, Firing, etc., and as detailed as we wish ... all the way from how we decide what to Bid, to who orders the paper clips. The paperwork flow can be spelled out. Who generates reports and summaries? Who receives the reports? How many hard copies ... how much remains stored on disks? What about backup procedures? The list goes on ... how do we load a truck ... how do we run the Finishing room ... how do we order material? Do we really want things to *"just happen?"* Understand, we don't spell out these details because we like to tell folks what to do. This isn't to be dictatorial. Consensus will be sought. We spell them out because everyone needs something to refer to, from time to time. And when a different person steps in to help out, they can quickly be at ease because answers are in place.

Particularly important are guidelines for response to emergencies, and other events which occur sporadically. All types of known emergencies should be discussed, and responses planned ... preferably before they

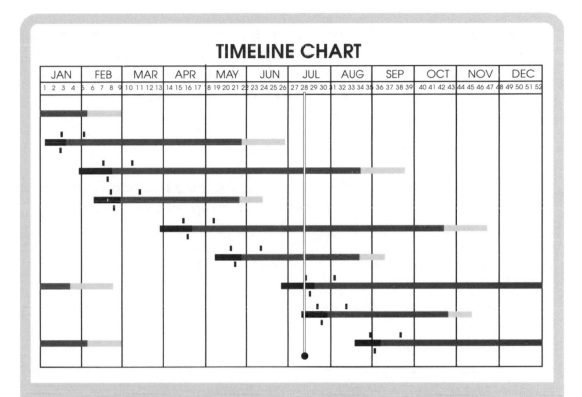

TIMELINE CHART

JAN	FEB	MAR	APR	MAY	JUN	JUL	AUG	SEP	OCT	NOV	DEC
1 2 3 4	5 6 7 8 9	10 11 12 13	14 15 16 17	18 19 20 21 22	23 24 25 26	27 28 29 30 31	32 33 34 35	36 37 38 39	40 41 42 43	44 45 46 47 48	49 50 51 52

The **TIMELINE CHART** is an excellent reference point when discussing Operations. In a sense the Timeline Chart is the center of ALL Operations. Everything we do involves: keeping it full ... keeping it Operating ... and clearing it out. Everyone is guided by the commitments which are so graphically displayed.

occur. (Sudden illness, injury, fire, storm, etc.) If not, have a policy meeting shortly after the incident and set down guidelines for next time.

ORGANIZATION CHARTS?

We don't need complicated Organization Charts. Our companies work without layers of Management. Management staffing will be determined by where we are in the transition of Management styles. Do all directions still come from a single source, or have we learned to delegate? The nearby Charts demonstrate the difference.

The Charts shown are deceivingly simple ... simple to draw, and simple to understand. The transition, however, is anything *but* simple. We wood-workers seem to make the first step ... from doing, to directing ... fairly smoothly. The next step ... on to directing folks who direct other folks seems to be difficult. We need to think about it, and work at it.

PLANT FLOOR EXAMPLES

"The Plant Supervisor has the responsibility for the whole Plant. He delegates responsibility (and authority) to various Leadmen. The Leadmen, in turn, train backups who will lead whenever Leadmen are absent."

"Individual Machine authority is similar. Principal Machines have a No. 1 Operator, and a No. 2 Operator, (and possibly a No. 3, in training). It is probable that some Operators are also Lead People. Lead People are responsible for Conduct, Output, Quality, Training, etc. Machine People are responsible for Operating and Maintaining the Machine." Point: the Operations Manual is the result of thinking things through, and writing them down. Everyone can know what's happening.

"A standing Safety Team is established, consisting of the Plant Supervisor, All Lead People, and all Lead Backups. The Team (along with other

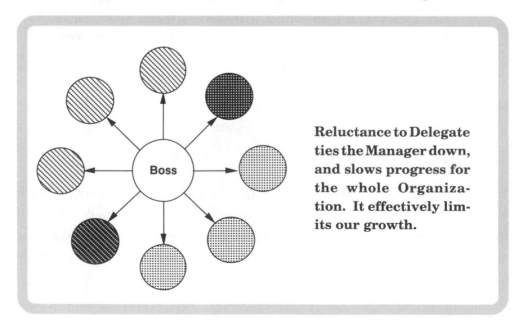

Reluctance to Delegate ties the Manager down, and slows progress for the whole Organization. It effectively limits our growth.

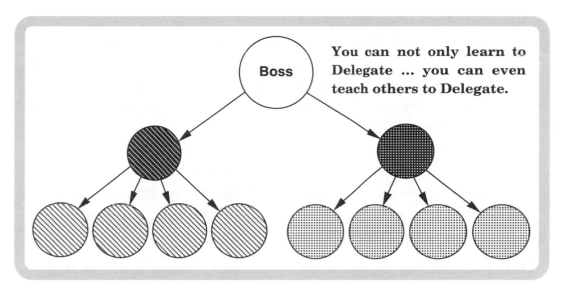

Boss

You can not only learn to Delegate ... you can even teach others to Delegate.

Managers and volunteers) develops and spells out Safety Rules for our Plant (using guidelines by our insurance company, along with state and federal safety agencies). Walk-around Inspections are made at least once a week (but at unexpected times) by a Team Member. (Position is rotated the first of each month.)"

"Another, similar, Team is established to review Manufacturing Methods. We believe many innovations can be discovered if our professionals have a means to communicate suggestions. Rather than risking everyone inventing all day long, we intend to encourage a structured approach. At regular intervals, all suggestions will be examined and considered. Participants will be recognized and coached toward bringing forth more sound ideas."

That's the idea. Write it down. Do it. If it doesn't work, change it.

BUT, WHY DO ALL THIS?

Look at it this way. If we can't write it down, do we really know what we want, or expect? If we don't know, how will we explain what is to be done? And, how can *we* tell if the job is done right? How can *anybody* tell? Employees deserve better and so do Employers.

There is much value in the process, as well as in the product. When you think it through ... write it down ... then think some more ... then write some more ... you will be amazed at the improvement in the methods. There will also be interesting discoveries. You will find that some jobs are done 3 or 4 different ways. You will find that some jobs have *never* been done correctly. There will be amusement, and amazement. Best of all, once it's written down it can be reviewed from time to time. Improvements will be made. We will discover things we no longer need to do ... or they can be combined with another chore. Everyone begins to have guidelines to measure performance. We can begin to discuss how much is being done ... and how much is being done *right*. Productivity is tough to measure. It's even tougher when there's nothing to measure.

Doing something "by the book" is not just a cliche ... it can really work.

20

People

People are great!

The marvelous human spirit has awesome strengths which remain under-appreciated and under-utilized (both by the individual, and by groups). The human spirit may well be the greatest natural resource around. Wouldn't it be great if our dealing with people had improved at the same rate as improvements in technology. In spite of the fact we deal with people every day of our lives, we seem to be in the early learning stage.

We need to break away from this strange stand-off. Management insists the Employee should make Management happy. The Employees insist Management should make them happy. Yet, neither of us knows for sure what would make us happy. And even when we know, we don't communicate it.

We *are* in the People business ... and the Teaching business. We didn't ask for it. But, there it is. We need people to perform the tasks and accept the responsibilities if things are going to happen. That puts us in the People business. There aren't enough good people trained and ready. That puts us in the Teaching business. It matters not whether there *should* be qualified people out there, or who should be providing them. If we're in the woodwork business, we're also in the business of recruiting and training employees ... for the whole plant. Office people, production people, estimating, machining, finishing, project managing, installing ... it runs the whole gamut.

Good People *are* available. Good People includes you and the ones beside you ... and there are plenty more. And our Team *can* find them. We can find them because they're looking for us, too. They need us as badly as we need them. Most People are intelligent, capable, and dependable. They want to work, and they want to learn. However, they will work better if they feel the work is important, and will learn better if the subject is well presented. People will apply their enthusiasm and energy gladly if their efforts are appreciated and recognized

The lesson: We should build on the symmetry. Whether we're the Employee, or the Employer, we should to look to see how we can best help the other party deliver what we need even as we deliver what they need. As Employers ... Team builders ... we need to know what we want and what we expect. Then, we need to be able to present the picture to others so that they can understand if there's a "fit". They should be able to see if they are what we're looking for, and if we are what they're looking for.

RECRUITING AND TRAINING

Draw on our company Operating Plan. It defines who we are, what we do, and what we're about ... and prepares us to communicate that position. It defines the industry, and our place in it. It contains facts concerning our products and our markets. It shows: where we are, how we got here, what we're doing and where we're going. Refer to our Spectrum of Events which describes the parts of the Transaction. It is a terrific checklist when examining the question of who we are and what we're about. We should define our policies and methods concerning each step. Use it as a "This-is-what-we-do-and-this-is-how-we-do-it" reference work which can be used in the employment interview, and from there on. It's a useful exercise for both old and new employees.

We already have Training experience. We're not introducing something totally new. We deal with new end products which require a different approach. We accommodate new raw materials. We become familiar with new machines. We already train current employees in all these things, plus new methods and procedures. New-hires are not too much different. This is the practical approach. Each work assignment should become an ongoing learning experience. Training and retraining is going on all the time. The workplace is probably the finest "finishing school", anyway. Many skills (on either side of the door) can be taught this way. Find some reasonable aptitude and a good attitude, and we can have productivity along with job satisfaction in a short while.

THE PART DELEGATION PLAYS

Delegating is not always understood as part of Training. Delegating is far more than handing out a one-time assignment. Effective Delegating involves these steps:

> 1. We know what we want done, and become proficient in doing it.

> 2. We teach someone else to do it.

> 3. Not long after, we have them do it.

> 4. As appropriate … they repeat the process by teaching someone else.

Let's take them one at a time.

> *1. We know what we want done, and become proficient in doing it.* This step is quite doable. We usually have strong opinions about what we want done. And woodworkers are "hands-on". Whether at a keyboard, a drawing board, machine setup, finishing room. We know how to do it.

> *2. We teach someone else to do it.* This tests us. Tests us quite a bit. We must develop patience. We must decide if anyone can *ever* do it as well as we. There may be a nagging doubt about whether we *really* know how to do it. Relax. You can do it. You *do* know how to do it. (If you don't you will learn the rest of the fine points as you teach.) And they *can* do as well. (Possibly better … which is what we really want, when it comes right down to it.) It gets easier with practice. You'll even enjoy it.

Teaching by example has special strengths. It is far more effective than simply telling, or having someone read about it. There *will* be reading, to back up the example and be handy for reference. Here, we have a great example of the What, Who, How, When, Where, and the Why. The Why is extremely important. The learning, growing, improving mode should always be our posture. If we don't stress the Why of our methods, we will miss opportunities to do it better. Both Student and Teacher will feel good about the whole process.

3. Not long after, we have them do it. We have set the stage for the Handoff ... real Delegation. Make clear to all parties involved: With the Task, goes the Responsibility. And with Responsibility, goes the Authority. Authority and Responsibility ... Neither give nor accept one without the other. And don't hover. Don't keep looking over someone's shoulder to "keep them from making a mistake". They will make mistakes. Let them. Mistakes are a part of the learning process. Letting them go "solo" is also the best proof you trust them. Mutual trust must develop for Delegating to work.

4. As appropriate ... they repeat the process by teaching someone else. Perhaps the toughest step of all. Even after we begin to accept the truth that someone else can *do* some of the things we do, it's still almost impossible to believe anyone might be able to *teach* them.

THE GAINS

The steps just outlined demonstrate the difference in the 2 basic methods of giving instruction to others *(touched on earlier in Operations Chapter)*. Here's what happens when we learn to do it.

1. We become more professional. We hand off the routine chores, and are free to explore new things, or apply our stronger skills more effectively.

2. The company can grow. No longer locked in to the existing knowledge and experience, our capabilities begin an ongoing expansion process.

3. People will feel needed and appreciated. No longer little robots going through the motions of doing what they're told ... now, they're an important part of what's happening. There is a stronger energy and enthusiasm. They discover the joy of learning and improving every day.

4. We now have backup capabilities. Every time we repeat the Delegating cycle, we have strengthened the company by improving the quality of substitute performers. Whether taking over for a leave day, a vacation, or a change of People ... the process provides capable, proven continuity. Of course the Teachers are superb backups, too. They haven't abandoned the tasks forever. How much better to use the experienced Managers as pinch-hitters instead of keeping them bogged down with day-to-day responsibilities. This is the most logical way to extend the effectiveness of talented People. The practical extension of all our skills and capabilities is accomplished even as the normal activities proceed. Of course, "cross-training" should occur, as well. The Training isn't just for new folks. Example: Estimators, Drafters, and Project Managers should be skilled in all 3 disciplines. It could be argued that until you understand all 3, you're not effective in any 1. More important, the company is strengthened immeasurably if we can step across the aisle and help in another area. Some days, we're all Estimators ... or we're all Drafters ... or Project Managers. In other words, take our marching orders from the Timeline Chart.

The 3 Key Managers mentioned before?

The Plant Manager will be given the authority to carry out all agreed upon policies and methods. Accepting the authority means simultaneous acceptance of the responsibility, as well. The Manager is handed the tools to make it happen, and agrees to be held accountable for the outcomes.

The Office Manager similarly accepts the authority and responsibility for what happens on the office side of the door.

The CEO then is free to make sales contacts, financial contacts and become a visible spokesman for the company. The CEO is also the logical backup, or substitute, for other key people. Note that none of these roles can be fulfilled if the CEO is armpit-deep in regular duties every day.

Given the average size of woodwork companies, we may well have described the entire organization for some. That's O K. In fact, it's theoretically possible to have the basic-three positions covered by two, or even one person. That's O K, too, for a start-up condition, but the basic-three must be understood, and covered, before you're really in business and can begin a sustained growth.

The remainder of the Organization consists of a few lead positions, plus the principal line performers. Any more layers merely clutter the communication and accountability process. Few woodwork firms are large enough to require another tier of management.

Accountability is expected at all levels. Some decisions will be made at all levels. Good communication will structure which decisions must be made at a higher level, and may further define and/or limit accountability. Every person is expected to have clear understanding of agreed-upon goals, the tools, training, and support to pursue the goals, some latitude to most effectively achieve, and the acceptance of accountability for outcomes.

We have just described the best organization currently known to profitably manufacture woodwork. We have also described the best structure currently known to teach and train people. And the best currently known method of creating a climate for team members to succeed … for achievers to achieve … for persons with career aspirations to learn and grow, both personally and professionally. And it won't hurt recruiting, either.

COMPENSATION

The fundamental employment agreement, or "contract", is a day's work for a day's pay. When I have done my day's work, and you have paid me … we're even. I must earn the right to be invited back for another day, and you must offer me sufficient reason to return. Whether your "sufficient reason" is wages, the other People, the Plant facility, good instructions, good material, good overall Management … in any combination … it's your offer, and I decide. If I have done the job (as it was described to me), been appropriately punctual, cooperative, have applied myself diligently, have shown any signs of having some intelligence, some future possibility, wanting to play on the team … in any combination, I may have earned the right to return. You decide. This can continue for a week, or 40 years. Each day, you can decide … each day, I can decide. If your Plant Supervisor is a dork, your machines are worn out, and you buy lousy material … I'm outta here! If I come in late, mis-machine parts, and refuse to take instruction, you wish me good luck on my next job!

Short term, only? Not at all. There is ample opportunity for the arrangement to acquire stability and continue indefinitely. As years go by, it is highly likely that mutual respect and trust grow. We will each have an investment in the package, and will be more inclined to keep it working. We will have become comfortable with making suggestions to one another about improving our respective performance. We will probably have grown to enjoy it … maybe enjoy it a lot. The size of our businesses, and the way we work, puts us pretty close to this concept. It may be useful to know this, but it won't make it into the Employee Manual.

One of the toughest ongoing questions top Management has is: How do we properly share improved profits? Do we reward Team members for their diligence and performance, or do we improve Machinery and Equipment, or do we invest in Marketing, or do we merely increase our reserve Working Capital to better ride out lean times. It's a tricky equation. We can't afford to under-invest in any area. Favoring any one area can undercut the others and disrupt the whole thing.

There can be no doubt … our Salaries and Wages cannot be far out of line with local standards. People won't even talk to us. The agreed on wage at hiring time will always be influenced by conditions of both Employer and Employee. Influenced by how badly the Employer wants to fill the position, and how badly the Employee needs the job. But, after the hiring, we need some measuring devices for further adjusting. If Management has hired too cheaply, an early raise may be in order. If Management has paid too dearly, it may be a while until the new-hire "grows into" the agreed on Wage.

I know of no pat formula. We can establish some guidelines, however. Extending the Operating Manual concept can help. When we have described all of our tasks, and then assigned them to respective Team members (possibly within their Job Description), we've made a good start. We can spell out standards for *quantity* of work, plus standards for *quality* of work. Periodic Reviews show whether the tasks are being done, or not. Observation will reveal whether the person needs help to get the work out, or if the person helps others in getting their work out. Ongoing Training and "cross-training" will be a plus. Assuming more responsibility (taking

ATTENTION ALL WHO ENTER ... GOOD DAY, AND WELCOME.

YOU ARE NOW ENTERING A VERY SPECIAL ENVIRONMENT.

AS THIS NEW DAY BEGINS, THESE PREMISES ARE CLEAR, CLEAN, UNSPOILED AND UNSULLIED.

PLEASE DON'T BE THE FIRST TO CHANGE THAT.

PLEASE CHECK ALL AGGRAVATIONS AND MEANNESS RIGHT HERE, RIGHT NOW.

THIS IS A FINE PRODUCTION FACILITY, WITH AN ABUNDANCE OF GOOD TALENT AND EQUIPMENT.

WE ARE A WELL MANAGED TEAM PEOPLED WITH SKILLED, EXPERIENCED PROFESSIONALS WHO UNDERSTAND THAT ALL PERSONAL PEEVES AND WHIMS ARE TO BE HERE SET ASIDE FOR THE GOOD OF THE TEAM.

WE ARE A FINE COMPANY PRODUCING FINE PRODUCTS FOR FINE CUSTOMERS.

THERE IS ABSOLUTELY NO REASON TO BE A GROUCH, HERE.

IF YOU MUST BE A SOREHEAD ... PLEASE DO IT

SOMEWHERE ELSE, AND ON YOUR OWN TIME.

WOULDN'T YOU LIKE TO SEE A SIGN LIKE THIS INSTALLED AT AN ENTRY SOMEWHERE?

over another task) is surely a plus. Assisting with the Training means another plus ... and, promotability. We don't want to force people, but we should encourage them. If they are content to just "do their job", we can accept it (in some positions). But we should encourage all Team members to stretch, and grow. When they do, they have something to talk about when it comes to a raise. I see no magic whatsoever in just "being around" 1 more year. But, if the year has been used to learn, and grow ... and we see more accomplished, then a raise may be considered. We should strive to establish measurements which can be seen by all parties. Goals and standards should be fair ... and understood.

Broadly, I would counsel paying People all we can possibly afford.
(We'll be discussing Cashflow, Working Capital, Machinery Upgrades, etc.
in the *Money Section* to get it all in context.) Companies who get their act
together make money by paying People well. If we provide the tools and
support to do the job, most People will earn their raise, and then some.

EMPLOYEE MANUAL

An Employee Manual helps everyone. It establishes the basics about
regular working hours, pay periods, holidays, etc., and can go on to outline
rules of deportment. Tardiness, absences, treatment of fellow employees
… we can spell out what is acceptable conduct, and what is unacceptable
conduct. Use a 90-day probation period. It's fair for all. (Then, make sure
there is a thorough Evaluation before the period is up.) Get current
guidelines (from books, or from disks) to get started. Give enough about
who we are, and what we do, to inform both the employee and the
employee's family (something to show the mother-in-law). Don't get too
flowery, and don't make promises we can't keep. Medical plans …
retirement plans … any benefits or features probably require qualifications
to the effect that whatever is here described is subject to change. Run it by
your barrister to make sure. Lots of predators out there trying to get rich
from what we say, or don't say, in a document such as this.

A similar caveat concerning Employment Applications and Interviews.
Things change too fast to keep up. Read up. Look up. Stay on top of it.

One note about Interviews: As the prospect is close to being hired, it is well
to ask the 3 Questions. After we've explained, "This is our Operation … this
will be your place in it …we've explained what you can expect from us …
this is what we expect from you."

> *"Do you understand?"*

> *"Can you do it?"*

> ***Will you do it?"***

Don't forget the third Question. It makes People think. And it prepares us for the next interview if the job isn't being done. We go through the explanation again, then ask the Questions again. Always ask, and always write it down. Then, about the third such discussion, we'll be talking termination. We've been fair ... we've been thorough ... we've been firm ... now we're done.

PERFORMANCE APPRAISAL

Performance Appraisal is our follow-up, and follow-through to gauge our People, plus our People procedures. Most of us agree that performance reviews should be done, but our own performance in this area is uneven. The Review may be a sit-down rational discussion every six months. It may be on a "demand" basis, when a disgruntled employee advises it's been much too long since the last raise and somebody better do something about it. And there's sure to be a review when something really dumb happens. Most will agree that a well-planned, well structured rational discussion is by far the best.

Few argue against the six-month plan. So why don't we do it? Well, the actual mechanics of it can get rather awkward. We get bogged down trying to decide how precise the "six months" period should be. Example: some employees think that if they started to work Monday morning, their review should be first thing Monday morning six months later. Or if it's postponed until 10:00 AM on that Monday morning, then it must recur at 10:00 AM on that Monday six months hence and so forth. Let's get serious.

To be effective, a Review must happen when time constraints and other pressures can all be shut off for the brief exchange. The supervisor who is to conduct the review should be prepared and be able to proceed without interruption. (NO interruptions.) The employee should also be prepared. (Which precludes a spur-of-the-moment call to the office.) It shouldn't be a lecture period. It shouldn't be a whining session. It should be a time for listening, and calm discussion. Are the goals and objectives still clear? Are the requirements too stringent? Is the Employee receiving everything (instruction, guidance, materials, equipment, etc.) to get the job done? Has a better way to do it been discovered or developed? A form should be developed and used. The appraisals should be discussed, written down, reviewed, and signed by both parties. *(See example Form nearby.)* If questions remain unresolved, another meeting can be set. Possibly others may be brought in for clarification and/or corroboration. To be useful exchange, all participants must agree that relevant points have been resolved. Everyone understands what is to happen next. The expectations are clear.

Option 1. Pick a morning or afternoon about once a month for reviews for all employees in a particular cycle. "Once a month" only if we have that many employees. (January and July reviews for folks hired in January and July, etc.)

Option 2. Schedule Reviews each Quarter.

Option 3. Better yet, have Reviews twice a year in May and November. Try to do everyone within a one-week period. Pick the period after reviewing the Timeline Chart and Production Planning Board so everyone is comfortable that we're not messing up our schedule. November is recommended, because the timing is right for year-end bonus evaluation (if there happens to be one) as well.

One time period must be taken very seriously. The 90-day (or whatever yours is) Probation Period. Shortly before the period is up, have that Review and make the decision whether the new-hire stays, or goes.

Another recommendation: Have a procedure whereby the employee (or the supervisor) can call for a Special Review. Obviously, conferences are called whenever there is an infraction of listed rules of conduct. But the Special Review should be available when the unexpected occurs. It could be extreme friction between employees, or a misunderstanding on rules interpretation, etc. When the need arises, it should be addressed quickly. Misunderstandings grow out of control much too rapidly.

EMPLOYEE PERFORMANCE EVALUATION

EMPLOYEE INFORMATION

NAME _____   Employed since (Date) _____

Classification _____   Current Rate of Pay _____

Advancement History

Classification_____	New Rate_____	Date_____
Classification_____	New Rate_____	Date_____
Classification_____	New Rate_____	Date_____
Classification_____	New Rate_____	Date_____

PERFORMANCE

ATTENDANCE: (Last 6 months)
Times Absent _____ Times Tardy _____

RATINGS	EXCELLENT	GOOD	ACCEPTABLE	POOR
SKILL	_____	_____	_____	_____
UNDERSTANDS TASKS	_____	_____	_____	_____
TEAMWORK	_____	_____	_____	_____
DETERMINATION	_____	_____	_____	_____
FOLLOW THROUGH	_____	_____	_____	_____
PUNCTUALITY	_____	_____	_____	_____
_____	_____	_____	_____	_____

REMARKS

ACKNOWLEDGEMENT

We certify that on this date we completed and thoroughly reviewed this EVALUATION.

Employee Signature_____   Company Evaluator_____

OTHER METHODS AND REWARDS

There are other methods in addition to the six-month sit-down Review. One "experiment" I know of is working well. It's an "Employee of the Week" bonus. That's right! A WEEKLY recognition for superior performance. Bonuses along with the weekly paycheck. It's been in place for several years now, and the enthusiasm remains high.

Some changes have evolved. Instead of only one craftsman receiving the bonus, there can be many. Starting with a "duplicate-in-place-of-tie" doubling up ... soon there were three, and since then there have been as high as eight recipients. Amounts can vary, too. Depending on the circumstances the bonus may be $20, or as much as $50. I'm told when things are really humming, the awards are higher and greater in number. When things slow down, so do the bonuses ... and no one objects.

Plant Supervisors note certain performance aspects on a daily basis *(see nearby chart)*. Then, on the day the checks are to be cut, the Supervisors sit down with the Guy who's going to sign those checks and the final selections are made. I've been encouraging this concept for many years, but my friend had the courage to extend it farther and do it better than I ever did. Think of some of these tremendous strengths this program brings:

1. Employees know absolutely and positively that someone's paying attention. It's a first for some newer, younger workers. Many are convinced management only notices screw-ups. Some suspect management even ignores the screw-ups.

2. It happens now! This has been called the "Now" generation. To the newcomer in the work-place, if it doesn't happen "now", it's never going to happen. Even the fairest profit-sharing plans have a element of "pie-in-the-sky-bye-and-bye." Particularly for entry-level folks and people new to the industry, the here-and-now incentive is much more tangible. Many haven't committed to being around at the end of the year. Recognition will help that.

```
┌─────────────────────────────────────────────────────────┐
│                  PERFORMANCE REVIEW                       │
│                                                           │
│  EMPLOYEE NAME _____ WEEK STARTING _____ │
└─────────────────────────────────────────────────────────┘
```

EVALUATION	MONDAY	TUESDAY	WEDNESDAY	THURSDAY	FRIDAY
ATTENDANCE					
PUNCTUALITY					
WORK QUALITY					
PRODUCTIVITY					
JOB KNOWLEDGE					
ACCURACY					
ADAPTABILITY					
INITIATIVE					
DEPENDABILITY					
ATTITUDE					

KEY: E - Excellent   VG - Very Good   AAV - Above Average
       AV - Average   BAV - Below Average   U - Unacceptable

COMMENTS:_____

_____

Signed:_____   Signed: _____

FORM USED FOR DAILY CRAFTSMAN PERFORMANCE REVIEW

3. Bonuses can be awarded from time to time before the permanent aspect of a raise. In most cases, the bonuses are eventually followed by raises. In the meantime, the craftsman is encouraged to learn and grow by the occasional bonus. A $20 bonus is like a 50 cent raise, except it's not permanent. But, it may well keep a rookie around long enough so he can earn the raise.

4. The level of productivity for the whole team rises considerably. Since the message is sent that management is paying attention, more effort becomes easier. Then it becomes fun. Then it becomes habit. Everybody wins.

5. Experience shows that turnover slows and recruiting becomes easier. Woodworkers talk to one another. Word gets around. Wouldn't you want to work where they were paying attention to performance?

Note that the rating sheet includes 6 levels of performance. It comes as no surprise ... tardiness or absenteeism automatically disqualifies.

What does all this cost? It's averaging $150 a week ($7,000 or $8,000 a year). $150 on top of a payroll of about $6,000 is not a big deal. The management is confident the money is well spent.

NEW HIRE ORIENTATION

Another good idea on follow-up and follow-through. The people who were involved with interviews, especially, but others as well should be involved. Introductions, beginning of training, Plant familiarity, even a sponsor (or special mentor) to get things comfortable. No more getting thrown into the deep end of the pool to learn to swim. When we have been thorough in explaining who we are, and what we are about ... we surely should also show by example, and show sincerity about Team building.

BE GOOD TO EACH OTHER

Manners are more important than laws. Upon them, in great measure, the laws depend. The law touches us but here and there, and now and then. Manners are what vex or soothe, corrupt or purify, exalt or debase, barbarize or refine us by a constant, steady, uniform, insensible operation like that of the air we breathe in.

-Edmund Burke

21

Money

There is a curious irony about the way we approach the subject of Money. We woodworkers are absolutely convinced of the *need* for Money, but we are astonishingly uninformed about the *workings and handling of* Money. We know that Money is vital to the functioning of our business. Why, then, do we not understand more about how to get it, and how to keep some of it? Making Money is NOT an option. And, if we're going to make money, we need to know some things about it. Some Basics:

1. Money is good, and does good. A business should create wealth for its owners. Don't fight it ... enjoy it.

2. With a few refinements, the standard Accounting process can give us better information with which to make management decisions.

This Section of the Book is designed to improve understanding of the subject. We'll try to gather up all the parts and pieces of the subject, and arrange them into a more logical picture.

Herewith, some brief introductions to the Chapters which will follow:

ACCOUNTING

Money neither appears, nor disappears by magic. It always comes from somewhere, and when it goes, it always goes somewhere. The tracking of the "coming" and the "going" is called Accounting. The systems account for each bit of revenue and each bit of expense. Properly set up, they can do much more. They can not only do a read out on the total operation, they can focus on each part. They can help us analyze, and they can help us monitor. They can tell us our past, and then add that information into the budgeting process to help chart the future. When we know where we've been, where we are now, and have a clearer picture of where we're going, there can be

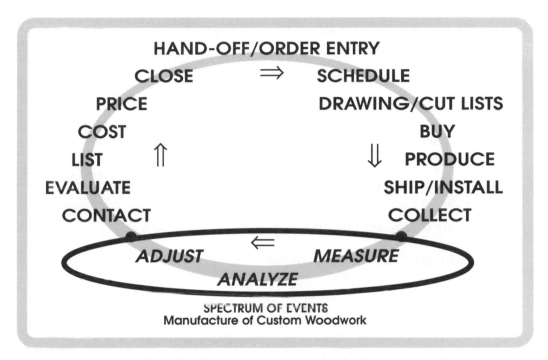

HAND-OFF/ORDER ENTRY
CLOSE ⇒ SCHEDULE
PRICE DRAWING/CUT LISTS
COST BUY
LIST ⇑ ⇓ PRODUCE
EVALUATE SHIP/INSTALL
CONTACT COLLECT
ADJUST ⇐ MEASURE
ANALYZE

SPECTRUM OF EVENTS
Manufacture of Custom Woodwork

no doubt … we will make better management decisions. And that is the ultimate goal of our accounting process.

Working Capital is the lifeblood of our company. We must understand what it is, how it is used, where it comes from, how to build it and conserve it.

JOB COSTING

We need monitoring and measuring of individual Jobs in addition to the standard Accounting. Job Costing is the integral part of the lower loop of the Spectrum … the "Measure" component of the Measure, Analyze, and Adjust triad. Correct Adjustments come from good Analysis, which begins with accurate Measurements. That makes Job Costing an extremely important function.

CASHFLOW

We've discussed other Flows, at length. We stressed the importance of the Flow of Information, the Flow of Material, and the Flow of Events in both the Managing and Manufacturing functions. Important as they are, they pale in comparison to the most important Flow of all … **CASHFLOW!** You will learn why we can run out of Money, even if what we're doing on a day-to-day basis is profitable. You will also learn steps we can take to prevent such an occurrence.

INVENTORY

We'll talk about the fact that tracking inventory in a woodwork manufacturing company is much different. The fact that the raw material completely loses its identity in the manufacturing process frustrates folks who attempt to track it with usual methods. But there is good news! … we know an easy way to handle the question.

MACHINERY PURCHASE

No one questions, for very long, the importance of keeping our Machinery and Equipment up to date. Machinery Upgrade is a normal part of our business. This Chapter suggests means to integrate the process into our normal "Cost-of-doing-Business", as well. We extend the concept of the Plant's approach to Machinery Upgrade, and get everyone comfortable with the Machinery Purchase Budget. Even our banker can appreciate the way we weave Machinery Purchasing into considerations of Net Worth, Debt Ratios, Cashflows, etc.

BUYING OR SELLING THE BUSINESS

We examine the financial aspects along with some of the practical considerations. Many of us woodworkers will have the question come up somewhere along the line. Counsel is provided for both Buyer, and Seller.

22

Accounting

Accounting is: *"the theory and system of setting up, maintaining, and auditing the books of a firm; art of analyzing the financial position and operating results of a business house from a study of its sales, purchases, overhead, etc."*

Accounting has been call the "Language of Business". It is a true statement. Unfortunately, not everyone speaks the Language. Many assume learning the Language comes automatically to all those in business. Many assume the Language is learned from a few conversations with an Accountant (or Banker, or Bookkeeper). **Those assumptions are incorrect.** This Chapter should help begin the learning of the "Language".

Mark these words: It is our responsibility, and ours alone, to learn the Accounting needs of our industry, and our individual business. No matter how knowledgeable and conscientious our professionals may be, it is highly unlikely that anyone can fully understand our business as we do. They set up our books in the prescribed manner, as they do for many different kinds of businesses. Standard Accounting practices do a fine job of keeping track of all our Revenues (Sales, etc.) and all of our Expenses (Costs) providing a record, and balancing the books … the same as they would for *any* business.

But we are *not* any business. **We're us.** We're different. But, our accountant can't know how different we are until we say so. And we can't say so, if we don't know. The better we can explain the differences, the more pleased our professional will be. The Charts of Accounts (which will be shown later) indicate the areas where custom woodwork manufacturing is different. The Charts of Accounts show much detail concerning both Income and Expenses. The various categories are then summarized in The

Balance Sheet and the Income Statement. The modifications we counsel are modest. We ask only a few more Line Items than would normally appear.

I see lots of Financial Statements. I don't see many good ones. Even the ones produced on time (indicating a certain degree of diligence, at least) don't tell the story the way they should. Which is why we need slightly different Charts of Accounts. We can't extract information that was never entered. And it can't be entered unless there's an Account for it. And there can't be an Account for it if it's not listed on the Chart of Accounts. And it can't be listed in the Chart of Accounts if the need has never been explained.

The weakness shows up in the area of Overheads, which are critical to developing our Markups (for Costing and Pricing). The weakness shows in allocation of Expenses. Installation Labor gets mixed in with Plant Labor. Supervisory Pay often ends up in the lump, too. And the weakness shows up in the area of Sales. If the Sales are not broken down, we can't determine which activities make money, and which ones lose money. Plant Processed Sales and Non-Plant Processed Sales are often mixed together. Sometimes Installation is included, too. Contract Labor (whether for Installation, Finishing, or whatever) might end up in the catch-all "Cost-of-Sales".

WHAT WE'RE AFTER

We need Measurements.

We need to Measure what we CHARGE for Goods and Services.

We need to Measure what those Goods and Services COST.

That way, we can know which Goods and Services MAKE MONEY for us … and which ones DO NOT.

When we know which is which … we can make appropriate ADJUST-MENTS.

If we sell more than one type of Goods or Services, we must Measure the SELLING PRICES individually.

We must also Measure the COSTS individually.

Let us proceed to examine the Balance Sheet, the Income Statement, and the 2 Charts of Accounts. As we do, we will note the steps to take to get us the Management Information we need.

BALANCE SHEET

A Balance Sheet is produced to balance all our Assets (what we *own*) against all our Liabilities (what we *owe*). The difference is what we're worth (Net Worth). The Balance Sheet and the Income Statement *(shown nearby),* have summarized the key categories of the Charts of Accounts.

Both Balance Sheet and Income Statement are typical for a custom woodwork manufacturer with annual sales of $1,000,000 ... of which $750,000 were plant processed.

The values and percentages are based on recent readings from custom woodwork manufacturers. They have been found to vary only slightly over quite a range of product mixes, as well as firms of varying size. However, each firm has its own special percentages and ratios which must be established ... and then monitored, carefully. We will show the recommended formulas for developing overhead factors, which then translate to correct Anticipated Costing for Bidding purposes.

INCOME STATEMENT

The Income Statement *(shown)* deals only with Plant Processed Sales. We have set this portion apart in order to isolate the critical categories used to develop Markups. The dollar amounts, and the percentages, include all of the Expenses (Costs) which were incurred in making Plant Processed Sales, including the proper portion of Administrative Overhead. Material is plant processed, only. Direct Labor includes fringe benefits and applicable payroll taxes, etc. Thus the Income Statement properly shows the Cost of Marketing, Managing, and Manufacturing.

BALANCE SHEET

ASSETS

	$	%
Cash	106,120	23.7
Receivables (Including unbilled)	129,600	28.8
Inventories (raw materials)	29,250	6.5
All Other	39,600	8.8
TOTAL CURRENT	**305,100**	**67.8**
Fixed Assets (invest. in property and equip, including leasehold improvements, net of accumulated depreciation).	131,850	29.3
Other Non-current	13,050	2.9
TOTAL ASSETS	**450,000**	**100.0**

LIABILITIES

	$	%
Notes Payable (portion due within 12 mo)	36,450	8.1
Accounts Payable	70,200	15.6
Taxes Payable	17,100	3.8
All Other Current	27,450	6.1
TOTAL CURRENT	**151,200**	**33.6**
Long Term Debt (due after 12 mo)	81,900	18.2
NET WORTH (capital and retained earnings, stockholder's equity)	216,900	48.2
TOTAL	**450,000**	**100.0**

INCOME STATEMENT

	$	%
PLANT PROCESSED SALES	**750,000**	**100.0**
Material	210,750	28.1
Direct Labor	173,250	23.1
Plant Overhead	123,750	16.5
COST OF SALES	507,750	67.7
Gross Profit	242,250	32.3
Admin. Overhead	129,750	17.3
OPERATING PROFITABILITY	**112,500**	**15.0**

Working Capital

Current Assets	$305,100
Current Liabilities	-151,200
	$153,900

(15.4% of sales - 20% ideal)

Current Ratio

$$\frac{\text{Current Assets}}{\text{Current Liabilities}} \quad \frac{\$305,100}{151,200} = 2.02$$

(O K Also, 2.0 Desirable)

Quick Ratio

$$\frac{\text{Cash+Receiv.}}{\text{Current Liabilities}} \quad \frac{\$236,250}{151,200} = 1.56$$

(O K Also - anything over 1.0)

Debt-to-Net Worth

$$\frac{\text{Liabilities}}{\text{Net Worth}} \quad \frac{\$233,100}{216,900} = 1.07$$

Return on Investment

$$\frac{\text{Oper. Incom.}}{\text{Net Worth}} \quad \frac{\$112,500}{216,900} = 51.8\%$$

Collections

$$\frac{\text{Receivables}}{\text{Sales}} \quad \frac{\$129,600}{* 1,000,000} = 0.13$$

365 x 0.13 = 47 days

Inventory Turn

$$\frac{\text{Inventory}}{\text{Total Material}} \quad \frac{\$29,250}{* 312,300} = 0.09$$

365 x 0.09 = 34 days
* Includes Non-Plant Processed

INCOME STATEMENT CHART OF ACCOUNTS

The nearby Chart suggests Line Items which work well for woodwork manufacturing Accounting. Our recommendations also create the means to differentiate Overheads. Certain expenses are distributed to a category called Plant Overhead. Remaining expenses are distributed to Administrative Overhead.

SOME LINE ITEM DEFINITIONS

PLANT OVERHEAD includes:

- Salaries (plus fringes and payroll taxes) for: Supervision, Detailing and Billing, Indirect Labor (maintenance, housekeeping)
- Shop supplies (including Finishing)
- Repairs and Maintenance
- Equipment Rental
- Heat, Light and Power
- Factory Insurance
- Rent
- Depreciation (Buildings, Machinery, Leasehold Improvements)

ADMINISTRATIVE OVERHEAD includes:

- Salaries (plus fringes and payroll taxes) for: Administration, Sales, Estimating, Clerical and Delivery People
- Commissions
- Advertising
- Travel and entertainment
- Utilities
- Professional services
- Taxes
- Office supplies
- Depreciation
- Rent
- Contributions
- Interest
- Bad debts
- Insurance
- Dues and subscriptions
- Professional activity and development
- Vehicle expense (including delivery)

CHART OF ACCOUNTS
INCOME STATEMENT

KEY INFORMATION IS ALL RIGHT HERE.

① SALES

② MATERIAL

③ LABOR

④ PLANT OVERHEAD

⑤ ADMINISTRATIVE OVERHEAD

These are the Fundamental Five Lines used to track the Performance of our Operation.

They are also the Fundamental Five Lines used to Develop and Check our Markups.

Note the Practice of Placing the Related Costs adjacent to their Types of Sales. This is quite useful in determining the Gross Margin for any Activity.

4400 SALES-NON-PLANT PROCESSED
5420 Cost of materials Sold
5499 Admin. Overhead Applied

① 4100 SALES - PLANT PROCESSED

② 5100 MATERIAL
5121 Material Purchased
5122 Inventory Adjustment

③ 5200 LABOR COSTS
5222 Direct Labor - Mfg
5223 Contract Labor - Mfg
5235 Payroll Taxes
5236 Workmen's Comp
5237 Employee Benefits

④ 5300 PLANT OVERHEAD
5324 Indirect Labor
5333 Plant Superv., Det.-Bill.
5335 Payroll Taxes
5336 Workmen's Comp
5337 Employee Benefits
5341 Shop Supplies
5343 Equipment Rental
5344 Equipment Repairs & Maint
5386 Insurance - Shop
5389 Rent - Shop
5391 Utilities - Shop
5393 Depreciation - Shop M&E
5394 Depreciation - Shop Improv
5395 Housekeeping
5396 Miscellaneous Expense

4600 SALES - INSTALLATION
5622 Direct Labor
5623 Contract Labor -Inst.
5635 Payroll Taxes
5636 Workmen's Comp
5637 Employee Benefits
5641 Supplies
5643 Equipment Rental
5645 Travel Expense
5678 Vehicle Expense
5680 Insurance Allocation
5693 Depreciation - Trucks & Equip.
5694 Miscellaneous Expense
5595 Admin. O'head Applied

⑤ 6300 GENERAL & ADMIN. EXPENSE
6321 Salaries - Clerical, Admin., Deliv.
6322 Salaries - Est./Sales, Proj. Mgmt.
6323 Commissions Paid
6324 Officer's Compensation
6335 Payroll Taxes
6336 Employee Benefits
6337 Workmen's Comp.
6341 Office Supplies & Exp.
6344 Dues & Subscriptions
6345 Travel Expense
6346 Meals & Entertainment
6347 Advertising & Promotion
6368 Contributions
6369 Professional Activity & Develop.
6381 Taxes - Sales & Use
6382 Taxes - Other
6384 Automobile Expense
6385 Delivery Vehicle Expense
6386 Insurance - Business
6387 Insurance-Officer's Life
6388 Housekeeping Expense
6389 Rent - Office
6390 Telephone
6391 Utilities - Office
6392 Bad Debt Expense
6393 Depreciation
6394 Bookkeeping Services
6395 Professional Fees
6396 Equipment Leases
6397 Repair & Maintenance
6398 Miscellaneous Expense

OTHER EXPENSE/INCOME
7040 Miscellaneous Income
7041 Discounts Earned
7042 Interest Income
7043 Rent Income
7045 Sales of Assets
8001 Interest Expense

OVERHEADS AND MARKUPS

Separating the expenses into 2 Overhead Categories ... Plant Overhead and Administrative Overhead ... gives us a useful option: Separate Markups. Experience has shown that the most effective method of recovering *all* overhead costs accompanying the manufacture of custom woodwork ... *and still remain competitive* ... is to apply separate developed Markups ... one for Material and another for Direct Labor. Why? Because each Job presents a different mix of Labor and Material. Some projects are Labor intensive ... some are Material intensive. We're not suggesting this is the only way to develop Markups. This method is recommended because it is uncomplicated ... it is straightforward ... and it works. The method also lends itself to the development of useful mathematical models ... as we will see.

The Operating Statement shows that as we develop correct Anticipated Costs, we must recover overheads totalling $253,500 (Administrative Overhead - $129,750 ... Plant Overhead - $123,750). *The most reliable method ... the one which can accommodate the variables ... and which has worked very well for many years ... is the one shown here.*

We're confident both woodworkers and their accountants can see the logic of spreading Administrative Overhead recovery across all operations that share administrative services, including the Plant, Installation, Buyouts and any other Special sales.

Since we're dealing with *Plant Processed* sales, we'll be recovering Administrative Overhead by applying Markups to *both* Direct Labor and Materials.

ADMINISTRATIVE OVERHEAD FORMULA

$$\frac{\text{Administrative Overhead}}{\text{Material} + \text{Direct Labor}} = \text{Administrative Overhead Factor}$$

$$= \frac{\$129,750}{\$210,750 + \$173,250} = \frac{\$129,750}{\$384,000} = .338$$

With the above calculation we have developed the correct markup for Material. Also we have part of the labor markup.

PLANT OVERHEAD FORMULA

$$\frac{\text{Plant Overhead}}{\text{Direct Labor}} = \text{Overhead Factor} = \frac{\text{Direct Labor}}{\$173,250} = \frac{\$123,750}{\$173,250} = .714$$

We now have the factors we need to markup Materials and markup Labor to produce correct Anticipated Costs.

LABOR MARKUP $1.00 + .338 + .714 = 2.052$

MATERIAL MARKUP $1.00 + .338 = 1.338$

Meaning that our Direct Labor times 2.052 develops our true cost (not selling price) of labor including overhead. And Material times 1.338 develops our true cost (not selling price) of material including overhead. Calculations should be done for your markups once a year ... blending the last three years with known near-future changes. Example: Insurance, Labor Rates, Payroll Taxes, Rent, etc.

Next question: a Factor of 2.052 applied to what? The Factor is applied to the Average Wage for experienced Craftswomen and Craftsmen ... plus Taxes and Benefits. (Take the average of the top 3 Wages.) If the Average is $13.00, and the Taxes and Benefits run 30%, ($3.90) we have a Direct Labor figure of $16.90. Applying the Factor: $16.90 x 2.052 = $34.68. That's Cost. If we're going for a 15% margin, a Labor Hour would sell for $40.80 (34.68 ÷ .85 = 40.80). *(This is NOT yours ... it is just for example.)*

INCOME STATEMENT

	$	%
PLANT PROCESSED SALES	750,000	100.0
Material	210,750	28.1
Direct Labor	173,250	23.1
Plant Overhead	123,750	16.5
COST OF SALES	507,750	67.7
Gross Profit	242,250	32.3
Admin. Overhead	129,750	17.3
OPERATING PROFITABILITY	112,500	15.0

MORE ABOUT THE BALANCE SHEET

Our Balance Sheet shows us much more than Net Worth. The Balance Sheet also shows a manager about:

1. Working Capital. You see categories called Current Assets, and Fixed Assets ... Current Liabilities, and Long Term Liabilities. The nearby Chart of Accounts indicates the sorts of items included in these categories. Current Assets include ready Cash, plus those items which are expected to soon convert to Cash. Similarly, Current Liabilities include all obligations which must soon be paid. **Working Capital** is defined as Current Assets, minus Current Liabilities. Assets which are Current consist mainly of: *Cash, Receivables, Unbilled Receivables and Inventory.* Liabilities which are Current include: *Accounts Payable, Short term Notes, Taxes Payable and any portion of Long Term obligations which will become due and payable within the next twelve months.*

BALANCE SHEET

ASSETS	$	%
Cash	106,120	23.7
Receivables (Including unbilled)	129,600	28.8
Inventories (raw materials)	29,250	6.5
All Other	39,600	8.8
TOTAL CURRENT	**305,100**	**67.8**
Fixed Assets (invest. in property and equip, including leasehold improvements, net of accumulated depreciation).	131,850	29.3
Other Non-current	13,050	2.9
TOTAL ASSETS	**450,000**	**100.0**

LIABILITIES	$	%
Notes Payable (portion due within 12 mo)	36,450	8.1
Accounts Payable	70,200	15.6
Taxes Payable	17,100	3.8
All Other Current	27,450	6.1
TOTAL CURRENT	**151,200**	**33.6**
Long Term Debt (due after 12 mo)	81,900	18.2
NET WORTH (capital and retained earnings, stockholder's equity)	216,900	48.2
TOTAL	**450,000**	**100.0**

INCOME STATEMENT

	$	%
PLANT PROCESSED SALES	750,000	100.0
Material	210,750	28.1
Direct Labor	173,250	23.1
Plant Overhead	123,750	16.5
COST OF SALES	507,750	67.7
Gross Profit	242,250	32.3
Admin. Overhead	129,750	17.3
OPERATING PROFITABILITY	**112,500**	**15.0**

CHART OF ACCOUNTS
BALANCE SHEET

Examples of Useful Information which may be derived from the BALANCE SHEET:

WORKING CAPITAL =
Current Assets
minus Current Liabilities

CURRENT RATIO =
Current Assets divided by
Current Liabilities

QUICK RATIO =
Cash + Receivables divided
by Current Liabilities

DEBT-TO-NET WORTH =
Liabilities divided
by Net Worth

RETURN ON INVESTMENT =
Operating Income divided
by Net Worth

To find NUMBER OF DAYS FOR COLLECTION:
Divide Accounts Receivable (from BALANCE SHEET) by Total Sales (from INCOME STATEMENT), then multiply by 365.

To find NUMBER OF DAYS FOR INVENTORY TURN:
Divide Inventory (from BALANCE SHEET) by Total Material Cost (from INCOME STATEMENT), then multiply by 365.

1100 CURRENT ASSETS
1101 Cash In Bank- Checking
1102 Cash In Bank - Savings
1109 Petty Cash
1111 Notes Receivable
1114 Interest Receivable
1116 Accounts Receivable - Trade
1117 Unbilled Receivables
1118 Allowance For Bad Debts
1119 Other Receivables
1123 Advances To Employees
1125 Advances To Officers
1131 Inventory - Raw Material
1137 Prepaid Rent
1138 Prepaid Insurance
1139 Other Prepaid Expenses

1200 FIXED ASSETS
1202 Shop Machinery & Equipment
1203 Acc Dep - Shop Mach & Equip
1204 Office Furniture & Equipment
1205 Acc Dep-Office Furn & Equip
1206 Autos & Trucks
1207 Acc Dep- Autos & Trucks
1210 Leashld Improvements-Shop
1211 Acc Amort - LH Improv-Shop
1218 Leashld Improvements-Office
1219 Acc Amort - LH Improv-Office

1300 OTHER ASSETS
1303 Deposits
1304 Organization Costs
1305 Accum Amort-Organ Costs
1308 Cash Surr Value -Life Insur

2100 CURRENT LIABILITIES
2171 Notes Payable
2172 Notes Payable-Stockholders
2173 Currnt Portn-Long Term Debt
2174 Unearned Income
2175 Accounts Payable
2181 FICA Tax Payable
2182 Federal Withholding Payable
2184 State Withholding Payable
2187 Acc Income Taxes Payable
2188 Acc Unemployment/
        Workman's Compensation
2189 Acc Salaries Payable
2191 Acc Property Taxes
2192 Acc Interest Expense
2195 Sales Tax Payable-State
2196 Sales Tax Payable-City
2197 Sales Tax Payable-Other
2199 Other Current Liabilities

2200 LONG TERM LIABILITIES
2205 Notes Payable (L.T.)
2300 Other Liabilities

3000 STOCKHOLDERS EQUITY
3001 Common Stock
3002 Additional Paid-in Surplus
3005 Retained Earnings
9000 Net Profit

2. *Financial Strength.* Financial Strength begins with an assessment of our ability to pay our obligations. Current Assets and Current Liabilities are used again, to produce what is called a Current Ratio. The **Current Ratio** is defined as Current Assets, divided by Current Liabilities.

Another Ratio, called the **Quick Ratio**, is similar, but even a bit more strict. For Current Assets, it leaves out Inventory, and other items which may take a bit longer to convert to Cash. It includes Cash and Receivables, divided by Current Liabilities.

Another item our bankers will be looking at (along with both the Current Ratio, and the Quick Ratio), is the relationship of our Debt to our Net Worth. You've heard the expression "leverage"? Well, this is one example. It essentially tells how much we have invested in our business, against how much others (lenders, suppliers, etc.) have invested in our business. **Debt-to-Net Worth** is Liabilities, divided by Net Worth.

INCOME STATEMENT

	$	%
NON-PLANT PROC. SALES	150,000	
Instalation Sales	100,000	
TOTAL	250,000	100.0
Non-Plant Proc. Cost	101,550	40.6
Installation Cost	67,700	27.1
Gross Margin	80,750	32.3
Admin. Overhead	43,250	17.3
OPERATING PROFITABILITY	37,500	15.0
PLANT PROCESSED SALES	750,000	100.0
Material	210,750	28.1
Direct Labor	173,250	23.1
Plant Overhead	123,750	16.5
COST OF SALES	507,750	67.7
Gross Profit	242,250	32.3
Admin. Overhead	129,750	17.3
OPERATING PROFITABILITY	112,500	15.0

Including both Plant-Processed and Non-Plant Processed Sales.

3. *Return on Investment.* The Return on Investment (you've seen it as R. O. I.) is measurement of how effectively we are using our financial resources. In other words, what are we doing with what we've got? **Return on Investment** is usually defined as Operating Income, divided by Net Worth.

4. *Collections.* To see how we're doing about collecting our Receivables, we look at another correlation … drawing from both the Balance Sheet, and the

Working Capital

Current Assets	$305,100
Current Liabilities	-151,200
	$153,900

(15.4% of sales - 20% ideal)

Current Ratio

$$\frac{\text{Current Assets}}{\text{Current Liabilities}} \quad \frac{\$305,100}{151,200} = 2.02$$

(O K Also, 2.0 Desirable)

Quick Ratio

$$\frac{\text{Cash+Receiv.}}{\text{Current Liabilities}} \quad \frac{\$236,250}{151,200} = 1.56$$

(O K Also - anything over 1.0)

Debt-to-Net Worth

$$\frac{\text{Liabilities}}{\text{Net Worth}} \quad \frac{\$233,100}{216,900} = 1.07$$

Return on Investment

$$\frac{\text{Oper. Incom.}}{\text{Net Worth}} \quad \frac{\$112,500}{216,900} = 51.8\%$$

Collections

$$\frac{\text{Receivables}}{\text{Sales}} \quad \frac{\$129,600}{* 1,000,000} = 0.13$$

365 x 0.13 = 47 days

Inventory Turn

$$\frac{\text{Inventory}}{\text{Total Material}} \quad \frac{\$29,250}{* 312,300} = 0.09$$

365 x 0.09 = 34 days
* Includes Non-Plant Processed

Income Statement. To find the **Number of Days for Collection** we divide Accounts Receivable (from Balance Sheet) by Total Sales (from Income Statement), then multiply by 365.

5. *Inventory Turn.* Similarly, to find the **Number of Days for Inventory Turn** we divide Inventory (from Balance Sheet) by Total Material Cost (from Income Statement), then multiply by 365.

Another important truth the Balance Sheet shows us is how much of our borrowing is Short Term, and how much is Long Term. This has a strong influence on our Ratios and, of course, our ability to meet current obligations. If we have too much Short Term borrowing, our day-to-day Cash requirements are extremely demanding. This would indicate it's time to transfer part of our obligation to Long Term.

THE NUMBERS

These financial statements have been synthesized from many actual statements. Therefore they are reasonable and valid examples of what any woodworker's financial information might resemble.

However, the ratios and relationships here shown and discussed are not held as goals, or ideals. Rather, the ratios and relationships are excellent "markers" which we can track to measure our Operational performance.

Balance Sheets and Income Statements, like those shown here are "snapshots". They accurately reflect the way everything was *at that time*. Various line items could be heavily influenced by conditions prevailing when the "snapshot" was taken. For us to understand (and be prepared to discuss the subject with anyone else) we need a "compared to what?" frame of reference. Example: The amount of Inventory shown is a bit higher than I would like to see at my Plant. However, if we just happened to bring in a large shipment because we're about to use it … and got the best price by doing it this way … it may well be sound business. The Inventory number will depend a lot on how we manage Inventory, too. And it is also possible our Plant is a bit off the beaten path, and we can't get prompt deliveries. We would certainly rather carry more Inventory, than run out of material. (This will be discussed further both in "Job Costing", and "Inventory" Chapters.)

What we need, then, is a method of "comparing to what?" that can give useful information … and at a glance. We can build comparisons of year-end information from past years. We can compare quarterly information … even month-to-month. As always, we counsel moving into the process slowly.

Start with yearly information. And line it up on one page so we don't have to flip back and forth. We introduced the idea of percentages, because they're often easier to compare than dollar amounts. This is the sort of task for a computer spreadsheet. This is why we remarked that a manager could justify having a computer just for this task. Production of Charts and Graphs is possible, too. Anything we can do to get meaningful information to our managers more quickly is worth a lot.

ABOUT WORKING CAPITAL

Working Capital … the life blood of the business … is not always fully understood, nor fully appreciated. It is a supply of money that continually rolls over ... shifting from payroll expense, raw material purchases and other operating expenses ... to accounts receivable ... then revenue ... then back around again.

It is the reserve that sustains us through the time period between the cash *outflow* required to manufacture and deliver products ... and the cash *inflow* from customers' payments. Working Capital must be defined, be understood, be methodically built up and preserved ... and must never be used for anything other than its stated purpose.

Understanding and monitoring Working Capital is particularly urgent during a growth period. From an overall business standpoint, we probably want to be growing, or at least poised for growth. A large order, or group of orders, which substantially increases our sales volume should be an important goal. However, processing increased sales can severely strain our Working Capital ... even jeopardize the stability of our business.

What to do? Once again ... understand it, monitor it, and prepare for that growth. Use a cashflow chart which anticipates expected expenditures and also expected income. A good cashflow chart should show both the how much and the when. Preparing for growth means both building up our capital from profits *and* developing our line of credit at the bank.

Keep in touch with the bank. Find a lending officer we can talk to. Share plans for performance including growth. Demonstrate to our banker that we know about Working Capital ... what it is, how it works, where it comes from. Then, let him demonstrate that he understands it, too. He can do so by systematically raising our line of credit as our sales and profits increase. *Note: Sales and Profits.* If we increase sales, but not profits, it's far more difficult to find something to talk about with the banker.

What determines the amount of Working Capital required?

First: Sales Volume. Consistent with our definition, its purpose is to cover all those expenses incurred in processing an order. It pays for the outflow until there's an inflow. The more orders we are processing, the more capital we need.

Second: Terms of the sale. Best condition ... deposit up front and remainder on delivery. Those terms would require the least amount of Working Capital. Worst condition ... nothing down, a reluctance to process progress payments, then slow pay at completion ... probably with retention.

Third: Terms of purchase. **Don't ever do it without asking** up front, but sometimes our suppliers will grant extended terms. Even as much as 60-90 days, on special projects. They understand our need to grow, and to take larger jobs. They also understand that we indeed have a sale ... a contract ... when we commence the work (as opposed to a manufacturer who is trying to fill a distribution network in the *hope* of selling the product). The supplier also understands that if we grow, he can grow ... and if we do well, he will do well. Extended terms could take this form: Our supplier brings in a large quantity of goods and gives us the accompanying volume price, but allows us to draw (and be billed for) the quantities needed on a month-to-month basis. Don't forget, he wants to make the sale ... so negotiate the best terms possible!

How much Working Capital is enough? *Optimum* is 20% of annual sales (about two and a half month's business). *Minimum* is probably 8 1/3% (one month's business). In other words, if we're doing $100,000 volume per month, minimum Working Capital would be $100,000. Optimum would be $250,000. Now, don't panic ... that doesn't mean all cash or a minimum bank balance. Remember, we said it included Receivables, Unbilled Receivables, Inventory plus any other Short Term investments which can quickly be converted to cash. And, there will be times when we go into our line of credit at the bank. But, let's not kid ourselves ... these figures are real. And the reason the guys down the street went belly-up last week was because they either hadn't been told ... or they didn't believe it. (The old "it won't happen to me" syndrome).

Sufficient Working Capital means paying bills on time and taking discounts. It's getting in on occasional special pricing on regularly used materials and supplies. (When a supplier needs to raise cash, or reduce inventory, he often offers special discounts. But, he knows there's no point in offering it to someone who can't pay for it). It's not having to take dumb jobs ... at dumb prices. It's managing the business with class ... and it's a whole lot more fun!

Where does Working Capital come from?

First: from stockholders investment.

Second: from retained earnings.

Third: loans or deferred salary draws from owners and officers.

Fourth: loans from our bank (line of credit or specific contract assignment). (Actually, not Working Capital ... rather a Cashflow assist.) In some instances, suppliers will also accept an assignment and allow large purchases on a "joint-check" arrangement. The customer makes out the check naming both us and the supplier. Maybe not the neatest arrangement, but not all bad. We can at least process the job properly. Then, too, with a large supplier's name involved, payment just *might* be made more promptly.

Historically, virtually all Working Capital growth for custom woodwork manufacturers comes from earnings. Also, historically, the woodworkers successful growth has been accomplished by working hand-in-hand with a good bank. Woodworkers who run a tight organization and consistently upgrade their performance in all areas can expect net profits of 10-15%. That will build Working Capital nicely.

Since the Working Capital is so essential, there is absolutely nothing wrong with prudent, respectful use of credit. But, it must be within the framework of a specific business operating plan and for a carefully defined purpose and a carefully defined time frame.

Most of all, the purpose must include **profitability!**

SETTING UP THE ACCOUNTING SYSTEM

This Chapter is about knowing the specifics about our Money. Balancing Revenues against Expenses ... knowing where every penny comes from, and where every penny goes. Plus, it is about the equally important part of generating useful financial information with which to make management decisions. We need to measure our performance, and see where we must do better. We should get some direction as to *what to do*, to do better. Then we must be able to measure the results of our efforts. I'm going to tell you the best way I know to set it up.

1. Go buy a low-cost ($200-$300) Accounting Application (Program) for your computer.

2. Install the nearby Charts of Accounts, (Balance Sheet, plus Income Statement).

3. Start Posting. If no one else will start, do it yourself. It will go so well, that the refusers will be embarrassed all the way to their next job.

I know we're talking drastic measures, here, but I'm serious! The measures are no more drastic than the need! This won't be easy. Many of your well-meaning advisors will counsel against it.

You'll hear: IT'S NOT POWERFUL ENOUGH! (Whatever that means). Maybe they're right. It will probably only have room for 5 bank accounts, each up to only One Trillion Dollars. It will handle multiple Companies, but probably not more then 5 or 6. One I'm looking at, right here, limits us to 8,000. 8,000 employees on the Payroll Account … 8,000 Vendors for Accounts Payable … 8,000 Customers for invoicing from Accounts Receivable. Clearly, we are limited.

You'll hear: IT'S NOT DOUBLE ENTRY! But it will be.

You'll hear: IT CAN'T WRITE CHECKS! But it can. Not only that, it will put the address on the check. Also, you can distribute the amount shown on the check to many other accounts … different invoices, different Job Numbers, etc.

You'll hear: IT WON'T DO EVERYTHING YOU WANT! Perhaps not. But, then what will? And how do we know until we get started?

You'll hear: AND THEN YOU'LL HAVE TO START ALL OVER!

WRONG!

After you have used the "starter" Application a while and can now evaluate the "better" options, you can try another. You can export all your Data from the old to the new, and also look at the Data through new Reports, Charts and Graphs. Once the selection is made, all entries can be imported into the new Application and we can get on with things! Yes you can!

Meanwhile, you can be experimenting with the various Reports and Graphs. There will be a bunch of them, but they may not suit. No problem. Export Data to your Spreadsheet and nudge it into any shape you want. This, too, will help shape the specifications for the "next-step-up" Application.

The main differences between Applications will be the various methods of extracting and reporting information. Other differences have to do with Payroll, Job Costing, and Forecasting. It is unlikely that any one of them will be the ultimate be all and end all for all time.

That's why the STRONG recommendation of starting small, inexpensively, and uncomplicated. The cost of "abandonment" will be extremely small, since the Data can be transferred.

FEATURES AVAILABLE

Some Accounting Applications can produce Invoices, complete with Addresses, etc. Each Invoice automatically becomes an "Accounts Receivable." You may even be able to "call up" each Customer Account, and see:

The Person to Contact.
The Phone Number.
The Fax Number.
All Outstanding Invoices (with their age).
Date of Last Payment, etc.

TRANSITION FROM WHERE WE ARE NOW

First of all, TURN OFF THE EXCUSES.

(nomenclature may differ from Application to Application), with Dates and Amounts. If a certain Payment is made the 12th of each Month, it can be set up that way and included in the Budget. If the Amount changes from Month to Month (Utilities, Phones, Etc.) ... no problem. The Date remains, plus a Budget Amount, but the Actual Amount may be changed when the Statement arrives. Some Applications have a "Reminder" Feature which tells which Checks are to be written, today. If we approve payment, the Checks are printed out ... with the various Accounts being Debited and Credited automatically.

Another Budget Report can be produced in which all of the highly detailed items (such as "Future" Checks) flow into summary categories and help us tailor our Performance Expectations. Income from Manufacturing. Income from Other Revenue Sources. Cashflow Charts. Many options are available.

BACKING UP

Important counsel: soon after you learn to turn on your new computer ... learn to "back up" what you do. As we begin to use the Accounting Application, get into the habit of Documenting what you do with printed copies *and* Backup Disks. Do more, rather than less, at the beginning. Hard Drives fail. Back up with Floppies.

I followed this advice and it paid off. I went for years without a single glitch with the Hard Drive. Backing up seemed somewhat silly, some days. But by then it was habit, so the process continued. So when a System-wrecking virus struck, we were we glad we had Backups on everything!

You'll soon learn what proportion of paper you need for peace of mind, and how much Disk Backup. You may get comfortable with a Monthly Report printout on most items ... Daily on some, printing Special Reports only as needed.

Keep the manila file folders handy. Put the Monthly printouts into a notebook. Keep the Backup Disks handy, too. Color coding is useful in quickly finding the right one. Many folks "rotate" several Disks ... one for Monday, one for Tuesday, etc. Others do with only two in rotation ... first: A, then: B, etc.

Start with more, then refine it down to a comfortable amount. It's certainly not so touchy that you need be intimidated by the process. After all, your "Posted" basket is still there. If that once-a-year "something" should wipe out the last three entries, you and the Company will survive. Try one of the useful Accessory Applications to assist in the process of "Saving" your work periodically, as well as the Backing Up chore.

SECURITY

There are means to use Passwords to access the Data. There can be different levels, so that clerks may make entries and/or look up certain parts of the Information, without being able to see other parts. You'll be able to find measures to match your concern. You'll be pleasantly surprised at how nicely this all works.

MATHEMATICAL MODELS

With our developed costs of Labor and Overhead, we can examine some more of the "what-if's" we face, as managers. It's fun to learn to produce, and experiment with, mathematical models. We know how to sketch out plans for a woodwork project. Why not learn the fun of sketching out financial plans? As the Accounting process becomes more familiar, we can apply the financial facts in other ways.

OVERTIME

A nearby Chart shows an example study of Overtime. The examination of Overtime is a prime example of costs which are "fixed" and costs which are "variable". Working a sixth day within a week whose Overheads are already "covered" presents some interesting possibilities. We see that the use of more Labor Hours always results in a proportionate increase in Payroll (the "variable"). However the increase in Labor Hours does NOT result in a proportionate increase in Plant Overhead. Many Overhead expenses are determined by calender influence. Rent is so much a month, regardless of how many hours we use the Plant. Other Expenses, as well, are paid by the month, or by the year … Insurance, certain taxes, fees, and permits, etc.

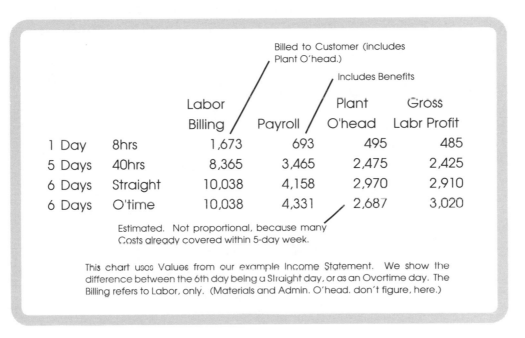

Billed to Customer (includes Plant O'head.)

Includes Benefits

		Labor Billing	Payroll	Plant O'head	Gross Labr Profit
1 Day	8hrs	1,673	693	495	485
5 Days	40hrs	8,365	3,465	2,475	2,425
6 Days	Straight	10,038	4,158	2,970	2,910
6 Days	O'time	10,038	4,331	2,687	3,020

Estimated. Not proportional, because many Costs already covered within 5-day week.

This chart uses Values from our example Income Statement. We show the difference between the 6th day being a Straight day, or as an Overtime day. The Billing refers to Labor, only. (Materials and Admin. O'head. don't figure, here.)

Things which change:

- Payroll 6.25 days instead of 6

- Light, heat, power

- Machine and tooling wear

- Use of supplies (glue, sandpaper, etc.)

Things which don't change

- Rent, taxes, depreciation

- Supervisor salaries

- Indirect (delivery, drafting, etc.)

- Insurance

Some of the assumptions are subjective and arbitrary. Usually, the Payroll figure would not be the full 6.5 days because many fringes have been accounted for within the first 40 hours. You will learn to calculate your own factors, here. Same with some of the "calendar" factors. Generally, though, Overtime is a good deal. (Theoretically, there might be some saving of Administrative Overhead, too, since we're processing more business in a shorter length of time.)

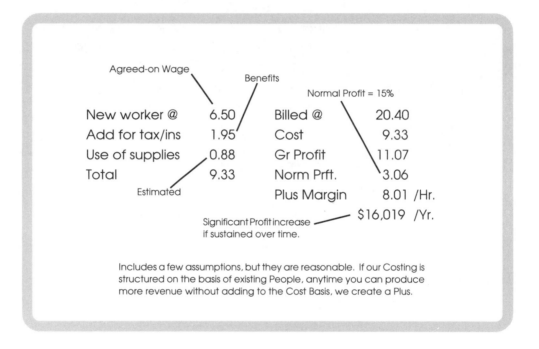

	Agreed-on Wage		Benefits	Normal Profit = 15%	
New worker @	6.50	Billed @	20.40		
Add for tax/ins	1.95	Cost	9.33		
Use of supplies	0.88	Gr Profit	11.07		
Total	9.33	Norm Prft.	3.06		
	Estimated	Plus Margin	8.01 /Hr.		
		Significant Profit increase if sustained over time.	$16,019 /Yr.		

Includes a few assumptions, but they are reasonable. If our Costing is structured on the basis of existing People, anytime you can produce more revenue without adding to the Cost Basis, we create a Plus.

This is a partial answer to the questions about what we can do to become more profitable. Any increase in Plant facility use will increase Profits. It is a function of Labor Hours. We can have the same People work more hours (as with Overtime), or we can hire more People. Any additional hours worked ... over and above the amounts calculated in our Overhead Mark-ups ... flow mostly to the Bottom Line. That is, *up to a point*. If we must add more Plant floor space, more Machines, or more Supervision ... any, or all ... the formula changes again.

NEW PEOPLE

Another nearby Chart examines the addition of a new employee. The results are similar, because we gain productive capability which can be billed. However, as long as we can add employees *without* adding more Machines, Supervision, etc., we have a definite plus.

23

Job Costing

Did we make money, or did we lose money? How much? How do we know? Do we know why?

Analyzing the financial performance of the individual Job is an essential step in determining how we're doing. First, we learn whether we made money ... or lost money ... on this particular Job. And, if we gather and organize the information well, we can begin to find out *why* we made or lost money.

The primary Accounting system tells if we're profitable. Monthly Income Statements show if we're gaining, or losing, on all operations combined. But individual Job Analysis can tell us much more. It can show performance on the particular job, plus offer clues about which components contributed pluses, and which ones produced the minuses.

Job Costing is the integral part of the lower loop of the Spectrum ... the "Measure" component of the Measure, Analyze, and Adjust triad. Correct Adjustments come from good Analysis, which begins with accurate Measurements. That makes Job Costing an extremely important function.

The Components to track:

      1. Labor.

      2. Material-Plant Processed.

      3. Plant Overhead.

      4. Administrative Overhead.

      5. (If needed) Material-Non-Plant Processed. (Buyouts)

      6. (If needed) Special Consideration categories. (Equipment rental, extra hauling, etc., to be charged directly to the Job.)

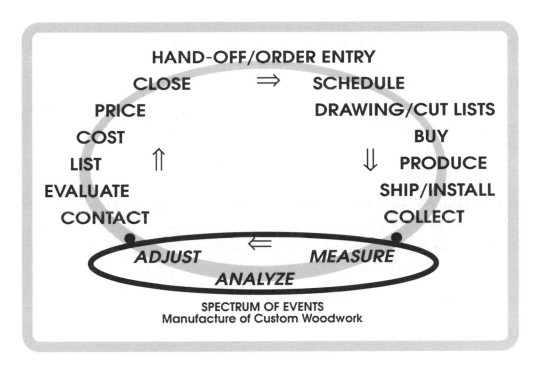

HAND-OFF/ORDER ENTRY
CLOSE ⇒ SCHEDULE
PRICE DRAWING/CUT LISTS
COST BUY
LIST ⇑ ⇓ PRODUCE
EVALUATE SHIP/INSTALL
CONTACT COLLECT
ADJUST ⇐ MEASURE
ANALYZE

SPECTRUM OF EVENTS
Manufacture of Custom Woodwork

OVERHEADS

We can assign both Overheads as a percentage of Sales as we begin to Cost our Jobs individually. The percentages will be the same ones we used in calculating our Markups. Of course, the Factor applied to Labor includes the combined Overheads. The Administrative Overhead Factor is applied to Material-Plant Processed, Material-Non-Plant Processed (Buyouts), and Special Consideration Items.

Broadly, the Overheads tend to be "fixed", whereas Labor and Material are "variable". "Fixed" meaning they change little with changes in Sales volume. (The Rent, Insurance, etc. remain the same, regardless of monthly Sales.) Labor and Material (both kinds) will vary a lot … rising and falling right with Sales (and in different proportion on every Job).

JOB COSTING BEGINS WITH ORDER ENTRY

The best Job Costing method we know combines neatly with an Order Entry system. As the "Hand-off/Order Entry" step of the Spectrum is executed, we set up a Budget for the Job. We enter Budgets for the various Components: Labor, Material-Plant Processed, Plant Overhead, Administrative Overhead and the others, if required. Then, as Material is purchased, we pay for it out of the Material Budget. As Timecards come in, and the payroll is processed, it is paid out of the Labor Budget. At any time, we can see what has been spent, and what remains in the Budgets. This information is quite useful for Progress Billing. Monthly Invoicing on all jobs will be easier.

Coordinate carefully with the Inventory system. Many invoices *could* be charged directly to a particular Job, and not even go through Inventory. If we use Materials which are always "carried" in Inventory (that is, always kept in stock for use on any and all Jobs) we can requisition it in much the same way we would issue a purchase order to a supplier.

ENTRY INTO A DATABASE

If we do the Budget entries into our computer database, it becomes even easier. And many more things can be done with the information base. The recommendation is to start with simple features, then add more, later. Trying to do too many things at once might make too much clutter, and make both setup and starting entries more difficult than they need be. The database can easily accommodate all our Jobs. The database can do all the calculations, automatically, and produce Running Totals and Summaries to suit our needs. The information can be printed out in several different appropriate formats.

But we still can consider a few of the features to look forward to, down the road. For example: ordering Material. If we ask for "Oak", a database can give us the total amounts of "Oak" we anticipate ordering in the next week (or two, etc., if we should wish to combine quantities), various Vendors (by 1st choice, 2nd, etc.) by Name, Address, Phone No., and the Contact Person (it can even dial the phone for us). Then we can cue up a Purchase Order Form, and enter the items we wish to order. (Can be done as we order, after we order, or before we order … in fact orders could be written ahead, then executed at the proper time.) Purchase Orders can be printed out and mailed, or they can be faxed right from the computer. Even if we don't actually mail or fax Purchase Orders, they can be entered into the computer

Job File. The Purchase Order information could be consolidated into a different form ... that is, combined with *all* outstanding orders. This is useful for tracking Cashflow (anticipating checks we will have to write), and it is also good information for our Receiving Dock. At the dock, information about incoming orders will reduce surprises, plus head off the possibility of accepting the wrong goods. The "Purchase Orders Issued" Form can be used by others, as well. Project Managers and others can review expected delivery dates, etc. It is a useful document to bring along to the Production Planning Meeting.

THE ANALYSIS

Variances from Budgets give clues which we must follow up. In the case of Material, the variances may indicate a difference in areas such as these:

1. Takeoff and Listing.

2. Waste Factors.

3. Material management while Machining.

4. Quality of Material ordered.

5. Quality of Material shipped.

6. Quantity of Material ordered.

7. Quantity of Material shipped.

Don't quibble over modest variations. Watch for patterns. Waste Factors move. Make sure we're not too casual in Listing, Purchasing, and checking deliveries ... both for quantity and quality.

There WILL be variances in Labor. It is the nature of our business. Yet, each must be considered. We need to keep tightening those "brackets" ... the allowable variations. The list of possibilities would include:

1. Assumptions made during development of Anticipated Cost.

2. Planning and Scheduling.

3. Methods used in Manufacture.

4. People used in Manufacture.

5. Machines used in Manufacture.

6. Drawings and/or Cutting Lists.

7. Combining, or not combining, Operations with other Jobs.

Make sure we compute Labor Costs consistently. If we have applied a computed percentage for Payroll Taxes and Benefits, make sure it's the same one used both in the Anticipated Cost and the Analysis.

Somewhere down the road, the Payroll Timecard entries can be extended further to include measuring and analysis of Manufacturing Operations. In addition to the Timecard stipulating which *Job* was involved, we can extend to which *Operation* was involved. Although the information will be extremely useful, it is a very serious step. If we don't set it up properly, it can generate far more aggravation than information. Some considerations:

1. Keep it simple … not too many categories.

2. Track the same Items used in the Costing (Estimating) process.

3. Ease into it when most everyone trusts it, and believes in it.

4. If the Codes for categories confuses people, consider bar codes and readers. It's likely to improve accuracy, plus save time and aggravation.

FURTHER ANALYSIS

Extend the process and the concept to answer other questions. Individual Job Costing will not only reveal which *types* of jobs make us more money. Other patterns may emerge, as well. It might be interesting if certain Contractors cost us more money. Or, certain Architects. Or certain of our own People might be better (or worse) at developing the Anticipated Cost, or Managing Projects. We all have our strengths, and our weaknesses. Better to be able to build on our strengths, and neutralize our weaknesses.

Measuring performance is good.

24

Cashflow

The most important Flow of all … **Cashflow!**

We've discussed other Flows, at length. We stressed the importance of the Flow of Information, the Flow of Material, and the Flow of Events in both the Managing and Manufacturing functions. But, Cashflow is *absolutely* the most important of all. We use the term, Cashflow, not merely in the technical sense as a part of after-tax profit, but as the Flow of funds in and out of our company. The Flow from payment of Rent, Payroll, and Material invoices, on into Receivables. The Flow from Receivables back into Cash, etc.

We've examined many of the steps necessary to generate Sales and Revenue. Every one of the steps is important toward inducing Cashflow. In fact, practically everything talked about in the Book focuses on developing a steady Flow of Cash. But, there are a few more steps which can be taken to improve the orderly Flow, and to better *anticipate* our Flows.

It is important to understand why we can run out of Money, even if what we're doing on a day-to-day basis is profitable. We need to know what steps we can take to prevent such an occurrence. While discussing Working Capital, we noted that the amount of Capital required depended a lot on the way we managed our Cash. First, by the terms of our contracts … but even more important, our follow-up and diligence in holding customers to those terms.

COLLECTIONS

Poor Collection is the foremost reason for not only *appearing to be*, but actually *being* Profitable, and still **running out of funds.** Our Income Statement and our Balance Sheet (which do not lie) may show us as profitable, and even reasonably "solvent". The difference is in two Balance

"This isn't a good time ... "

"Maybe the next Quarter ... "

"Maybe we should wait 'till the Year-end ... "

THE TIME TO DO IT IS RIGHT NOW.

"We'll have to have more people to do that ... "

WRONG, AGAIN! IT MAY WELL TAKE FEWER PEOPLE.

Consider this: Regardless of who actually prepares our Financial Statements, we already do practically all the work.

Who produces and posts all the Invoices we send?

Who posts all the Invoices we receive?

Who matches them with the Delivery Tickets?

Who logs all the Purchase Orders outstanding? The List goes on. As long as we are doing the work anyway, why not be able to go ahead and print out the Reports?

PAYROLL

Not all modestly priced Accounting Applications include Payroll. But, some do. Others have Payroll as an add-option. Even if Payroll is now done by someone off-premises, we still have to do all the tallying and correlation from the Timecards. As we do that, why not do it in a Base from which we can extract other information? We could Cost by Job Number. We could Cost by Operation (checking the efficiency of both the Technician and the Equipment). Since Accounting Applications can produce Payroll Checks, assist with Job Costing, Operations Costing, and proceed on to producing the various Tax Report Forms, we may find that we can do the whole thing faster, and more economically, right in house.

BUDGETING

Computer Accounting Applications can assist Budgeting in several different ways. Checks to be written can be set up as "Future Payments" pricing on regularly used materials and supplies. (When a supplier needs to raise cash, or reduce inventory, he often offers special discounts. But, he knows there's no point in offering it to someone who can't pay for it). It is also not having to take dumb jobs ... at dumb prices. It's managing the business with class... and it's a whole lot more fun!

PURCHASING

We can give our Cashflow a little help by timing some purchases. While continuing to weigh the critical factors in the timing ... not running out of materials, and buying at the right price ... sometimes a few days difference can help Cashflow. Know the "closing" dates of our suppliers. Sometimes, ordering on the 27th, instead of the 26th, moves us up a month ... giving us another 30 days use of someone else's Cash.

CASHFLOW CHART

The Monthly Cashflow Chart can be one of the best guides the woodwork manager has. It should be used more. Maybe it *will* be used more if its value and ease of use become better understood. As mentioned, Cashflow is different from Profit and Loss. We always look knowingly at the "bottom line" to see if we made as much profit as we hoped. But, even if the news is satisfactory (and timely) it doesn't warn of the actual Cashflow picture. We could be processing a large job quite profitably, and quite satisfactorily, but run out of Money.

Essentially, a Cashflow Chart shows our best information available concerning:

1. Money in the till, now. (Checkbook balance)
2. Expected cash receipts. (Reliable Receivables)
3. Obligations to be paid. (Accounts Payable)
4. Remaining Cash. (Which will become next Month's Start)

The nearby form may be copied and used to get Cashflow Charting started at your plant. This example Chart works well. Get involved, yourself. Work it out with the person doing the posting, but it's your decision-making

MONTHLY CASHFLOW CHART

	YEAR	JANUARY		FEBRUARY	MARCH	APRIL
		EST	ACT	EST	EST	EST
CASH AVAILABLE	Cash on hand (beginning)					
	Cash receipts					
	Other					
	TOTAL CASH AVAILABLE					
CASH PAID OUT	Material					
	Payroll					
	Plant Exp. (rent, util, supp, etc)					
	Insurance					
	Taxes					
	Repairs and Maint.					
	Dues and Subscriptions					
	Accounting and Legal					
	Note or Loan payment					
	Miscellaneous					
(List any items which need tracking for a time or unusual one-time expenses, etc.)						
	TOTAL CASH PAID OUT					
	ENDING CASH POSITION					

tool and you must be in on its development. Somewhere down the line we will make the transition to a computer spreadsheet but we can start with pencil and paper, right now.

3-4 months ahead is our critical Cashflow period. However, the concept can evolve into many different sizes and shapes. We will quickly want one that stretches out for a full year. A year's projection becomes somewhat more "iffy", but (particularly after some practice) reasonable projections can be made for all Items. Even without absolute precision, it's much better than "flying blind." (I have even used a detailed one-month Cashflow chart, showing checks to be written on the 5th, 15th and 25th along with the expectations in between. An excellent procedure when things are really tight.)

KEYS TO THE CHART

1. Cash on hand. (Beginning Balance)

2. Cash receipts. (Receivables, plus Cash Deposits, etc.)

3. Other. (Draws on Line of Credit, etc.)

4. Total Cash Available. (What we have to work with.)

5. For the Cash Paid Out section, list all anticipated expenses. We pretty well know from Invoices in house, plus Orders placed, what Material will be in the next month or two. We know what our current Payroll is. We can "plug in" figures from last Year (along with known adjustments) for most other Items. Find and insert all those sneaky annual, semi-annual, and quarterly payments. Log all Notes coming due. And, don't forget the 5-payroll months. It's when several of those "surprises" hit at once that things get exciting. Remember: ANTICIPATE!

Once again, the strength is in *anticipation*. We need to put down everything we can reasonably expect. Then when we have all the "knowns" and the "probables" set out, we'll have a good picture and can begin to consider some options. Options are great, but they diminish with time. We have options, today, which will be gone, tomorrow. And tomorrow's options will be gone, next week. Therefore, we gain options with every day's jump we can get. Even if the precision is lacking, if we chart carefully and consistently, we can pick up the signals when our Cashflow is drifting off course.

Can you believe some woodworkers are still startled by a 5-payday month. How can we forget that each 3 month period contains a 5-payday month. (Even February can be a 5-payday month in a Leap Year.)

The Cashflow Chart is a key tool for discussions with our banker, too. Along with the rest of our Financial information, this piece is extremely important. The document itself is important, but so is the fact that we have one … and that we understand it. And as we develop a pattern of showing our Charts, using them, and verifying their reasonable accuracy … conversations with the banker will become easier.

So, get to know your Cashflow. Use the Form. Get the jump on what's coming. Take charge, and *have a Happy positive Cashflow!*

MONTHLY CASHFLOW CHART

	YEAR	JANUARY		FEBRUARY	MARCH	APRIL
		EST	ACT	EST	EST	EST
CASH AVAILABLE	Cash on hand (beginning)					
	Cash receipts					
	Other					
	TOTAL CASH AVAILABLE					
CASH PAID OUT	Material					
	Payroll					
	Plant Exp. (rent, util, supp, etc)					
	Insurance					
	Taxes					
	Repairs and Maint.					
	Dues and Subscriptions					
	Accounting and Legal					
	Note or Loan payment					
	Miscellaneous					
(List any items which need tracking for a time or unusual one-time expenses, etc.)						
	TOTAL CASH PAID OUT					
	ENDING CASH POSITION					

25

Inventory

Inventory management for woodwork manufacturers is different. Let's examine how much different, and why. Then, let's talk about managing Inventory the sensible, easy way. Too many well meaning folks encourage too much work keeping track of material.

Accountants properly believe everything must be accounted for. So do Woodworkers. The difference is in the approach. Many of the strong beliefs concerning Inventory and its accounting carry over from retail and/or wholesale operations. In *that* world everything that comes in gets counted and put on the shelf, then counted again when it's taken off the shelf, repacked, and shipped. And, that's fine. If I were in that sort of business; I, too, would want a running tally of every item. Then, I would have accurate counts and accurate values … which is the whole idea.

A Woodwork manufacturing operation, however, is different. We don't have a shelf. (At least not in the aforementioned sense.) When we have a firm order, we're ready to start production. We buy raw material for a particular Job, and then proceed to cut it up.

That's an early clue. The materials we use get vastly changed. We can count items as they come in, but we can't count them when they go out, because they have been transformed. And then there are the waste factors. Panel goods have waste factors upwards of 20%. Hardwood lumber waste factors begin around 50%. In view of that, tracking material through every step with two decimal point accuracy becomes impossible.

The question becomes: how can we best account for incoming and outgoing material with reasonable accuracy, and without the process costing more than we gain from it?

Our recommended method: Rely on quantities calculated during the Anticipated Costing (Estimating) process, then refined during the "Hand-Off." Why have production people scaling lumber, counting panels and part panels, and messing with all that arithmetic, when the process will not produce more accuracy?

Believe what was estimated and ordered. Let production people produce.

Let's understand there are two levels of Inventory tracking and measuring. One consists of the paperwork and the money. The other consists of the large lump of goods which must be received, then cut up. (Of course, with proper consideration to storing, staging, and management of offal.) Recommended for paperwork and the money:

1. Enter Raw Material by dollar value. This month's beginning dollar inventory figure is last month's ending inventory figure.

2. Add each invoice, as received, to the inventory figure. Inventory keeps building all through the month.

3. Reduce Inventory as each project is billed. The figure is ascertained from the quantity of material originally estimated … plus or minus any adjustments made at the hand-off stage.

Most of this can be determined as part of the Accounting process. The Invoice provides quick dollar confirmation on material purchased for a specific Project. As materials are requisitioned out of stockpiles of items we keep on hand for all Jobs, they will be "charged" to our specific Job. These dollar numbers will be used by Project Managers and Accounting folks when determining Progress Billing amounts. As we Invoice, we also stipulate an "Out of Inventory" dollar amount of raw material inventory used.

The procedure is not difficult, and produces the greatest possible accuracy with the least time and money spent. Review: Beginning Inventory (dollars), plus Invoiced Raw Material (dollars), minus Material (dollars) taken out as Customer is Invoiced = Ending Inventory (dollars).

Keeping track of the "Lumps" consists mainly of using the material well, and also using it for the right job. When a certain order comes in, tag it with the job number. Then cut carefully to avoid waste. Keep track of all remnants ... particularly if it's a material we don't use on a regular basis ... and be prepared to retrieve the material for additional work, should a change occur.

Actual physical inventories must be taken from time to time, to adjust the "real" dollar inventory figure. Most people (and many, many people use this system) take inventory once a year, at close of fiscal year.

At that time, adjustments can also be made concerning the worth of "leftovers." Many raw materials have a specific shelf life. Even though we have saved some items (and used parts of those items), and they have a dollar value included in our inventory figure; there comes a time when they must be written down, or written off. Doing this as a part of the physical inventory makes good sense, and shows just one more reason why a "perfect" inventory value is elusive.

Folks who have learned to use this system claim high accuracy. Mine used to require about a 5% adjustment, each year. Others claim even better accuracy ... and in extremely large amounts of material.

Controls? That term comes up from time to time, and I'm not sure I understand it. Measuring and Monitoring, I understand. But, "Control" suggests further action beyond studying a printout.

My method of Control? Making sure the estimators can count and can properly apply waste factors. Making sure good Cutting Bills are produced and followed the get the best yield from the material. And discouraging folks from backing up to the door with a truck and adjusting my inventory that way. If I don't have to order more of something ... then, it's under Control.

That's better "Control" than a fancy system which produces reams of numbers concerning how many panels and boards we're supposed to have out there, today ... while driving everybody crazy with counting panels, and scaling lumber.

26

Machinery Purchase

We made a strong case for good Machinery in the *Manufacturing* Section. It follows, therefore, that we should develop a plan to help us acquire, (and maintain and upgrade), a group of fine Machines. It's easy to convince the hands-on woodworker in us to buy Machines. Machines, to woodworkers, are like toys to kids. But, the prudent business person in us knows there's more to it than buying toys. We need prudence, and caution. Where is the line? When are we being prudent, and when are we too cautious. We're talking about serious Money, so if we can develop some guidelines we'll be much better off. We can move closer to some answers if we apply some of the facts learned from the accounting process.

THE "REAL VALUE"

One of the things we learned was the depreciated "value" of our current Machines. We use quotes around "value", because it is not necessarily the "real" value. Real is also in quotes, because "real" is as elusive as "value". The "real value" of anything is best judged at the time it changes hands. At least, at that moment … and under those circumstances … someone wrote a check for a certain amount, and someone else accepted it. At least at that moment it's real to two … the Buyer, and the Seller.

But, having a better sense of the "value" is important. We're talking about a plan … a course of action … and whenever we start out on a course, it is useful to know where we are now. We have some good news. Historically, woodworking Machines retain reasonably good value. Therefore, it is possible to make reasonable assumptions for studies such as we're doing, here.

I'm going to demonstrate such a reasonable assumption. It is uncomplicated, and has been used for many years. It begins with the assumption a

This Table shows a practical method of determining a reasonable Resale Value of our Machines as they grow older. While the Table is unlikely to be precise at any time on any one machine ... it's pretty good when applied across all Machines of all ages. You may use it as shown, or adjust up or down to suit. But use something to establish a Value Line.

Start	$10,000	Yr 7	$2,800
Yr 2	$8.800	Yr 8	$1,600
Yr 3	$7,600	Yr 9	$1,600
Yr 4	$6,400	Yr 10	$1,600
Yr 5	$5,200	Yr 11	$1,600
Yr 6	$4,000	Yr 12	$0

ESTABLISHING THE VALUE OF AGING MACHINERY

Table 1

good Machine has a useful life of 100 months (8 1/3 years). It seemed realistic, and it simplified the arithmetic. It would depreciate at 1% per month, and the "real" cost of a Machine would be $10 per month per $1,000. To carry the assumption a step further, why not say it depreciates at 12% per year, and chart it like this: 88-76-64-52-40-28-16 For easier charting, we've gone to years instead of months. The depreciation is still 1% a month, or 12% a year. After 1 year the property is valued at 88% of original price, after 2 years: 76%, etc. The further assumption is made that the value levels off at 16%. Premise: If the piece is still around after 7 years, it must be doing a job. If it's still doing a job, then it's worth 16%. This method of depreciation is used in the charts which follow, and is referred to as "Real" value.

Understand, this is not intended to reflect the selling price (or even the asking price) of an individual Machine at any given time. But, applied broadly over our whole group of Machines, it's not so bad. And, at any rate, it's realistic enough for use as a "baseline" approach to our Machinery assets. If the assumptions don't fit your situation, they may be modified to suit. However, I think you can agree with the soundness of the methods of this approach. It should also be noted: this has nothing to do with the other, more traditional methods of depreciation used for accounting and tax reporting.

INTO A LONG RANGE PLAN

We're suggesting a new approach. Apply the "baseline" approach to track the Worth of our Machines over the years (and thereby, our relative Equity in them). Then, use the information as part of a long range Financial Plan. Let's explore the possibility of setting a specific dollar amount to be invested each year. Let's examine what it does to our Cash position ... what it does to our Cashflow ... and also our Debt-to-Equity position. What kind of obligation will it take? How does the equity position look after 3, 4, 5 years? Can we be comfortable with it? Can the Banker be comfortable with it? Let's examine what happens when we put some numbers to the process and establish a Workable, Flexible, Long-range Money Plan.

The recommendation is to Budget a serious amount of Money to be spent each year on Machinery and Equipment. If a certain amount is stipulated, then planned for, much of the consternation is removed. We don't have to wonder if Money will be spent ... only when. Plant People know upgrades are coming. Our Banker is aware of the plan and is not surprised. Everyone becomes more comfortable, and better decisions are made.

The ensuing pages show a MASTER WORKSHEET, plus several Tables showing backup information. Our Mathematical Model demonstrates the advantage of a consistent Buying pattern.

The MASTER WORKSHEET is taken from a Computer Spreadsheet. In fact, most all of the Charts and Tables are taken from the same Spreadsheet. Only Table 2 shows the typical Spreadsheet Rows and Columns with letter and number designations. We have elected to omit the typical grids, letters, and numbers from the other Charts and Table. Yes, the Charts come from the same Spreadsheet, too.

Spreadsheets allow us to "call out" certain rows or columns and construct a Chart based on their relationships. That's how Charts A and B were formed.

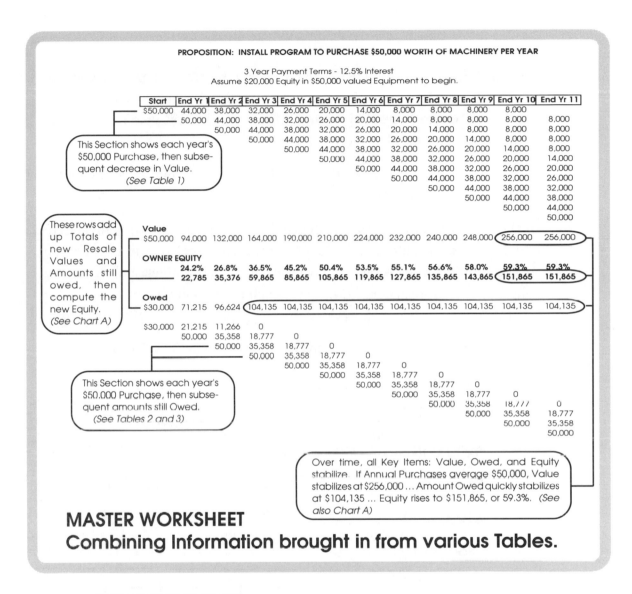

PROPOSITION: INSTALL PROGRAM TO PURCHASE $50,000 WORTH OF MACHINERY PER YEAR

3 Year Payment Terms - 12.5% Interest
Assume $20,000 Equity in $50,000 valued Equipment to begin.

	Start	End Yr 1	End Yr 2	End Yr 3	End Yr 4	End Yr 5	End Yr 6	End Yr 7	End Yr 8	End Yr 9	End Yr 10	End Yr 11
	$50,000	44,000	38,000	32,000	26,000	20,000	14,000	8,000	8,000	8,000	8,000	
		50,000	44,000	38,000	32,000	26,000	20,000	14,000	8,000	8,000	8,000	8,000
			50,000	44,000	38,000	32,000	26,000	20,000	14,000	8,000	8,000	8,000
				50,000	44,000	38,000	32,000	26,000	20,000	14,000	8,000	8,000
					50,000	44,000	38,000	32,000	26,000	20,000	14,000	8,000
						50,000	44,000	38,000	32,000	26,000	20,000	14,000
							50,000	44,000	38,000	32,000	26,000	20,000
								50,000	44,000	38,000	32,000	26,000
									50,000	44,000	38,000	32,000
										50,000	44,000	38,000
											50,000	44,000
												50,000

> This Section shows each year's $50,000 Purchase, then subsequent decrease in Value.
> *(See Table 1)*

> These rows add up Totals of new Resale Values and Amounts still owed, then compute the new Equity.
> *(See Chart A)*

Value

	Start	End Yr 1	End Yr 2	End Yr 3	End Yr 4	End Yr 5	End Yr 6	End Yr 7	End Yr 8	End Yr 9	End Yr 10	End Yr 11
	$50,000	94,000	132,000	164,000	190,000	210,000	224,000	232,000	240,000	248,000	256,000	256,000

OWNER EQUITY

	Start	End Yr 1	End Yr 2	End Yr 3	End Yr 4	End Yr 5	End Yr 6	End Yr 7	End Yr 8	End Yr 9	End Yr 10	End Yr 11
%		24.2%	26.8%	36.5%	45.2%	50.4%	53.5%	55.1%	56.6%	58.0%	59.3%	59.3%
		22,785	35,376	59,865	85,865	105,865	119,865	127,865	135,865	143,865	151,865	151,865

Owed

	Start	End Yr 1	End Yr 2	End Yr 3	End Yr 4	End Yr 5	End Yr 6	End Yr 7	End Yr 8	End Yr 9	End Yr 10	End Yr 11
	$30,000	71,215	96,624	104,135	104,135	104,135	104,135	104,135	104,135	104,135	104,135	104,135

	Start	End Yr 1	End Yr 2	End Yr 3	End Yr 4	End Yr 5	End Yr 6	End Yr 7	End Yr 8	End Yr 9	End Yr 10	End Yr 11
	$30,000	21,215	11,266	0								
		50,000	35,358	18,777	0							
			50,000	35,358	18,777	0						
				50,000	35,358	18,777	0					
					50,000	35,358	18,777	0				
						50,000	35,358	18,777	0			
							50,000	35,358	18,777	0		
								50,000	35,358	18,777	0	
									50,000	35,358	18,777	0
										50,000	35,358	18,777
											50,000	35,358
												50,000

> This Section shows each year's $50,000 Purchase, then subsequent amounts still Owed.
> *(See Tables 2 and 3)*

> Over time, all Key Items: Value, Owed, and Equity stabilize. If Annual Purchases average $50,000, Value stabilizes at $256,000 ... Amount Owed quickly stabilizes at $104,135 ... Equity rises to $151,865, or 59.3%. *(See also Chart A)*

MASTER WORKSHEET
Combining Information brought in from various Tables.

STARTING VALUE

We assumed a starting Value of $50,000, with a $20,000 Equity. We also arbitrarily picked the $50,000 Annual Investment. We picked $50,000, not because it was necessarily the ideal number. Actually, it's probably the minimum. Your ideal number may be 2, 3, or even 5 times this amount. We haven't received enough feedback from readers and clients to pin down an "Annual-Machinery-investment-per-craftsman" figure. An educated guess would be at least $5,000 per year, per craftsman. (And that would be after a plan is established. Growing and/or "catch-up" periods might double that.)

Sheet Line Items: Cash and Receivables. If our Current Assets (including our Profits) consist of Receivables, but no Cash … we can't write checks.

Collections don't begin after the last shipment and the last delivery, they begin clear back in the Evaluation process on our Spectrum. Even before we offer a Proposal, we should try to get a reading on the paying habits of the prospect. Even when we get the Order, diligence must be the rule. A critical part of "perfecting" the Contract is ascertaining both the understanding, and the intent, the customer has concerning our terms. Does the customer understand the terms? Does the customer see any problem in meeting those terms? "Slow-pays" destroy capital management, but they are out there and must be handled …a fact of life that can't be ignored.

Recommendation: Use the deposit / C.O.D. technique whenever possible (a must for smaller jobs … especially retail type transactions, designers, and such) Don't be afraid to ask for it … just explain our policy. You'll be pleasantly surprised at your success. You'll be amazed at what you can get just by asking for it. Try it. With other accounts (GC's, etc.), be sure to use clear, specific language in proposals so everyone knows what's expected. No surprises! Everyone must agree on what's going to be delivered, where and when … including the money!

The essentials haven't changed … there are two parts to the transaction:
1. We deliver fine woodwork, as agreed.
2. The customer delivers money, as agreed.

Boards for dollars! We'll have the boards there when he needs them … he'll have the dollars here when we need them. Not too complicated. If the customer won't respect that … dump him! Let him become someone else's problem. Alert woodwork manufacturers who write clear proposals, insist on fair response and then follow up on due dates get receivables down to 40-45 days. That keeps the Cash Flowing, and Capital requirements reasonable.

When we have sufficient Cashflow and Working Capital, it means paying bills on time and taking discounts. It means getting in on occasional special

The Top Section of the WORKSHEET charts the $50,000 annual Machinery Purchase, then the subsequent diminishing Value, year by year. A "stair-step" effect is created as we continue to add next year's purchases, plus Future Values, clear across the row.

The Lower Section of the WORKSHEET shows the Amount Owed entered in a similar fashion. (See Table 3)

In the Center Section of the WORKSHEET, we asked the Spreadsheet to add up the accumulation of Values from the Top Section, and also, add up the accumulation of Amounts Owed from the Lower Section. Then we asked for a computation of Equity for each progressing year.

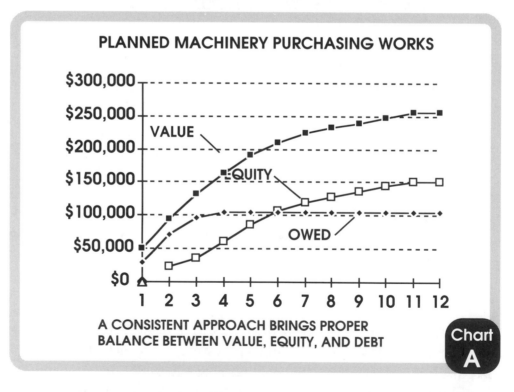

Those 3 Lines were selected to form the Chart A. Chart A shows the same information, but in a pleasing and (for some) more readable presentation. Both WORKSHEET and Chart show us that the Owed Amount quickly levels off at $104,135 as Value grows to $256,000 and Equity climbs to $151,865 (or 59.3%). Clearly a sustained plan's benefits.

	C	D	E	F		G	H	I
53	LOAN ANALYSIS					Interest	Monthly	Total
54						Rate	Payment	Interest
55	Down Payment	None					1,112	16,733
56	Interest Rate	12%				12.0%	1,112	16,733
57	Term	60				12.5%	1,125	17,494
58	Loan Amount	$50,000				13.0%	1,138	18,259
59	Monthly Payment	1112.22				13.5%	1,150	19,030
60	Total Interest	16733.34				14.0%	1,163	19,805
61						14.5%	1,176	20,585
62								
63	1112.22	60	48	36				
64	12.0%	1112	1317	1661				
65	12.5%	1125	1329	(1673)				
66	13.0%	1138	1341	1685				
67	13.5%	1150	1354	1697				
68	14.0%	1163	1366	1709				
69	14.5%	1176	1379	1721				

LOAN ANALYSIS

Study of Monthly Payment Required ... set up to take into account various Loan Amounts, Down Payments, Interest Rates, and Number of Payments. For Master Worksheet, we selected $50,000, No Down Payment, 12.5% Interest and 36 Payments (3 Years).

Table 2

Principal	50000
Annual Interest Rate	0.125
Term	3
Periods	12
Monthly Payments	1672.68
No of Payments	36

PAYMENT SCHEDULE

No	balance	Interest	Principal	Balance
1	50000	520.83	1151.85	48848
2	48848	508.83	1163.85	47684
3	47684	496.71	1175.97	46508
4	46508	484.46	1188.22	45320
5	45320	472.08	1200.60	44120
6	44120	459.58	1213.10	42906
7	42906	446.94	1225.74	41681
8	41681	434.17	1238.51	40442
9	40442	421.27	1251.41	39191
10	39191	408.24	1264.44	37926
11	37926	395.07	1277.61	36649
12	36649	381.76	1290.92	35358
13	35358	368.31	1304.37	34053
14	34053	354.72	1317.96	32735
15	32735	340.99	1331.69	31404
16	31404	327.12	1345.56	30058
17	30058	313.11	1359.57	28699
18	28699	298.94	1373.74	27325
19	27325	284.63	1388.05	25937
20	25937	270.18	1402.50	24534
21	24534	255.57	1417.11	23117
22	23117	240.80	1431.88	21685
23	21685	225.89	1446.79	20239
24	20239	210.82	1461.86	18777
25	18777	195.59	1477.09	17300
26	17300	180.20	1492.48	15807
27	15807	164.66	1508.02	14299
28	14299	148.95	1523.73	12775
29	12775	133.08	1539.60	11236
30	11236	117.04	1555.64	9680
31	9680	100.84	1571.84	8108
32	8108	84.46	1588.22	6520
33	6520	67.92	1604.76	4915
34	4915	51.20	1621.48	3294
35	3294	34.31	1638.37	1655
36	1655	17.24	1655.44	0

A Payment Schedule is essential to good Financial Planning. This Schedule is also the Basis for the "amounts still Owed" Section of the MASTER WORKSHEET. (Note shaded portions at Payments 12, 24, and 36.) *(See, also, Table 2)*

Table 3

FLEXIBILITY

We don't really expect a Woodworker to spend exactly $50,000 on the last day of each fiscal year. But once the Spreadsheet is set up, unlimited options are available. And each "what-if" can be tested well in advance of the commitment. No more mysteries. No more wondering. Each purchase can have Financial ramifications carefully studied. The influence on Net Worth, Cashflow, Debt-to-Equity, etc. will be known ahead of time. Various financing options can be studied even as we refine our Priority List and the various Machinery Buying Checklists.

PAYMENTS AND DEPRECIATION

PAYMENTS

YEAR	1	2	3	4	5	6
30,000	1004	1004	1004			
50,000		1673	1673	1673		
			1673	1673	1673	
3 year				1673	1673	1673
payout					1673	1673
						1673
PAYMENTS	1004	2676	4349	5018	5018	5018
DEPRECIATION	833	1667	2500	2500	3333	4167

DEPRECIATION

	1	2	3	4	5	6
	833	833	833			
		833	833	833	833	833
			833	833	833	833
				833	833	833
					833	833
						833

Payments (See Tables 2 and 3) plus Depreciation (5yr Straight-line) amounts are entered into a corner of our Spreadsheet. Entries follow the "stair-step" pattern like our MASTER WORKSHEET. The comparison is shown in the Center Section, and again in Chart B.

Table 4

Chart B and Table 4 round out our Financial charting. Both Table and Chart show how the Cashflow-Equivalent of Depreciation almost makes our Monthly Payment. ($4,167 out of $5,018) This type of systematic, consistent, long-range Planning will bring us much closer to the Ideal Machinery Purchase: The Right Machine, at the Right Time, at the Right Price, and with the Right Financing.

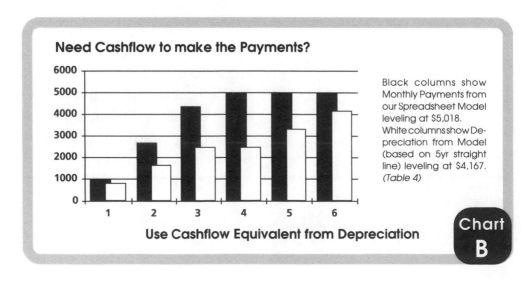

Need Cashflow to make the Payments?

Black columns show Monthly Payments from our Spreadsheet Model leveling at $5,018. White columns show Depreciation from Model (based on 5yr straight line) leveling at $4,167. *(Table 4)*

Use Cashflow Equivalent from Depreciation

Chart B

THE LENDERS

The business of a moneylender ... has nowhere, nor at any time, been a popular one. Those who have the resolution to sacrifice the present to future, are natural objects of envy to those who have sacrificed the future to the present. The children who have eaten their cake are the natural enemies of the children who have theirs. While the money is hoped for, and for a short time after it has been received, he who lends it is a friend and benefactor. By the time the money is spent, and the evil hour of reckoning is come, the benefactor is found to have changed his nature, and to have become the tyrant and the oppressor. It is an oppression for a man to reclaim his own money; it is none to keep it from him.

-Jeremy Bentham, in his 1787 "Defense of Usury"

The knowledge from Tables and Charts will help us when talking to bankers. This is important. Or course, we don't develop these Tables and Charts *just* to impress the banker, or anyone else. We use them to better inform ourselves and our colleagues, first. But, as *we* become convinced through knowledge, so we will be better prepared to convince others. And, even as we must develop a good working banking situation for our Line of Credit, so we need to be on the same page with someone when it comes to Machinery Purchase. Even a modest woodworking operation soon requires Machinery valued at $150,000 or more. Most woodworkers don't have that much lying around in petty cash. Sooner or later we'll be talking to someone who lends money.

As we try to make our needs known to the Banker, let us be aware of the Banker's needs. *What are they looking for?* Recently, a loan officer from one of the big downtown banks told us that many lenders still often follow the old, tried-and-true basic 5 C's: Character, Capacity, Capital, Collateral, and Conditions.

1. Character. An assessment of the integrity, intent, attitudes, values and determination of the people who will be repaying the loan. Their history of general conduct. What kind of people are they?

2. Capacity. Some options: Earning capacity, Production capacity, Capacity to understand the import of the obligation. Mostly, the Capacity to generate cashflow and profits : and repay the loan.

3. Capital. Total Assets from the financial statement, Working Capital, etc.

4. Collateral. Whatever the order, nobody's going to ignore Collateral. A sensible relationship between money owed on Machinery loans, and the Machinery's "Real" Value is key to any discussion on the subject.

5. Conditions. Could be a long list. Timing. Amount too big? Not big enough? Part long term, part short term? Prudent expansion plans, or "stayin'-alive" money? But essentially: How much is needed? ... for what purpose? ... for how long? ... repayment terms, etc. How does it fit into an overall strategy and the Business Plan?

Look for a lender who looks the *dynamics* of the financial picture ... a study of the Income Statement ... looking at our money-making machine. Some seem to prefer focusing on the *statics* ...looking at the Balance Sheet ... and asking, "What are they worth dead?" The emphasis ebbs and flows. Some years it's "Asset-based lending". Other times it's all "Cashflow". We should be able to handle either, since we're going to focus on both.

Let's not be paranoid about personal guarantees. They are a part of lending to any closely held company, particularly in the early years. The lenders position is: If the applicant isn't willing to back the proposition, why should we? However, we have the right to get some of our personal guarantees released as we reach certain benchmarks. The Banker should have sufficient collateral, but he shouldn't tie us into a straight-jacket to keep us from talking to anyone else. That's a sorry way to try to keep our business.

27

Buying or Selling the Business

"What's a woodworking business worth, anyway?"

"Are we buying or selling?"

"Why do you always answer my questions with another question?"

"Do I do that?"

"You just did it, again! Answer the question."

"Well, it depends."

"Thanks a lot!"

Sound familiar to you? Me, too. Let's take the discussion a little further, this time.

We can all agree that the true worth of something is attested at the time the item is sold. At that moment, both buyer and seller agreed the price was correct. We forget that those conditions … same merchandise, same seller, same buyer, same conditions, will never occur again. So, even if we happen to know the price of some other deal, we still have to approach our own deal our own way.

Truth is, the "price" would be different for each individual buyer. I put price in quotation marks because terms and conditions are a part of price, too.

Yes, it does make a difference (in viewpoint) whether we're buying, or selling. But, reconciling that difference is what makes the deal. If you want to deal, that's where to start.

The negotiating process involves studying, understanding, then meeting (or modifying) the perceived needs of both parties. Perceived needs are seldom *completely* met, but everyone has to come away with a reasonable percentage, or the deal won't go.

The transaction often becomes awkward because of lack of experience. *It may well be a once-in-a-lifetime experience for both buyer and seller.* They both want the best deal they can get, but with very little idea of what they really want, or what they can really get.

The evaluation process usually stumbles on the "going-concern" value. There are pretty good guidelines on the value of real estate; machinery and equipment; and materials. It's the value of all those things *in place* that gets the scrutiny ... and the debate.

Best advice to both Buyer and Seller: Be realistic. Be sensible. If possible, talk to someone who's been there.

Well, what are the differences. Why? Who's right?

Typical positions we can understand, *but also question:*

Seller: *"This is a terrific business, and it's my whole life. It makes a lot of money and I'm not going to give it away. I want my price, and I want it in cash up front."*

Buyer: *"Well, he can forget that. I know it's a terrific business, but I can start up, myself, for one-fifth of what he's asking. I can bid to the same people he bids, so why should I have to pay so much? Besides, if I had the kind of money he's asking ... I could retire instead of having the hassles."*

Those positions are not unreasonable, nor are they false. The problem with those statements is that they're true and correct, *up to a point.* **They just don't tell the whole story.**

To the **Seller**, I say: I haven't even heard your asking price, but I can still argue your last sentence. There is no way you're going to get as much cash up front as you can get with a sensible term sale.

And it can be far better for you tax-wise, as well. Also, you can get interest in addition to the principal.

To the **Buyer**, I say: You apparently don't realize how long it takes to build a business. Just the time lost "looking" is incredible. I mean "looking" for everything. Plant facility, Sales Contracts, Money, People, Equipment ... the list goes on and on. Even if money's no problem (I've never seen it, but it may be possible), an incredible amount of time will be consumed just getting everything together. If you're any kind of woodworker, you've observed materials coming in ... people and machines making things happen ... and product going out the door. But there's an 89% chance you've no idea how long it takes to get there from a dead start. ***And there's a 99% chance you've no idea how long it takes to get the money in after the product is shipped, nor how much operating money it takes to keep the whole thing afloat.***

If you, as Buyer, are shrewd enough to buy a "going concern" you can get everything in place and humming. And you can have cash inflow the first month, instead of 6, 9, or 12 months down the road. (And possibly keep about an extra year of your life). Trust me, there will still be plenty of excitement ... *your life will still include many thrills.*

STATIC AND DYNAMIC

I use the terms "Static" and "Dynamic" to refer to two distinct values for the business.

I call the "known" or "discernible" values of Inventory, Real Estate and Equipment the Static Value. *(What's it worth shut down and padlocked, or what can we get if we have to cash out by a week from Tuesday?)* Some banks look at us that way. *(What's the salvage value?)*

The "Dynamic" value is what it's worth under way and producing cashflow and profits. (Functioning as a money-making machine.)

That portion of the value of a business is sometimes referred to as "goodwill" or "going-concern value." *(The buyer may also refer to it as Blue Sky.)*

Goodwill has real value, but it's hard to pinpoint. It can be related to historical Profits. A good place to start, but not definitive. Economic conditions may have made the picture worse (or better).

Biggest question mark is whether the new owner's team is as capable as the old one. Indeed, one of the most important questions is how much of the present team will remain intact.

The personal influence of the owner may be enormous. His charm, knowledge and experience may be the company's greatest asset. He may have a gift of dealing with people which is seldom found. He may be able to get more money for our work and still have happy satisfied customers. He may have the ability to get better prices and service from suppliers. He may have the respect and loyalty of employees. He may get outstanding performance at modest wages.

The new owner may not be able to duplicate all those things. *The new owner may not be able to duplicate any of those things.* In other words, the current owner may be a tough act to follow.

Which means the business can make money for him, hence is valuable to him. *But that, by itself, won't make it valuable for someone else.*

But, there is a corollary. Those special touches may have slipped in recent years. If an owner has begun to "burn out" from keeping customers and employees happy, plus dealing with more and more bureaucracy, things could be slipping. Some grouchiness may be creeping into various transactions. If so, the "goodwill" value may have slipped, as well.

Question for Buyer: *How much of the strength that has built this company and produced the historical profits is <u>really</u> transferable to me?*

Answer: Tally it up. There will be pluses and minuses. List them and add it up. And forget the rose-colored glasses. This is the time to be a realist. (Maybe "slightly optimistic" can be permitted.)

Question for Seller: *Should I take the trouble to screen the buyers and select the ones most likely to build on what I've built and continue my success?*

Answer: It's worth taking time to think about. Try to honestly answer questions like this:

Do you really want to twist someone's arm hard enough to extract a certain size check, and then split?

Have you already bought a condo on Maui, and could you care less what happens to your baby after closing the deal? Or, do you intend to continue to live here where family and friends are ... in the community you've been a part of so many years?

I suspect most Sellers do care what happens. Most of us would like to believe we're capable of building an enduring entity. We'd like to think that we have put the right people and the right procedures in place, and have fashioned something of quality. How can we abandon the labor of years so easily?

The screening process might be a good idea. It might be a way to accomplish several things. If there is likelihood of continued success, you will have provided the continuity of a stable community entity. You will have provided for a smooth transition for customers, employees, and suppliers. You can continue to observe your creation as a positive and viable force in the world. There may well be measure of satisfaction in that. Good News: The hard-headed business reality says this is also the best way to get the most money out of what you've built. Why? Because it benefits the buyer enough to make the business much more desirable and therefore more valuable to him/her.

If we're looking to buy, what do we look for?

What we want is a money making machine. Our options are:

> ***Find one ready to go.*** Not too likely, but we can establish our parameters and begin the search.

Build one from scratch. Already touched on. Time consuming. Takes more dollars than you think. Healthy profits slow to arrive.

Find one worth fixing up a little. A realistic way to go.

Sort through the strengths and weaknesses, add up the pluses and minuses to arrive at a reasonable worth and try to buy it.

What we want is a well managed company. Not too big. Room to grow. Good people on both sides of the office door ... experienced, capable and hard working. A good plant facility with a long term, low priced lease. Equipment pretty well up-to-date and well maintained. Good Profits. Good Cashflow. Good Backlog. Good financial information, including job costing, so our accountant can sort out the particulars for us. Good pay habits and good contracts, along with good contract performance, so our lawyer won't have trouble with real and/or potential liabilities. (Oh, yes, we will use an accountant and a lawyer. We "believe" what we see and hear, but we still check everything out.) Last, but not least ... we want all team members to be ecstatic with our approach. Everyone will stay to ensure continued success (theirs and ours). The price is low, and the terms are great.

That's what we're looking for, but it's not very likely we'll find it. I see a lot of woodwork manufacturing companies, and I've never seen one that totally fits the description. *If we find about half of that, we probably have something to talk about.*

What do we look at first? Let's start with a walk-through. We can tell a lot about the Equipment, the efficiency of the Plant Layout, and also (if the Plant is in operation) something about the mood of the people. Is there confidence, or hesitation? Do we see smiles, or scowls? What about the quality of the work? If it's a "happy" place with a sense of order, that's a good sign. Production workers respond if given good equipment, good instructions, and good materials. They respond, and they stay. If there is a surly mood, we may have already lost some good people. The good ones don't have to stay around and put up with a bunch of crap. However, if we see any good signs … Plant facility, Equipment, or People, we keep looking.

We want to see Financial Information. The owner may not want to show everything right off. He wants to be sure we're serious. And, after all, the information is sensitive. But, he also knows a serious buyer won't stay around long if such information is withheld.

Let's not get into terms, yet. Use a "poker" face. Don't show either delight or dismay. The posture is "matter-of-fact" … we're interested, we know what we're looking for, we know what we're doing, we can swing it, and his isn't the only business available. Of course, he might have a strategy, too. He may act as if he has three other buyers all lined up and waiting, and we'd better hurry and snap up his offer. I don't counsel game-playing, but we must be prepared for a bit.

Tax returns for the past three years should be examined. They won't indicate the maximum profits possible. They will show a trend, and are less likely to have been enhanced. Here's where our accountant comes in. If things don't add up, we must find out why, or we walk away.

We must examine items on the Balance Sheet, as well. *(See nearby Table A.)*

The Operating Statement will reveal important aspects of the business, too. A line-by-line study can help spot areas where changes by a new owner can improve profits.

Depending on the sophistication of the buyer prospect, much can be learned from an examination of Receivables and Payables. Payables can indicate if we're buying from the right people, in the right quantities, and at the right price. Also, we'll find out if the company discounts, or if we're on C. O. D. Receivables will show whether we're doing business with good accounts, or a bunch of dead-beats.

These facts may be moot, if we're merely buying the assets. It may be the seller's responsibility to collect the Receivables, and also to pay the

Balance Sheet

ASSETS

Cash	22,680
Receivables (Including unbilled)	112,804
Inventories (raw materials)	69,234
All Other	7,461
TOTAL CURRENT	212,178
Fixed Assets (invest. in property and equip, including leasehold improvements, net of accumulated depreciation).	83,260
Other Non-current	1,003
TOTAL ASSETS	298,422

LIABILITIES

Notes Payable (portion due within 12 mo)	27,156
Accounts Payable	59,088
Taxes Payable	11,340
All Other Current	2,686
TOTAL CURRENT	100,270
Long Term Debt (due after 12 mo)	48,344
TOTAL LIABILITIES	148,614
NET WORTH (capital and retained earnings, stockholder's equity)	149,808
TOTAL	298,422

Income Statement

PLANT PROCESSED SALES	682,400
Material	207,450
Labor	188,342
Plant Overhead	124,197
COST OF SALES	519,989
Gross Profit	162,411
Admin. Overhead	128,291
OPERATING PROFITABILITY	34,120

The Financial Information in this Chart reflects recent Industry Averages, which vary slightly from year to year.

Receivables are high. Also borne out by collections calculation. Check to see if some are too old and/or no good.

Collections

$$\frac{\text{Sales} \quad \$682,400}{\text{Receivables} \quad 112,804} = 6.05$$

$$365 / 6.05 = 60 \text{ days}$$

Inventory looks high. Unless Plant is away from delivery opportunities, or special material has been brought in for a particular job, that's more inventory than a firm doing this volume needs. Maybe it's material that can be returned for credit, or maybe it can be worked down. Check it.

Inventory Turn

$$\frac{\text{Total Material} \quad \$207,450}{\text{Inventory} \quad 69,234} = 3.00$$

$$365 / 3.00 = 122 \text{ days}$$

The Machinery and Equipment Asset figures are unusually low. Some machines may be almost fully depreciated. Have a machinery dealer help with a "real" value.

Theoretically, the actual value of a Business. Worth looking at, but certainly not absolute. Even after adjustments are made for fair Machinery values, Inventory, Receivables, Payables, etc. The Buyer still has to determine what the Business is worth to *him.* **The past, and the present, are relevant ... but the new Owner is looking at, and betting on the future.**

Note that the Operating Profitability is only 5% of sales. Will figure in discussions of Value of the Backlog. If he's only getting 5% out of his backlog, there's no way it could be worth more than that. In fact, I wouldn't give anything for it, unless I estimated it myself (or possibly, the gal or guy next to me).

Table A

Payables at time of Closing.

On the other hand, we may want to assume the Payables as part of the financing plan. (Buyer pays out of normal Cashflow, and the seller keeps more of the Closing proceeds.) The other significance has to do with the Goodwill aspect. If the company is known as "slow-pay" what's that "Goodwill" worth?

WHO OWNS THE BUILDING

Who owns it now? Who will own it? What will the rent be?

We need to examine the lease to prevent surprises. Is the lease transferable? Renewable? At what price? Is its length sufficient to cover the time of payout terms? We certainly don't need the excitement of a move during the critical acquisition period. This question will be asked by financing people, too.

We need to look at all other contracts, too. Here's where we need our lawyer, again. If the lease, or other contracts are not readily transferable, it may change the way the purchase is handled. Instead of just buying assets, perhaps the entire corporation will be purchased. This will give continuity to all contracts, but also open the door to any future liability claims. This must be considered most carefully and proper safeguards must be put in place.

OTHER CONSIDERATIONS

We might consider other items which will be transferred, and, indeed, the actual mechanics of transfer as we sort out the value of the business.

Insurance:
Can we take over the present policy or must a new one be found? At what cost difference?

Deposits:
With Utility companies or other. Transferable? At what cost? How about deposits from customers for current or future projects?

Taxes:

Payroll, Sales, Use, or other. What's due? What do we adjust?

Fringes:

How about the vacations coming up? Medical plans? Sick or Personal leave obligations?

Licenses and Fees:

Once again. Transfer and adjust? Do they have to be renewed? Or a new application?

When we think through the various aspects of values, the past, the future, the knowns, and the unknowns ... we may see a pattern emerging. A Going Concern has far more value to someone who knows it well. Even if there are certain deficiencies, someone who understands will better know how to address them.

Which tells us that a Seller probably should be looking at his own people for good prospects. A well managed company is always developing managers and leaders. If we, as owners have been doing our job, we should have developed some managerial leadership which is worthy and capable of ownership. *Why not start there?*

Conversely, a Buyer would do well to look to his/her own store, first. Sure, we know about all the warts, and the rest of the shortcomings. Do you really think you'll find a company with no blemishes? At least, at home we know just how bad it is. We probably have a pretty good idea of how to correct the shortcomings, too.

On the previously mentioned Table we referred to the value of the Backlog. *(Some prospects may not know what a Backlog is.)* If you or I bid most of the Backlog and the work-in-process, it surely has more value to us. Present team members also know which machines and which people work, and which ones don't.

Biggest hang-up here? I've heard Owners say, *"You mean, let 'em buy me out with profits from my company? ... You've got to be crazy!"*

But wait, let's analyze that statement. *First of all, when it's sold, it's not "my" company anymore.* Second, profit is gained mostly from hard work, not some sort of gift. Third, that entity you refer to as "my" company ... the part which you built ... had a value placed on it, and you're getting paid for it. Last, but not least, if the new owners can't expect to pay for the business out of future profits ... **why in the world would they want to buy it?"**

As we think through the idea of a deal struck by "staying home," that is, current employees buying the business they know ... their own place of employment. Indeed, they helped build it. They know the strengths and weaknesses. We should also consider that the best deals are made with good terms. Good terms, meaning longer payouts and smaller sums up front. Reasonable enough to assure a successful acquisition without crippling the new team with oppressive terms which hamper operations and choke off any growth possibilities.

It's not a one sided affair. It works for the Seller, too. It's much easier to get top-dollar with more lenient terms.

But we still haven't answered the question, "What's it worth?"

RETURN ON INVESTMENT

People nearly always consider the "pay-back" for any endeavor. We don't necessarily think of it as "Return on Investment."

But that's really what it is. Whether we're deciding to buy some stock, or deciding to go bowling, or put in a garden ... there's a similarity in the equations. What will it really do for me? What will it cost? Is it worth it?

What are we going to put out in terms of Time, Talent, Energy, Money, or other items of value ... and then, what do we expect in return?

"Return on Investment" is a useful measurement when determining the value of a business.

What do we mean by "Investment?"

It can include whatever we're willing to invest.

If we're talking about the MONEY, only, then we make the comparison on that basis. Is a woodworking business better than CD's, Money Market Funds, Real Estate, Treasury bills … whatever.

But, that's not the whole question. A business owner invests much more than money. There's the Time, Talent, Energy already mentioned. It doesn't stop there. **A business owner invests everything.** His/her whole being … the future … perhaps the whole family's future. That's the reality.

If that's too difficult to commit, perhaps ownership shouldn't be considered.

That kind of investment had better return much more than the average savings account.

What else do we want? How about:

- A job with a salary.

- Some profit on top of that.

- The Joy of Accomplishment.

- Financial stability for the business.

- Financial stability for the family.

- Making a contribution to Good Order.

Complete your own list and then check the symmetry of the expectation versus the investment.

RETURN ON TOTAL ASSETS

Arguably a realistic measure of operating efficiency, as it considers use of all available resources … money, inventory, equipment. *Probably should include gross value of machinery and equipment, instead of net after depreciation.* After all, we do indeed have the use of the equipment.

Also, it is a realistic expectation of equipment replacement. Replacement is *not* an option. It *will* happen.

RETURN ON NET WORTH

Some say the "Investment" is the Net Worth. Certainly a useful method. Measures both return on net investment, plus return on operations. Most useful in analyzing ongoing operations, but should be considered at time of purchase, as well.

RETURN ON BUYER'S COMMITMENT?

I think "Investment" might include whatever has been borrowed to make the business run. As buyers we may want to compute a return on our commitment, or what we have "at risk." In other words, the cash we put up *plus* the obligations we incur. We may decide that we must recover the cost of the business in 3 yrs ... 4 yrs ... 5 yrs ... whatever makes us comfortable. In the negotiating process, that may well be our "go - no-go point." We continue discussions as long as this pay-back looks realistic.

If the new owner's main thrust is getting that production machine humming, there must be a balance in selling as well. That big production machine is a hungry animal. It requires a good diet, and a steady one.

Conversely, if the new owner is a super-salesman, he'd better match it with a super-production capability.

USE PROFESSIONALS

Both Buyer and Seller should have sound counsel. Accountants to verify the numbers and the soundness of the approach. Lawyers to make sure we do and say what we *think* we're doing and saying, as well as preclude any surprises from outside sources. There are many regulations regarding a transaction such as this, and we want to do it right. Example: Complying with Bulk Sales Act of your state. Don't forget, the accountant and the lawyer need guidance from us. They know *their* business, but they don't know *our* business until we instruct them. If we're not sure about advising our professionals, we can call a woodwork business expert to review the proceedings.

Balance Sheet

ASSETS

Cash	22,680
Receivables (Including unbilled)	112,804
Inventories (raw materials)	69,234
All Other	7,461
TOTAL CURRENT	212,178
Fixed Assets (invest. in property and equip, including leasehold improvements, net of accumulated depreciation).	83,260
Other Non-current	1,003
TOTAL ASSETS	298,422

LIABILITIES

Notes Payable (portion due within 12 mo)	27,156
Accounts Payable	59,088
Taxes Payable	11,340
All Other Current	2,686
TOTAL CURRENT	100,270
Long Term Debt (due after 12 mo)	48,344
TOTAL LIABILITIES	148,614
NET WORTH (capital and retained earnings, stockholder's equity)	149,808
TOTAL	298,422

Income Statement

PLANT PROCESSED SALES	682,400
Material	207,450
Labor	188,342
Plant Overhead	124,197
COST OF SALES	519,989
Gross Profit	162,411
Admin. Overhead	128,291
OPERATING PROFITABILITY	34,120

The Financial Information in this Chart reflects recent Industry Averages, which vary slightly from year to year.

Based on the figures shown, here, the business owner might ask this Price:

Machinery and Equipment	$165,000
Inventory	69,000
Good Will	183,000
TOTAL	$417,000

He arrives at these numbers by determining that his Machinery and Equipment is about one-half depreciated. He assumes the Inventory is worth dollar-for-dollar what is shown on the Balance Sheet.

He calculates the Good Will is worth Profits x 5 = ($171,000), plus 5% of a $240,000 Backlog ($12,000).

We touched on that Backlog value idea earlier. I still feel that unless someone I know bid that Backlog, I don't think much of its value. *It might just as well be a liability.*

However, if you reach for it, even a "break-even" Backlog might have some value.

- It gives everyone something to do.
- It continues the flow of activity.
- It will produce Cashflow.

In short, unless it was really badly bid, it is far more of a plus than a minus.

But, since every bid ... even the best ... have unknowns, a Buyer should be very wary of them. A Seller should understand.

The notion of Profit x 5 being used as a value is not outrageous. It suggests a 20% return, and can be considered. Before embracing it, however, compare several things:

THE TREND

Has the Profit been growing? ... shrinking? What has changed in the "neighborhood?" Is business falling off? What about competition? Is a new kid on the block ripping up the market with stupid prices?

Good answers will move us a step closer.

CONTINUITY

What's going to change, and how will that change the Profits? If the Seller's skill and personality had a significant effect ... and he's leaving ... what good's the equation?

Table
B

Bring in the professionals early. Before we get serious about the price, and before we make any offers. Here are some examples of considerations in working toward an offer:

TAX CONSIDERATIONS

Depreciate again, if assets purchased … not, if corporation is purchased. A Tax loss carry-forward would be a consideration, in some instances. Seller and Buyer look at stated Goodwill price differently …each trying to prevent higher taxes. Seller and Buyer should reach agreement, so I. R. S. doesn't get to decide it for them.

PURCHASE PRICE INCLUDES:

Should be itemized. Inventory; machinery and equipment; supplies; goodwill; real estate. (Nearby Table B points out some methods to determine a value on various items.)

METHODS TO FINANCE

Banks. Leasing companies (for some, or all, of Machinery). Owner carry. Payables. Suppliers (special terms during "start-up").

TERMS

Banks: 3 to 5 yrs … Seller may go 6 or 7 at lower interest.

Example:

Bank: $100,000 @ 14%   60 payments of $2327 for a total of $139,610.

Owner: $100,000 @ 12% 80 payments of $1822 for a total of $145,751.

$500 a month in cashflow might make quite a difference.

QUID PRO QUO: GOOD FOR BUYER AND SELLER

Many changes in ownership occur when the more experienced (older) professional decides it may be time to do more fishing and less dealing. The dues have been paid … the contribution has been made … the right to relax has been earned. *Why not! Let's let go, and let the youngsters have at it. We've left some pretty good marks for them to shoot at. Let's see what they can do.*

And the youngsters ... the new owners ... get their shot. *Now we'll show the world how it should be done.*

A fair price serves both well.

The community is also well served by a smooth transition. Employees, customers, suppliers ... everybody wins when a good business is allowed to continue its course without undue trauma.

The acquisition period should be a high point in the lives of the purchasers. The level of excitement ... plus the level of energy and enthusiasm makes the experience grand. But it requires a tremendous concentration of thought and effort which needs some understanding. The participants may have an inkling of what's involved, but sometimes the families don't.

Much is written about entrepreneurs and entrepreneuring, mostly by writers and not entrepreneurs. Somehow, the glamour comes through without proper explanation of the back-breaking effort. They usually get around to mentioning a millionaire, or two, by the third paragraph. And they may not mention the start-up mortality rate at all. (In construction related industries ... which includes us ... the overall *mortality rate* for entities, large and small, started from scratch is 95%. Of course, it's nowhere near that when a going concern changes hands.)

It's perfectly healthy for the families to have dreams of affluence. *I maintain that any business should create wealth for its owners.* But no business can create wealth for foolish spenders. Mark it down ... you and your family *can* look forward to comfortable incomes down the road. *But only if the first years are performed with strict discipline and frugal conduct.* Obligations must be paid off. Operating capital must be built and maintained. Equity must be established and not be highly leveraged.

Once this solid base is established, we can relax a bit. We can finally enjoy that vacation. Normal owner draws can be established and the owner's family can proceed with investments for everything from kid's college, to a second residence ... or any prudent expenditure for comfort and enjoyment.

But remember ... spend later earnings, not the working capital. The wrong road taken, here, may not have a chance for a return.

Recommendation: Structure this period for 5 years. Then try to do it in half that time. But be specific about the size and shape of your base. And back off from the extra effort only when it is achieved ... no fudging!

Fixed Assets (invest. in property and equip, including leasehold improvements, net of accumulated depreciation). 83,260

From our previous example ...

That's the Net.

But, is it an investment of $92,511 which has been reduced by 10%?

or is it an investment of $416,300 which has been reduced by 80%?

GETTING DOWN TO THE FACTS

As the prospective buyer, consider this approach:

1) Pin down the tangibles.

Get as close as possible to the real value of Machinery and Equipment. Look again at the value stated on our example Balance Sheet. It shows NET Fixed Assets of $83,260. But it doesn't tell us whether it's an original investment of $92,511 depreciated by 10%, or an investment of $416,300 depreciated by 80%. Learning that will help us determine the true value, plus allow some idea of how intensive our machine upgrading will be during the next few years. (Important influence on our Pro Forma).

Add in the "real" value of the Inventory, plus real estate, etc.

2) *Place a value on the intangibles.* Analyze the sellers justification for value of intangibles. How much will remain after the deal is closed? (If strengths in marketing, financial connections, and overall good management instincts rest solely in the Seller … they'll be gone, and therefore of little value). However, a lively and alert Team, coupled with a good plant facility and equipment, along with a well-costed backlog, certainly *does* have value.

MOST IMPORTANT: With the help of your accountant, put together your own *pro forma* financial statement *(a pro forma financial statement is a forecast of results if a particular budget or plan is followed)* … a strict, comprehensive budgeting of all revenues and expenses anticipated. Be realistic. Project from recent history. Then, sensibly blend in all expected changes. Cover the years involved in completion of the buyout. (Include both Balance Sheets and Operating Statements).

3) *Structure the Financing.*

Keys: Terms are a part of the price, so financing may well be a part of the proposal. The expected Profits indicated by the *pro forma* should pin down the value of the business TO YOU. It may be a function both of what it's worth, and what you can afford. Know where you are before you make a proposal.

How much cash can you put up and still be certain of retaining adequate Working Capital? This is not a 2 + 2 type equation. It's much more complex. It will depend on which of the assets and liabilities are to be acquired. It will depend on Backlog strengths and weaknesses (is the cash going to be flowing in, steadily?). It depends on personal sacrifices you are willing, *or able* to make (low or no Owner Draws for a time).

The bank's involvement is fundamental. Determine what the bank can (will) do (hopefully a large part of the "tangibles" at a sensible interest rate). Then, see what the Seller is willing to carry, and at what interest rate. Use these numbers to adjust the Pro Forma. The interest paid will definitely influence the Profits. The payment obligations will definitely influence Cashflow. Don't take on more payments than you can handle, but don't starve the Working Capital. Some extremely sensitive trade-offs, here.

The tone of this Chapter has been stressing the idea of the Seller making the terms somewhat easier, both to get the best price, and to help make the deal.

We have not meant to imply, however, that the Buyer should waltz right in with no sacrifices. On the contrary, we respect the truth … there is no free lunch, and there is no free ride. The Buyer must either come up with serious cash, or be willing to pledge personal assets and live quite frugally until the high-leverage situation is relieved.

HURDLES

Family and friends who aren't in business. There'll be loads of free advice available for the decision on whether to become an owner, or not. Most of the free advice will have the same value as the cost. Zero. Well meaning friends who haven't been owners have no basis on which to comment. Dire warnings of impending disaster reflect their own fears, possibly tinged with a bit of wistful jealousy. It's not the best for your self image when a friend dares to do that which you do not. They're not bad people. They're probably great people. But, ignore their advice.

The family is different, especially members of the immediate family. Their opinion is crucial. Best approach: reduce the "unknowns." We all fear "unknowns" far more than "knowns." Unlock the mysteries. Help them to understand the complexities.

True, we'll be buying and selling … hiring and firing. True, there are genuine responsibilities to customers, employees, and other associates and agencies. But we are responsible professionals, well versed in those aspects. And, we have probably already been functioning in those areas. Spell it out. Take it slow. Be patient. Listen. Carefully address each apprehension. It'll be easier now, than later.

And don't forget, there are enormous pluses to being business owners. The joy of accomplishment. The opportunity to achieve. The chance to have more say in career direction. And the chance to accumulate wealth. There'll be work, sacrifice, triumphs and disappointments. But there'll be fulfillment and tremendous satisfaction.

Still, it's not for everyone. Some individuals, and some families, are quite comfortable with the trade-offs of risk and gain. Some are not. Try to get an understanding, and a consensus that it's the right thing to do.

PROTECTION FOR SELLER:

Language in the Contract can structure assurances buyer won't run the business into the ground. (Maintain value of inventory, and/or machinery value, for example.) Stipulate personal backup (mortgages, shares, personal guarantees, etc.) to cover difference above what bank covers.

PROTECTION FOR BUYER:

Indemnity from customer claims for past work. Unless Buyer is taking over the whole corporation, there should be no liability for Seller's past performance. It's reasonable to get an agreement not to compete. (Must be sensible, or it's unenforceable). If, in the actual mechanics of things, Buyer is collecting the receivables. (Could be they were acquired, or they're still owned by Seller and new crew is sending out the statements as part of smooth transition). Either way, there will come a time when they revert to Seller, with appropriate monetary adjustments.

DON'T MOVE TOO FAST

Keep the Trade Name, if it's feasible. Maintain the identity. Don't rile team members, customers, or suppliers. The new owner's style and personality will make their mark quite soon. It needn't be rushed.

GETTING READY TO CLOSE

Set up an arbitration method in the agreement. Stipulate how any unexpected differences will be resolved. Agree on adjustments for events between signing of agreement and actual closing. (Changes in Inventory, Receivables, Payables, whatever).

Refer to the list developed early on concerning items which transfer, such as: lease, name, phone numbers, utilities, insurance, liabilities for employee benefits, etc.

Close as soon as possible after agreement. Just enough time to arrange financing.

Think it through. Plan it. Do it.

We wish the best for both Buyer and Seller.

28

Make it Happen

A great pleasure in life is doing what people say you cannot do.

Position Report: We've been reading the Book. We have a new sense of Who we are, and Where we are. We're energized to make some changes. Where do we start?

Start by making a list. There is more strength than we realize in the simple process of writing down the What, Where, When, Who, How, and Why.

We are talking about establishing priorities, we are talking about planning, and we are talking about making things Happen. The place to start is to learn to write. Write it down. Sketch it out. Think about it. Change it. Show it to all those who will work on it. Rewrite it. You can believe it, **great accomplishments begin as a list.**

There is a magic in lists. Life can be so much simpler and more satisfying when we learn to use lists. We are wrong to insist making lists is time consuming, and *trying to operate without them is not.* Lists are everywhere. But, we take them for granted without realizing their power and their magic.

First of all, a list defines something. And when we have defined something, we can act on it effectively. It begins by defining the boundaries and shows the size and shape of the subject.

Second, a list allows us to break down a complex subject into pieces and parts which can be understood … and then communicated to others.

Third, since we now have discernible items; we can put them into sequence, grab one, and do it. Or grab a bunch and hand them to others to do. What a marvelous opportunity for Delegation.

How much time we waste trying to attack the whole lump, when we should systematically process the parts. We worry over this massive project which really is only pieces and parts ... just more of them. The dictionary says: define *(di fin´) v.*

1. to state or set forth the meaning of
2. to explain or identify the nature or essential qualities of; describe
3. to fix or lay down definitely; specify distinctly
4. to make clear the outline or form of

Aren't those great! Don't we wish all questions in our lives (personal and professional) could be "defined?"... that we could know the meaning, the nature, the qualities, the boundaries and see the clear outline? WOW! But, that's part of the magic. Putting it on paper can help us do *all those things*.

When we have definitions (Lists), we have something we can work with.

1. We have something we can study, and think about.
2. We can add to, or delete from.
3. We can assign proper priorities.
4. We can merge with other lists, or, as we have just done, set out a sub-list.

When a project begins to slow down, or has been interrupted, it is of tremendous value to have written, structured guidelines for reference. If the assigned team's vigor and enthusiasm has begun to fade, the guidelines are needed to pinpoint the frustration and get things back on track. The written record is even reassurance for the originator of the idea. Some doubts creep in, even with the best of concepts.

But, with a written plan ... which everyone has studied and had opportunity to amend ... we can expect performance, and the non-performer will have a tough time coming up with an excuse.

Learn to break the List into other Lists. Example: A main list: Goals and Objectives, divides into: Personal and Business which divide into: Long Range and Short Range, etc. Each step defines the questions more precisely and makes effective action more doable.

There will come a day when your enthusiasm for lists takes a great leap forward. It will be that day when you list a particularly awkward task only to discover that it's not nearly as difficult as you thought. The list turns out to be much shorter that you expected.

So, we're energized and eager … and we want to start a List? How about the major categories of the Book? Marketing, Managing, Manufacturing, Operations, and Money? Pick the weakest link, and start to work on it. Usually, one or two worrisome areas come to mind. Don't try to do everything at once. Pick the area most needing attention … define the deficiency … define the remedy … and make the assignments, along with the budget and the schedule. Make certain of the follow-up and follow-through, then address the next Item.

Too urgent to wait for the whole listing process? No problem … get right on it. Call a huddle of all those involved in the decision, and in its execution, and do it! Spell out the What, the How, the Who, the Where, the When, and don't forget the Why. They'll do it better, and quicker, if they're convinced of the Why. And they need a clear understanding of all (What, How, Who, Where, When, Why) if they are to work around obstacles and know when to come back for further instructions. **All of which spells out the main reasons things don't get accomplished.** Encourage *everyone* to start writing things down. While some Team members are executing the first plans, others are still collecting and refining the Lists. A Weekly review will receive progress reports, requests for further assistance, review of schedules, following up with a review of Priorities.

Don't forget Checklists. Checklists may well turn out to be your favorite lists. That's where we have a list of all the items critical to the success of a particular endeavor, and check it thoroughly and methodically before we begin. Whether it's leaving on a fishing trip or business trip, or starting to interview an employee prospect, or getting ready to open a meeting. Having a complete list of things to prepare, or to bring up, or to make sure we've packed, increases the odds of success dramatically. The knowledge that whatever needed to be done has been done does wonders for the "peace of mind", too.

Reduction of stress is dramatic. Doubt and uncertainty are replaced with assurance and confidence. The function and importance of checklists was emphasized many years ago when I was a military pilot. That checklist was read, and each item was checked, before every flight. No matter what the distraction … bad weather, lack of sleep, pitch darkness … you don't have to worry and wonder … just read the list. The list remains the same. Regardless of your condition or other conditions, use the list and relax … knowing that everything has been done to assure good conditions for operation. Aircraft operated without checklists would be an invitation to disaster. Operating a business without checklists also invites disaster.

The Checklist for our business? The Operations Manual we discussed back in *Operations*.

Lists are but one way to get ideas on paper. Pictures, and Spreadsheets (with their Numbers) are also excellent tools to: Define, Study, Refine, *and* Communicate. Many more good things will Happen as we, and all our colleagues, learn to sketch out the first glimmer of an idea. Just do it! Don't worry about perfect form, or appearance, or acceptance. Sketch it out, then put it away. Look again, the next day. Put it back, again … or redo it … or throw it away. Both the idea and the Process improve each time we do this. And, it is key to making things Happen. The computer is great for this process. Revisions are quick and easy. Many versions may be kept, if appropriate. Many presentation formats are available.

Whether our individual responsibility is to "Make it Happen" for our own selves, our Area of the Plant, or the whole Company … the process is essentially the same. Determine what we want to Happen, the Sequence of events, and the remainder of the What, How, Who, Where, When, and Why.

Spell it out. Do it. Now.

The Business Plan

29

The first, and best, way to prove we have the right to be in business is to be able to present a Business Plan. And prior to presentation, the ability to produce it. Actually, we need to develop 2 Business Plans. The first, and most important, is our "internal" or "in-house" Business Plan. The second is the one we prepare to present to others.

The internal plan is confidential, and we can be completely candid about our hopes and dreams, apprehensions and frustrations, dumb competitors, etc., if we wish. It should be flexible and free of limitations in its comments. But, out of all those characteristics, it still *must be reduced to specific marching orders for us all* (primarily through the Operations Manual). It's just that we can leave more doors open for refinement and modification when the time is right. We can not only permit changes, we encourage them. Of course, the key parts become the basis for the "presenting" Business Plan.

I urge a 1-page Summary … regularly updated … for both the internal Plan, and the Formal Plan.

I particularly encourage a Summary for the Formal Business Plan, for these reasons: We are presenting something for their evaluation, and judgment. Part of their evaluation will certainly be based on our ability to spell out … thoroughly, but succinctly … what we have to say. Many may conclude we don't know the subject if we can't Summarize. And we must be prepared to Summarize verbally, as well. When presenting, we must remember: some people are "readers", others are "listeners". "Readers love to pore over the pages, and study all the details. "Listeners" don't have time for that. They make their judgments by what they hear (or possibly by the way it's presented). Some may be "readers", but they still want to hear how we say it. Understand, in some cases, we either do this … or the document never will be considered. In short: If we don't have something to catch, and hold, their interest our possibilities for consideration are near zero.

This is not to suggest that a good Summary will get us all the way. Not so. We may make a fantastic presentation to a "listener" and the "listener" is all smiles. But, you can be sure there are plenty of "readers" behind the "listener" who expect to comb through every detail … so the detail had better be there.

It is excellent discipline for us to know, and believe, all the details of our Business Plan. We should know it well enough to summarize, or verbalize, with ease.

The amount of detail, even the form of the plan for presentation will depend on the needs of those receiving it. Venture capital people, or other investors, might expect more detail than some lenders. A start-up, or huge expansion program, will require much more information then the company with a track record.

The Business Plan begins with basic facts, such as:

Company Name and location.

Products and Services

Principals. (Their qualifications, experience, possibly short biographies),

Company History. (Years in business, growth, successes, etc.)

Objectives. (Growth Plan, etc.)

Historical Financial Data

Proforma Balance Sheet and Proforma Income Statement

They may wish to know our thoughts on overall Business Strategy, such as:

1. What business are we in?

2. What do we offer that is better?

3. Do we understand business?

4. Do we know our Market?

5. Does our Market know us?

6. Where are we now?

7. Where do we want to be?

8. How do we intend to get there?

If we're asking for money, they'll test our comprehension, and our presentation, of how we are going to use the money, how it will influence our ratios and risk, and how we are going to repay it. Our Business Plan recipients may also wish to know about:

Competition (Who are they, and why can we compete?)

Marketing Plans

New Products and Services

Growth Plans by Year

The document may grow to the point where we must add an Index. Adding detail can be useful. We should certainly include many details in our own "internal" plan, so we can come up with then, if required. However, many details should be remain confidential. We can't be sure who all may get a look at our document. And, some items thrown in to impress may be construed as promises to be kept. Our policy should be to keep all promises, but also be slow to make promises … or make statements which could be considered promises.

The main idea is to have a Business Plan we understand, believe in, and are in a position to expound on it. Next step is to put it into a form that is thorough, succinct, and pleasing in appearance. Do it for *us,* first. But, be prepared to make it available to others.

30

Government

What is the species of domestic industry which his capital can employ, and of which the product is likely to be of the greatest value, every individual, it is evident, can, in his local situation, judge much better than any statesman or lawgiver can do for him. The statesmen who should attempt to direct private people in what manner they ought to employ their capitals would not only load themselves with a most unnecessary attention, but assume an authority which could safely be trusted, not only to no single person, but to no council or senate whatever, and which would nowhere be so dangerous as in the hands of a man who had folly and presumption enough to fancy himself fit to exercise it.

-Adam Smith in The Wealth of Nations.

We need governments. We don't always need what governments do. A democratic form of government is widely accepted as viable, and can be quite effective at times. Its value is considerably diminished by career politicians. Their effectiveness seems to decline in direct proportion to the number of years they hang around with others of their kind.

In a way governments give business a backhanded compliment. When burgeoning bureaucracies fail to deliver the promised happiness, they turn to business. Business is called upon to provide: Full Employment, provision for Health Care, Pensions, Holidays, Vacations, Sick Leave, a Clean Environment, absolute Safety, Overtime Pay, Tax Collection, Unemployment Compensation, Immigration Control, Drug Rehabilitation, Bill Collection, plus new areas of Education, Quotas, Day Care, and Family Leave. The amazing part: business takes all this in stride.

Our concern is the pattern of things. With more demands for happiness, accompanied by more promises to deliver happiness, we (in business) are vulnerable to being caught in the middle. The other part of the pattern is the penchant for central planning. Although central planning is a proven failure, worldwide, some insist on implementing more. The notion that central bureaucracies can design sensible uniform rules for diverse industries and diverse situations across thousands of miles of a vast country is not only absurd, it is a little frightening, too. Another concern is the weakness of review processes. There is is an ominous reluctance of any bureau to review either the fairness, or the effectiveness of their rules (or their implementation). A regulation may not accomplish the original intent, at all. But, it stays. And enforcement can be uneven … tough, one month … but more relaxed, the next.

Having said all that, we can stop the whining and discuss the subject. It is not useful to waste time with the would be, could be, should be. We need to deal with what is.

WE CAN HANDLE IT

What we have is a plethora of rules and regulations, from several levels. City, County, State, and Federal regulations will apply to much of what we do. We need to be aware of regulations, but shouldn't panic because of them. Most all regulations stem from legitimate concerns. Their basic objectives are sensible, reasonable, and do not conflict with our intentions at all. We understand that a good business is a good citizen. We understand that fair treatment for employees, and the providing of a safe workplace is in everyone's best interest.

If we proceed on such a basis, we'll be fine. Many communities now have small business centers which can give good information. Our accountant can keep us abreast of tax laws … those we pay, those we withhold, and those we collect. Each has a set of reports which go along with the passing of money. (Here, again, is an outstanding area to use computer capability.)

CONTINUE TO REVIEW

Many regulations don't apply to the smallest of small businesses. But, there is no consistency, and they keep changing. They can "kick in" at 100 people, 50, 20, 10, or even 5. We need to be particularly alert to the possibility of growing into a whole new set of rules. Or the rules can reach down to us because the employee number changes the first of next month. Establish a review process with the help of our accountant, our lawyer, any small business "assist" center, trade associations, the libraries, trade publications, and the newspapers. With enough lookouts up in the tower, we should keep abreast.

31

You!

We saved the most important subject until last.

You!

As a woodworker, you make an important contribution to good order. You deserve to do well. We sincerely hope these writings about other woodworkers' methods will prove useful to you. Nothing written has meaning until it helps you.

No matter where you are in the scheme of things, whether you are running the whole show, or quite a bit further down the totem pole … we trust you now have a better frame of reference. Knowing how your responsibilities complement the efforts or other team members should make your work more meaningful, and more enjoyable. Understanding the many facets of this great business of woodwork manufacturing should help your career, no matter where you are now, or what your ultimate goals might be.

Most woodwork business people fit the definition of an Entrepreneur. An Entrepreneur is: *"one who undertakes, or engages in, an enterprise."* And further defined as, *"one who organizes and manages any enterprise, especially a business, usually with considerable initiative and risk."* And Enterprise is further defined as, *"a project undertaken, especially one that is important or difficult or that requires boldness or energy."* And, again, one who has Enterprise has *"…readiness; adventurous spirit; ingenuity."*

The Entrepreneur seems to better understand risk and gain … to take a bright, new idea and make it work. The balance of brains, guts, and determination seems to make things happen. Entrepreneurs are quicker to learn the joy of accomplishment. They get "hooked" on achieving things, and therefore work harder.

Most woodworkers fit those descriptions. And, I see many similarities between the crafting of a woodwork project and managing the business (or parts of the business). Each "undertaking of an enterprise" is "important" and involves "initiative and risk" … each is enhanced by (and sometimes requires) "boldness, energy, readiness, adventurous spirit, and ingenuity". In fact, the same characteristics of resourcefulness, ingenuity, flexibility, intelligence, and determination translate very well into management.

Don't worry about becoming a stuffy "suit". Learning about paperwork, learning about People, and learning other business practices does not change you from being a woodworker. It's still woodwork, and it well utilizes your skills and knowledge. It merely stretches you to a greater dimension. And your talents become more marketable.

As you grow in ability to handle transactions and situations, continue to grow as a person, too. Conduct yourself with integrity. Integrity isn't just a word, it's a way of life. Move away from pettiness. Disavow bitterness and bickering. Forget gossip, and playing the game: "Ain't it Awful". Don't join the whiners, and the critics.

Continue to gain strength, but with compassion. We need strength in courage and convictions. We need strength to meet adversity, and strength to persevere. But, we can retain kindness and gentleness. Being tough enough to meet any situation doesn't equate to being mean.

We will need to be tough. There will be situations which call for toughness and resiliency. We need to resist being pushed about, but that does not say we should push. We don't push, we just stand firm. Hold your anger. Anger does nothing but corrode all parts of the angry person. We will, on occasion, be righteously indignant. Some occurrences are outrageous enough to call for a response. We will find battle necessary, sometimes. But, we don't do battle at the drop of a hat. Instead, we pick the time and the place where our resources will be most effective. And we learn to avert most such occurrences, and make them few and far between.

Be of good cheer. We will never be free of annoyances, but we shouldn't succumb to them. There will always be a few rascals and fools, but most of us are good people. And, when something aggravates us, shrug it off. Don't allow the aggravation to affect our next conversation … and don't take the aggravation home. People wonder why their offspring are reluctant to follow in the business. In some cases, it could be because over the years family dinner tables have heard renditions of all the awful things that happen in the business. Your kids aren't stupid. Tell them things are awful, they'll believe it. Tell the good news, too, or you'll sound like the network news.

You're in the right place. Stay in woodwork. Retain the love and reverence for this unique and marvelous material. Learn the business, too. Learn to provide quality and service. Keep growing … getting smarter, and richer. Learn, Work, Prosper, and Enjoy!

Press on. Nothing in the world can take the place of Persistence. Talent will not: nothing is more common than unrewarded talent. Education alone will not: the world is full of educated failures. Persistence alone is omnipotent.

-Calvin Coolidge

Books to Read

GOOD READING FOR GOOD MANAGERS

MANAGEMENT • Tasks • Responsibilities • Practices
By Peter Drucker (Publisher - Harper & Row)

The Time Trap (Paperback)
By R. Alex Mackenzie (Publisher - McGraw-Hill)

What They Don't Teach You at Harvard Business School
By Mark H. McCormack (Publisher - Bantam Books)

The Supermanagers (Paperback)
By Robert Heller (Publisher - McGraw-Hill)

Tough Minded Management (Paperback)
By Joe D. Batten (Publisher - AMACOM)

Shirt-sleeve Management (Paperback)
By James E. Evered / J. Erich Evered
(Publisher - AMACOM)